The Witness of Preaching

The Witness of Preaching

THIRD EDITION

Thomas G. Long

WJK WESTMINSTER
JOHN KNOX PRESS
LOUISVILLE · KENTUCKY

Third edition
Published by Westminster John Knox Press
Louisville, Kentucky

16 17 18 19 20 21 22 23 24 25—10 9 8 7 6 5 4 3 2 1

Book design by Sharon Adams
Cover design by Allison Taylor
Cover art: Let Everything That Have Breath Praise the Lord, *1978 (stained glass), Chagall, Marc (1887–1985) / Chichester Cathedral, Sussex, UK / Photo © Neil Holmes / Bridgeman Images*

Library of Congress Cataloging-in-Publication

Names: Long, Thomas G., 1946- author.
Title: The witness of preaching / Thomas G. Long.
Description: Third Edition. | Louisville, KY : Westminster John Knox Press, 2016. | Includes bibliographical references and index.
Identifiers: LCCN 2016013581 | ISBN 9780664261429 (pbk. : alk. paper)
Subjects: LCSH: Preaching.
Classification: LCC BV4211.3 .L66 2016 | DDC 251--dc23 LC record available at https://lccn.loc.gov/2016013581

Most Westminster John Knox Press books are available at special quantity discounts when purchased in bulk by corporations, organizations, and special-interest groups. For more information, please e-mail SpecialSales@wjkbooks.com.

For my brother Bill,
maker of good music
and rich laughter

Contents

Preface to the Third Edition

When I wrote the first edition of *The Witness of Preaching* in the late 1980s, I was trying to do both something old and something new. The "old thing" was to create yet another basic textbook on Christian preaching, both as an introductory resource for beginning students and as a refresher for more experienced preachers. Since at least the fifth century and the appearance of the homiletical portion of Augustine's *On Christian Doctrine*, every generation in the church has produced manuals of instruction on preaching, and *Witness* was simply one more entry in this very long line. Hundreds of basic textbooks preceded this one, and a good number of new ones have appeared since this book was first published. What sets *Witness* apart from the others is that I have tried to allow the theological image of bearing witness to the gospel to govern and organize every aspect of the process of creating a sermon from beginning to end—from the interpretation of a biblical text to the oral delivery of the sermon.

The "new thing" was to create a textbook that was in direct conversation with other voices and opinions in the field of preaching. For much of its history, the discipline of homiletics was viewed, like the other so-called practical fields, as *applied* theology. What this meant was that "real" theology was acquired in the systematics class or in Bible courses, and preaching class was consumed with the process of learning the pragmatic skills and techniques needed to apply this theology, already worked out elsewhere, in the form of sermons. Thus, most homiletics textbooks were manuals written by master preachers who shared secret recipes, techniques, and nuts-and-bolts wisdom about their methods for fashioning effective sermons. These books were often very sage and helpful, but they were for the most part quite self-contained and largely unaware of other voices and other views. They said, in effect, "Here is how I do it. Imitate me."

As the first edition of this book was being written, however, a sea change was taking place in the understanding of practical theology, including homiletics. Instead of thinking of practical theology as merely applied theology, practical theology was beginning to emerge as a generative theological discipline in its own right. The actual lived experience of faithful people—as individuals, in churches and other communities, through their religious rituals and practices, and in their engagement with society—was increasingly being seen as a *source* for theological knowledge and not just as a *target*, the place toward which one shot doctrinal arrows sharpened somewhere else. We began to recognize that the ways the church preached over its history, as well as the ways it celebrated the Lord's Supper or showed hospitality to the stranger, were not just applied theology; they *were* theology—lived theology, theology in action, theology embedded in practice. So, practical theologians, instead of simply packaging and retailing formal theology for the mass market or giving helps and hints for surefire results in the church, now understood themselves to be directing traffic in the middle of a busy three-way intersection, with knowledge coursing back and forth among dogmatics, the practices of the church, and "secular" disciplines, each with its claims and effects on the other.

One of the results of this redefinition of practical theology was that homiletics began gradually to develop a highly creative and theoretically sophisticated literature. By the late 1980s, homiletics had many lively disciplinary and interdisciplinary conversations going, with a host of scholars engaging the debate, and we had moved well beyond the point where another "here is my method" cookbook would be sufficient. We needed, I felt, a textbook that acknowledged there is a field of homiletics out there to be reckoned with and one that explicitly put the reader in the middle of the game on the field. Readers of a basic text in preaching should know where an author stands on the homiletical map, of course, but they should also become aware that there is, in fact, a map, a wide territory full of contrasting opinions and important options. Books like that in homiletics were not unheard of, but they were rare enough and recent enough to merit being called "new," and creating a basic textbook in this genre was the "new thing" I tried to accomplish in *Witness*.

By the time that the second edition of *Witness* appeared in 2005, a decade-and-a-half after the first, many fresh issues and voices had entered the homiletical arena, and that edition constituted an attempt to catch up with the field, to address some of those new forces and factors, to reflect the current state of the homiletical conversation, and to introduce not only the best methods for preaching but also the sort of theological thinking needed to do good preaching. The homiletical party had gotten more crowded, more interesting, and a good bit louder, and the second edition attempted to capture some of that excitement.

Now, another decade has gone by, and the rate of change in the field of homiletics has not abated. But perhaps the greatest shift reflected in this edition of *Witness* is in the context of preaching. In North America, seemingly unshakable understandings of the church are now being deeply shaken. Many congregational membership rolls have dramatically declined, numerous church buildings have been abandoned, and the Sunday assemblies in many places look noticeably greyer and smaller. Will Herberg's mid-twentieth-century classic *Protestant—Catholic—Jew* described a religious establishment that is now shattered, and the voice of Christian witness today takes place amid a global marketplace of religious expressions and traditions. Preachers still hold forth in old country churches and neo-Gothic sanctuaries, but they are almost as likely to be found in taverns and movie theaters, storefronts and living rooms. Experiments in church life and structure abound, and preaching is a part of this inventive ethos.

Some might well say that, in the midst of all of this change, diversity, and experimentation, the time for preaching textbooks has passed. No single vision of preaching can possibly speak, it could be argued, to the dazzling array of today's Christian communities. This third edition of *Witness* stands as a wager that this is not the case. But the wager depends not on advancing some totalizing vision of preaching borrowed from an earlier day but rather on discerning the essential practices of Christian preaching that still shimmer in the diversity of expressions. Whether Christian worship occurs in a Puritan-style meeting house, a retrofitted warehouse, or a borrowed hookah bar, and whatever that worship may look like, eventually the hunger for the Word will emerge. And then someone must speak that Word, which means that someone must listen closely to hear the testimony of ancient

Scripture and then to seek to find the language and the forms needed to allow this testimony to find a new hearing. These are the essentials of preaching that nimble preachers must labor to enact in settings ever new.

So, this new edition of *Witness* remains, in a basic way, what it was from the beginning: not a manual for preaching in a church established and at rest but instead a guidebook for a church always on safari or, to employ a biblical allusion, for a church that, like Abraham, has set out not knowing where we are going. I have attempted to keep this volume relatively brief, simple, and uncluttered by peripheral squabbles and secondary concerns—in short, something that can be figuratively carried in a backpack. I hope this book will help nimble preachers prepare more faithful sermons, even when those sermons are preached in surprising places and to listeners who are perhaps only loosely tethered to the Christian faith. But my most fervent prayer is that this book will encourage preachers to become self-critical about their preaching so that wherever the Spirit may take them and the community of faith, they can become their own teachers and remain faithful to their call to bear witness to the gospel.

Thomas G. Long
Bandy Professor of Preaching, emeritus
Candler School of Theology
Emory University

Introduction

Because I am a teacher and not currently the pastor of a congregation, most of the preaching I do these days is as a "guest preacher." Guest preachers, because they are, well, guests, unfamiliar with the local customs, are almost inevitably given an elaborate list of instructions before the service begins. Sit here, stand there, be sure to turn on your microphone, use one of the band's music stands for your notes, say "trespasses" instead of "debts" in the Lord's Prayer, go to this door—that sort of thing. Especially when we are preaching in an older, more traditional building, one of the most important pieces of information we guest preachers receive, curiously enough, is a set of directions for entering the place of worship. Getting into the pulpit may seem like a simple matter, but church floor plans are notoriously complex, and a wrong turn can easily send an embarrassed visitor into the choir loft or a broom closet instead of the chancel.

Finding the Entrance

How a preacher enters the place of worship is not just a practical matter; it is a theological issue. Look closely for a moment at how this actually happens in various settings. In some churches, the minister appears, almost unnoticed, through a side door during the playing of the prelude, unobtrusively moving to a seat near the pulpit. In other churches, the minister joins the choir in a processional down the aisle during the opening hymn. In churches built to resemble theaters or music halls, the preacher emerges, almost magically, from the darkened wings at the preaching moment. In still others, the entrance

1

of the clergy is a moment of high ceremony, marked by prayers and hymns. Notice, however, that in every one of these cases the clergy come from somewhere *outside*; the preacher comes from somewhere else into the place where the congregation waits.

Logistically, this makes sense, since ministers typically spend the last few minutes before the service in the study fiddling with their sermon notes, or in the sacristy pulling on vestments, or pacing around trying to memorize how the projected images supporting the sermon will be woven into the spoken word, or in the music room meeting for prayer with the choir, or in the hallway being tugged on the sleeve by someone who wants a quick word with the pastor. Theologically, though, another picture appears. Regardless of where the worship leaders emerge physically and architecturally, theologically it is crucial to remember that we come from within the community of faith and not to it from the outside. Whether we use this door or that one, process down the center aisle or modestly glide to our chairs, it is not nearly as important as remembering that, even though we will now be the leaders of worship, we have come to this task from the midst of the community of faith and not from the outside.

If we were putting this theological conviction into strict practice, worship leaders would not enter from outside the place of worship at all. We would come from the pew to the pulpit, from the nave to our place in the chancel, from the middle of the congregation to the place of leadership. For most church settings it may seem somewhat far-fetched to imagine a minister rising from a pew to give the call to worship or to preach the sermon, but this is precisely the picture of the Christian church at worship portrayed by Jürgen Moltmann in *The Church in the Power of the Spirit*:

> [W]e can take our bearings from the simple, visible procedure: the community gathers to hear the proclamation, or for a baptism, for the common meal, for the feast and to talk together. Then one person or more gets up in front of the congregation in order to preach the Gospel, to baptize, to prepare the meal, to arrange the feast, and to make his contribution to the discussion. These people come from the community but come forward in front of it and act in Christ's name. It is not they as "office bearers" who "confront" the congregation; it is Christ. What they

do and say is in the name of the triune God. How, then, are we to understand the position of these people with their particular charges or assignments? They come from God's people, stand up in front of God's people and act in God's name.[1]

What is at stake here is not a liturgical quarrel over the mechanics of how worship leaders get into place. Local circumstance, architecture, and tradition will always dictate that. What is at stake is the more urgent matter of how worship leaders, including preachers, *understand* themselves and their leadership roles in relationship to the whole community of faith. This is a book about preaching, and we will soon turn our attention to that particular ministry and to the many tasks involved in creating sermons. It would be a mistake, however, to jump immediately into that undertaking, as if sermons had no context and preachers had no community.

Preachers come to the pulpit from *somewhere*, and unless we can name that place, we risk misunderstanding who we are and what we are supposed to be doing. When we who preach enter the place of worship and find a congregation waiting there for us, it is easy to forget that we come from these people, not to them from the outside. We are not visitors from clergy-land, strangers from an unknown land, ambassadors from seminary-land, or even, as much as we may cherish the thought, prophets from a wilderness land. We are members of the body of Christ, participants in the worshiping assembly, commissioned to preach by the very people to whom we are about to speak.

From the *Pew* to the *Pulpit*

Whether we realize it or not, most of us who preach act out in our own ways this business of coming to the pulpit from the pew, from the midst of the congregation's life. Regardless of how we physically navigate those last few steps into the pulpit, dynamically we come fresh from engagements with the community of faith. We may have spent the previous hour in prayer for ourselves and for the others who will worship, or with a blue pencil, still trying to find just the right sermon words for these people on this day. We may have attended an educational class or taught one, gathered with a small group, listened with care to a person in distress or been listened to ourselves, met with the church leaders as they prayed and then made a decision about the budget, drunk a cup of coffee with some people in the fellowship hall, been given a last-minute announcement about the pancake breakfast, or heard the choir or musical group rehearse. Whether we have been praying, talking, teaching, preparing, or listening, we have been immersed in the lives of these people to whom we will speak, which is another way of saying that, symbolically at least, we rise to the pulpit from the pew.

Moreover, we have been involved with these people, in ministry to and with them, throughout the week, in hospital rooms and living rooms, in town halls and school auditoriums, in kitchens and factories. Perhaps our work has strengthened the faith of others; perhaps we have found our own faith strengthened. Even if we do not do so literally, we stand up to preach from our place in the middle of this community's life, not from a point above it or at its edge. Moltmann has it right; preachers "come from God's people."

Preachers "come from God's people" in another and more basic sense as well. Those who preach are baptized Christians. Because preachers are people who have been baptized into Christ, they are *members* of Christ's body, the church, before they are its *leaders*. Sometimes we tend to think of "the call to preach" as a rather isolated event that happens to a few select persons. The finger of God somehow falls upon the chosen ones, summoning them to preach and sending them into pulpits. Some preachers have indeed had dramatic experiences of personal calling, but it is simply misleading to speak of the preacher's call apart from God's calling of the church as a whole. "What matters," writes Moltmann, "is that public preaching and the preacher should not be isolated from the simple, everyday and matter-of-course language of the congregation's faith, the language used by Christians in the world."[2]

The fact that the sermon, the proclamation of the Word, is a central event in worship echoes the fact that proclamation is a central activity of God's people. The sermon in worship stands, as it were, at the epicenter of the speech acts of Christians in the world. When a congregation takes a public stand for humane treatment of prisoners, insisting that they, too, are children of God, the entire church is preaching the gospel. When a church school teacher tells the stories of Jesus to children, the gospel is proclaimed. When a congregation opens its fellowship hall on winter nights as a shelter and provides hospitality for the homeless, it bears witness to the gospel. When, in the name of Christ, members of the congregation bring words of comfort and encouragement to the sick and those in prison, pray for and with those in distress, and welcome the stranger, they announce the good news of the kingdom. God calls the whole church to proclaim the gospel, and every disciple of Jesus Christ is a part of this calling. The whole church proclaims the gospel, and the preaching of sermons is but one part of this larger ministry. So when a preacher stands in the pulpit, reads the Scripture, and preaches the sermon, this act of speaking the gospel ripples out into the world as the church continues to speak in a thousand places and ways.

Those who preach not only participate in the church's common ministry, they are also shaped by it. Years ago, seminaries were sometimes jokingly called "preacher factories," and the assumption still lingers that the task of theological schools is to take people and fabricate them into ministers. This is not the case at all. Ministers are not "made" in seminaries. Seminaries and other programs of theological education *train* ministers; ministers are made in and through the *church*. Women and men may for a season engage in formal theological education to gain deeper knowledge of the Christian story, but they were first taught that story and they are sustained in that story by Christian people in the church. They come to schools to wrestle with the great theological ideas, but it is the church's theological heritage they will encounter. They come to places of theological training to acquire the skills of guiding, teaching, counseling, and speaking, but they come because the church, in some way, has already discerned in them gifts for leadership. They leave seminaries not to create the church but to take their places of service in its ongoing ministry. People do not stand up to preach because they needed a job and have answered a want ad on a website, but because the church prayerfully set them apart for this ministry. They have been entrusted with a ministry that does not belong to them but that belongs to Christ and is given to the whole church.

A *Lonely* Place

Despite this brave talk about the ministry of preaching belonging to the whole church, every honest preacher knows something of the loneliness of the pulpit too. As Moltmann's picture implies, we who preach get up from our place in the midst of the congregation, and then we walk to the pulpit and stand in front of the people. There is a distance between *us* and *them*, and often we feel this distance keenly. We want to speak the gospel to them, the gospel of grace and demand, and yet we sometimes stand there looking out at people who could hardly seem less receptive. Because we come from them, we know them, know their apathies and divisions, know their broken places and their dull ears—which are, of course, ours, too. We stand there and look out at the man who is even now cheating on his wife, the parents who are pressuring their children into lives of frenzied overachieving, the couple who just purchased a new home to escape an integrated neighborhood, the single mom who just lost her job and is deeply frightened for herself and her children, and the merchant who recently pulled a fast one on the Internal Revenue Service. As we stand there, we see the restless teenagers in the back playing with their phones and texting to each other, the church leader who is doing her best to undermine our ministry, and the man who is already asleep, and the place where we stand feels like a lonely place.

Part of this feeling comes because we allow our theology of the church to grow slack. We know better, of course, but it is always tempting to hold the gritty reality of the church up against some romantic image of the community of faith, vibrating in perfect pitch with the music of the Spirit. We adjust our carefully prepared sermon notes, clear our throats to begin, look up at the odd assortment of people out there who dare to call themselves a congregation, and wonder, "Can this be the church of Jesus Christ?" A realistic theology of the church must always begin with the frank acknowledgment that, as Craig Dykstra has claimed, "A basic reality of congregational life is that we are engaged in socially acceptable (indeed, socially celebrated) patterns of mutual self-destruction."[3] Dykstra goes on to say:

> Furthermore, the mere presence of the story, vision, and language of the faith is no guarantee that these powerful patterns *will* be overcome. The patterns easily survive in congregational life, no matter how much that life may be filled with talk about sin, crucifixion, the love of God, or the grace of the Lord Jesus Christ.[4]

This is where our theology of the church must begin, but it is not where it may end because there is more to the story. It is true that the church is tarnished by the same failings that stain every human organization, but congregations continue to say and do things that point to another truth about themselves, namely, that what is most important about their life does not spring from within but from God who calls the church into being. Worship, as Dykstra has observed, is the central event by which the church points beyond itself to God. "In worship," he states, "the congregation is a congregation. Through worship, patterns of mutual self-destruction become redemptively transformed."[5]

What does it look like for a congregation to point beyond its own institutional life in worship? One place we find this happening is in prayers of confession. These prayers may seem at first to be rather unremarkable features of the liturgy, but they are quite remarkable indeed when we contrast them to the rituals of the rest of society. Lofty words are spoken at the dedication of a civic center or a country club, but no one confesses sin. Prayers uttered before football games and corporate banquets are devoid of confession. In Christian churches every week, though, people say in one form or another, "We have erred and strayed from Thy ways like lost sheep. . . . O Lord, have mercy upon us." Week after week Christian people repeat words like these, and by them they celebrate the freedom that belongs to those who know that what is truly good in human life does not finally depend upon our capacity to manufacture it.

One can also discern a congregation pointing beyond itself as they share the bread and wine at the Lord's Table, as they gather to witness the marriages, as they sing songs of the resurrection at graveside, and as they pray for the needs of people all over the world. By doing so, they confess that they belong to a fellowship larger and deeper than their own making, greater even than their own desires. They testify that they have been made brothers and sisters to people they might otherwise pass by with a shrug of indifference. Through the words of worship, they are beckoned to speak, however haltingly, the language of a world that transcends self-interest and self-reliance; and even their children, just learning the rhythms of this language, begin to sense the difference between "When you wish upon a star" and "Now I lay me down to sleep; I pray the Lord my soul to keep."

The fact that the church in its worship points to, hopes for, and expects the reality of God beyond itself is the reason that William Willimon has insisted that the church, in its worship, retreats *to* the real world and not *from* it. "This is the 'function' of the delightfully non-functional world of Sunday worship," he writes, *"to withdraw to the real world where we are given eyes to see and ears to hear the advent of a Kingdom that the world has taught us to regard as only fantasy."*[6]

This is also the reason that the preacher rises from the midst of the assembled people and then stands in front of those people to preach. The preacher comes from God's people and thus is not outside the people or above them. But the preacher stands in front of the people because what the preacher is about to do is not of the people's own making or, despite all the work of sermon preparation, of the preacher's own making. As Moltmann puts it, "It comes from their God, in whose name they speak and act. After all, the commissioned and commissioning community does not want to listen to itself and project its own image of itself; it wants to hear Christ's voice, celebrate his fellowship, and have the assurance of his commission."[7]

So there we stand, we who somehow find ourselves in the pulpit with the commission to preach. We know, now, from where we have come, and it is from the congregation of Christ's people, both faithful and faithless, of which we are a part. They have taught us the "old, old gospel story" and have sent us now to this place to tell it anew to them; to recount its cherished word of hope; to remind them, because they have often forgotten, of its power; to call them, because they are prone to resist its claim, to take on once again its yoke, which is easy, and its burden, which is light; to comfort them, because they are frightened and doubting, with its unfailing grace; and to reassure them that, no matter how far they have strayed from home, it is still, and ever will be, the story of God with and for them.

A Sense of *Mystery*, a Sense of Humor

No discerning person can stand in this place in front of the community of Christ without a deep sense of awe and responsibility. It is also true that no one should stand in this place without a deep sense of humility and a healthy sense of humor. We come to the place of preaching, we have been insisting, from the congregation, and we share their faith, but we also share their failings. We have no more right to be in the pulpit than anyone else in the congregation; indeed, we have no "right" to be there at all. As fully as anyone present, we have our doubts and our patterns of disobedience about the very gospel we are to proclaim. It is good to be there in the pulpit, but we are not there because we are good. That the group of people from which we come could be called the body of Christ, and that we, of all people, could stand before them to preach the gospel in Christ's name, is humbling and, in its own way, humorous. As Karl Barth once remarked concerning those who speak of God:

> We can and must act as those who know. But we must not claim to be those who know. . . . [The power of God's self-revelation] consists in the divine act of majesty in face of which those who really know will always find and confess that they do not know. The attitude of those who know in this power can only be one of the greatest humility. . . . It is just because they can have no doubt as to the liberation which is quite outside their own control that those who are really free to know this matter can never lose a sense of humor in relation to themselves.[8]

"Never lose a sense of humor about yourself." Perhaps that line ought to be engraved on a plaque and placed on the back of the pulpit alongside the traditional quotation from the Gospel of John, "We would see Jesus." The verse from John would remind us to take the task of preaching the gospel of Christ seriously; the phrase about a sense of humor would encourage us not to take ourselves too seriously while we are doing that task. Moreover, a sense of humor in worship is not only a sign of humility but also of the gospel's liberating power. "With Easter," states Moltmann, "the laughter of the redeemed . . . begins."[9] Because God in Christ has broken the power of sin and death, Christian congregations and their preachers are free to laugh at themselves, and they can also laugh at the empty gods of pride and greed. They can mock hell and dance on the grave of death and sin.

When I was a child, my family worshiped in a small clapboard church set in the red-clay farming land of rural Georgia. We were a congregation of simple folk, farmers and schoolteachers mainly, and our ministers led worship wearing inexpensive and ill-fitting dark suits, believing that robes were a too-fancy sign of ostentation. The heavy summer heat of that region settled in at sunrise and gathered intensity through the day, so that Sunday worship in the hot months was punctuated by the waving of funeral-home fans and the swatting of gnats. All the windows of the church, and the main doors as well, were opened wide to accept whatever merciful breezes might blow our way. On some Sundays, however, it was not a draft that blew in the church door but a neighborhood dog, a stray hound of indecipherable lineage who somehow found our service irresistible. He was not there every Sunday by any means, but his summer appearances were frequent enough that some joked he had a better attendance record at worship than many of the officers.

The ushers knew better than to try to run him off, the one and only attempt at that having driven him bounding toward the pulpit. So, while we sang the hymns, the cur would sniff curiously at the ankles of the worshipers. Deacons would step around him on their way to take up the offering, and during the pastoral prayer the dog would wander aimlessly around the room. He was an endless source of mirth for us children, and he occasionally served as a handy and spontaneous sermon illustration in such references as "no more sense of right and wrong than that dog over there."

Looking back on it now, I realize what a trial it must have been for our ministers to attempt to lead worship and to preach on those Sundays when this mongrel was scampering around the building and nuzzling the feet of the congregation. I confess I do not covet the experience for myself, but there was something wonderful about those times as well. Whatever else it may mean, a dog loose in worship unmasks all pretense and undermines false dignity. It was clear to us all that the grace and the joy and power present in our communion, and these were present in abundance, were not of our own making. We were, after all, people of little worldly standing who could not keep even our most solemn moments free of stray dogs. I want to believe that even our dark-suited, serious-faced ministers were aware of the poetic connection between a congregation of simple farmers and teachers in their Sunday best with a hound absurdly loose in their midst and a gathering of frail human beings astonishingly saved by the grace of God, grace they did not control but could only receive as a gift. If so, then in some deep and silent place within them they were surely taken with rich and cleansing laughter—and if they were, they were better preachers of the gospel for it.

1

What Does It Mean to Preach?

> Whether in the mode of thanks and praise or of lament, preaching is a calling on the mystery of the transcendent God who alone can save us.
> —Mary Catherine Hilkert, *Naming Grace*

> I don't understand preaching, but I believe in it deeply.
> —Ian Pitt-Watson, *Preaching: A Kind of Folly*

Sometimes people assume that anyone who is preparing for ministry is eager to take on the work of preaching. After all, being a "preacher" is one of the most striking and public of all ministerial roles, and, in the popular mind, anyone who feels called to the ministry must surely be the sort of person ready and willing to preach, one who earnestly covets the "preacher" role. The truth, however, is that the preacher's mantle rests more comfortably on some shoulders than it does on others. Preachers, regardless of whether they happen to be beginners preaching their very first sermons or experienced ministers who have preached more often than they can recall, approach the work of preaching with a wide spectrum of attitudes and feelings, from zestful anticipation to downright reluctance, from enthusiasm to paralyzing fear.

Getting Started

Some pastors come to preaching eagerly. In fact, some come to preaching almost too eagerly. Because they relish the visibility of the pulpit or overlook the complexities involved in preaching the gospel or mistakenly indulge themselves in visions of the "authority" of the preacher or possess a naive confidence in their ability to stir up a congregation, they stride into the pulpit without heeding its dangers, unmindful of its fearful heights and deep responsibilities. "I used to preach better," one minister said facetiously, "before I understood the issues." He was pointing to the truth that the more one understands about the task of preaching, the more respectful one becomes of its challenges and the more aware one becomes of one's limitations. Preaching is a wild river, wide and deep, and one of the goals of this book is to encourage the modesty and caution needed by all who navigate its white-water currents.

Other pastors, however, far from being eager to preach, instead find preaching to be a heavy and at times unbearable burden. Simply standing up and speaking to a group can be a fearful experience. Despite the prevalent assumption that all ministers are free from the pains of shyness or the terrors of stage fright, this is simply not so. What is more, some who feel the call to ministry have been told by their churches, explicitly or implicitly, that they have no right to preach at all, and they consequently doubt their own authority to speak.[1] Still others perhaps began their preaching ministry with zest and excitement, but now they find themselves just basically worn down by the unrelenting schedule of regular preaching. "Sundays come toward the preacher," quipped the well-known preacher Ernest T. Campbell, "like telephone poles by the window of a moving train." Week after week the pressures to be solidly prepared as well as interesting and creative take their toll.

Sometimes perceptive pastors can feel overwhelmed by the sheer size and weight of preaching, because they know how essential good preaching is for the larger mission of the community of faith. Congregations may be satisfied when sermons are simply lively, engaging, and not boring, but wise pastors know that congregations desperately need preaching of substance, preaching that is more than mere religious entertainment. Pastors with a clear understanding of the power of preaching in the life of the Christian community, pastors who have seen the people sitting there in the congregation hungry for a truthful word that clarifies and compels—sometimes not even aware how hungry they are—know that preaching is serious and urgent business. These same pastors, however, are pushed and pulled by the many demands of ministry, and they wonder where they will find the energy and the time, not to mention the courage and the powers of insight, necessary for the task. "I confess," a minister admitted, "that sometimes I wish they weren't listening. I can tell you, as a preacher, that I bear a terrible burden when people listen, really listen, from the depths of their souls."[2] Such preachers understand well why the respected student of preaching Joseph Sittler would have titled one of his books *The Anguish of Preaching*. They also know why Karl Barth once wondered, "Who dares, who can, preach, knowing what preaching is?"[3]

Nevertheless, it is another of the aims of this book to present preaching as a ministry of exceptional joy. To discover joy in the work of preaching does not mean whittling down its size, hiding from its demands, minimizing its perils, or even eliminating its anguish. What it does mean is strengthening our grip on the truth that the announcing of the good news of Jesus Christ in human words is an inestimable gift from God. To have our own lives, our own work, our own words, our own struggles and fears gathered up in some way into that event is an occasion of rich and joyful grace. To be a preacher is to be entrusted with the task of speaking the one word that humanity most urgently and desperately needs to hear, the glad tidings of God's redemption through Jesus Christ. To be a preacher is to be a midwife of the word, and the midwife, as Theresa Rickard describes,

> . . . has to be comfortable in the labor room; she is skilled and compassionate in the bringing forth of life. The midwife does not create the child; the child has already been formed. The babies she delivers are not her possession, but a gift that she hands over. The midwife listens attentively to the heartbeat of both the mother and the child. . . . The new mother has the opportunity and responsibility to embrace and nurture her gift.[4]

Indeed, we do not create the word; we do not establish the time of its arriving; we cannot eliminate the labor pains that surround it; but we serve with gratitude at its coming and exclaim with joy at its birth.

Can preaching really be learned? People often wonder that, especially when beginning a first course in preaching. Many of the most dynamic preachers, the ones people seem most to admire, often appear to have a certain innate flair, a knack for using words and delivering sermons that seems more like a gift than a set of learned skills. What is more, some of these superb preachers seem to be naturals. Maybe they have never taken a class in preaching, perhaps never read a single book on homiletics. They just seem born to the task rather than instructed in the craft. We admire their abilities, but they make us wonder about ourselves. Is the capacity for effective preaching within our reach? Is good preaching something we can learn, or is it reserved just for those born with the gift?

It is true that some preachers do have extraordinary gifts for preaching, a rare measure of talent and charisma that sets them apart. It would be wrong, however, for the rest of us to envy them and theologically shortsighted to set them up as the one and only standard of effective preaching. The church is blessed, of course, by the rare preacher of exceptional ability, but the church is sustained most of all by the kind of careful, responsible, and faithful preaching that falls within the range of most of us. In this regard, preaching is a little like cooking. There are, to be sure, a few five-star chefs whose gourmet meals dazzle and delight. We can learn from them and be inspired by their gifts, but no one eats a steady diet of five-star meals. Instead, what truly sustains is daily bread—food lovingly, ably, and carefully prepared. So it is with preaching. God's people are nourished most not by the five-star preachers but by those preachers who, week in and week out, lovingly, ably, and carefully prepare the "daily bread" of sermons, and the art and craft of this kind of preparation can indeed be learned. To use another image, learning to preach is a little like learning to play the piano. Some basic musical ability helps, of course, but most of all it is a matter of mastering the scales, studying the fingering techniques, learning the music, and practice, practice, practice.

Effective preachers are gifted people, but the gifts needed for good and faithful preaching are different from those of the electrifying speaker or the charismatic entertainer. Faithful preaching requires such gifts as sensitivity to human need, a discerning eye for the connections between faith and life, an ear attuned to hearing the voice of Scripture, compassion, a growing personal faith, and the courage to tell the truth. These are gifts of the Spirit, and although gifts of the Spirit cannot be taught in the classroom, they can be named, developed, encouraged, shaped, and given direction and focus.

Through centuries of Christian preaching, the church has learned much about what counts for good preaching, what makes a sermon faithful or not. Thus, yet another goal of this book is to draw on this wisdom and to present as much good information as possible about how sermons are created, crafted, and delivered. Along the way we will make use of the insights of many writers in the field of homiletics. Almost as long as Christians have been preaching, there have been others who reflected on this activity, tried to understand what makes for responsible preaching, and sought to make available for preachers the best wisdom from rhetoric, psychology, sociology, and other pertinent fields of knowledge. As a result, books and articles in the discipline of homiletics are plentiful. Not all of them are good, of course. Homiletics has suffered its share of fads and gimmicks, but much that is solid and fruitful as well has been learned through the years. As you read this book, you will recognize that my own voice and views form the main threads of the discussion, but others will frequently be brought in as conversation partners, even sometimes as debate partners. There are many good ways to approach preaching, and there are often disagreements over which is the best tack to take on certain matters. So you will have choices before you and decisions to make for your own preaching ministry.

The Event of Preaching

What is preaching? That sounds like a simple question, but the more we think about it, the larger and more complex it becomes. Indeed, the event of preaching is so multifaceted we will never understand it fully, but we need to take a stab at naming what it is. We need to fashion some broad understanding of the nature of preaching, because if we are not aware at least in some general way of what we are doing when we preach, it makes little sense to talk about the practical steps needed to create a good sermon. We have no way of judging whether a piece of practical advice about some aspect of preaching is good or bad, wise or foolish, until we have a frame of reference in which to assess it, a fairly clear picture of what it is that we are attempting to do when we preach. So what is preaching? One possible way to try to answer that question would be to come up with a concise, dictionary-style definition, but such a definition would inevitably disappoint because it would miss much of the richness and mystery of preaching. A better approach is not to reduce preaching to a formula but to focus on the actual *event* of preaching, to look with a probing and theologically discerning eye at what actually takes place when someone preaches.[5] Moltmann's rather simple picture of this, given in the introduction, is again helpful:

> One person or more gets up in front of the congregation in order to preach the Gospel. . . . These people come from the community but come forward in front of it and act in Christ's name.

The crucial ingredients of preaching are all here:

1. First, there is the *congregation*, the *assembly*, the people who will hear the preaching. A congregation is, of course, a gathering of people, and they have been gathered from somewhere, assembled for something, and eventually they will be dispersed to the place from whence they came. In other words, the fact that the event of preaching involves a congregation, a gathering, already implies two other realities, namely the *world* from which the congregation is called out and to which the congregation will be eventually be sent, and *worship*, the reason for which the congregation is gathered.
2. Then there is the *preacher* (or preachers—it doesn't have to be only one). The preacher must be seen from two perspectives. First, the preacher is in every way a part of the congregation, a member of the assembly who rises from the midst of the gathered people to perform the task of preaching. But notice that the preacher moves to a new position, getting up from the congregation to stand in front of the community. Something has changed. The preacher now is not simply one of the members of the assembly but is one who stands before the community in some new role, some new relationship to the others. Looking purely at the event of preaching, this new position of the preacher is not so much a change in status but a change in place and function. The preacher is still a member of the assembly, but now the preacher has moved to a different place, the preaching place, because the preacher is about to do something that, for the moment at least, the others do not do. The preacher will act and speak a particular word, a sermon, in the name of Christ.

3. Then there is the *sermon*. Because we are describing the event of preaching, we must be careful not to confuse the sermon with what the preacher may have written down beforehand or even with the words the preacher has in mind to say. The sermon is action; the sermon is what the preacher enacts in performed speech (words, voice, and body) joined with what the rest of the congregation hears and receives. The preacher may have notes or a manuscript, of course, but this is not the sermon. The sermon is an event of speaking and hearing, performed by the preacher in Christ's name.[6]

4. Finally, there is the *presence of Christ*. To say that the preacher "acts in Christ's name" is more than simply claiming that the preacher has authority or that the preacher is a local agent for a distant God. Preaching that happens "in Christ's name" is preaching in which the risen Christ is truly present here and now. Preaching is a human activity but not merely a human activity. Christ is present in the church, with the church, for the church, in the world, with the world, and for the world through preaching. In the power of the Holy Spirit, Christ speaks God's word in the human and frail words of the sermon. As Mary Catherine Hilkert has said, "Depth words—the words of the poet, the preacher, the priest—effect what they signify. They are audible signs of inexpressible realities. In the end we return to Augustine's insight: sacraments are visible words; words are audible sacraments."[7]

We have to admit, of course, that many sermons are boring, incompetent, or faithless. Jesus, the living Word, was crucified, and the preached Word can be crucified too. There is little to stop a preacher from preaching sermons that are trivial, destructive, and demonic. In fact, even the best sermons are not so pure and holy that they could on their own strength merit being spoken "in Christ's name." So, to say that preaching happens "in Christ's name" is not first a sign of the quality of a sermon but of the graciousness of God's promises. God has chosen to meet us in the event of preaching, promised to be present there, and this is not because our sermons are good but because God is good. Or, to put it another way, we strive to make our sermons good and faithful in response to make them fit dwellings for the word of God,

We are not so vain, then, to think that when we stand up to preach, our eloquent speaking somehow forces God to act. Preaching does not cause Christ to be present, and just because somebody stands and says, "I have a word from the Lord," that does not whistle Christ into the room. Christ is not present because we preach; we preach because Christ is present. Preaching, like all other actions of the church, is joining in on what God is already doing, and we dare to preach because we believe that Jesus Christ is already speaking to the church and to the world. Preaching in the name of Christ is possible only because Christ is already present, because Christ has already decided to be with us, because Christ has already chosen to meet us in the spoken word of preaching. To preach is to join our human words with the word that God in Christ in the power of the Spirit is already speaking to the church and to the world, and to speak in Christ's name is to claim Christ's own promise, "Whoever listens to you listens to me" (Luke 10:16).

So the pieces are all here—the congregation, the preacher, the sermon, and the presence of Christ—but how do these pieces fit together? What are the connections and linkages among these various elements of the event of preaching? What sort of relationship, for example, should the preacher have to the congregation? Should the preacher talk like a peer or a leader or a servant? What voice should the preacher take? The voice of a counselor, a teacher, a prophet, a trusted friend? Or what about the relation of the sermon to the congregation? Should it assume a particular form? Should it be a conversation between the preacher and the hearers, a prophetic oracle on the lips of the preacher, a story about Jesus, a beautifully written essay about God, or perhaps a meditation on the presence of Christ? And where should the words of the sermon come from? The preacher's imagination? The Bible? The everyday life of the congregation? All of the above?

We have named the parts of the preaching event, but these are moving parts. We need to see them in operation, and to describe how each piece relates to the others. In order to do this, we have to stand somewhere in the solar system of preaching in order to be able to see the relative positions and movements of the other planets. Hypothetically, we could assume the perspective of any one of the elements and see how it relates to all the others. One vantage point is potentially as good as another. The obvious place for us to stand, however, is in the preacher's spot. We are learning how to be preachers, so if we can stand where the preacher stands and describe the role of the preacher in a comprehensive manner, we will necessarily also describe all the other relationships and dimensions of preaching. In other words, we can elaborate our answer to the question "What is preaching?" by focusing our attention on a related question, "Who is the preacher?"

Images of the Preacher

Most ministers have in their minds a general understanding of who they are and what they are doing as they go about the work of ministry. In other words, we do not just go out and do ministry. As we go, we carry with us pictures of what we think ministers ought to be and do, pictures of who we believe ourselves to be as ministers.

Sometimes the picture we have is vague (occasionally even incoherent), and often the minister is not fully conscious of its presence, but it is there nonetheless, exercising a high degree of control over the patterns and practices of ministry. If ministers picture themselves as "shepherds" or "prophets" or "enablers" or "teachers" or "evangelists" or "spiritual entrepreneurs" or "servant leaders" or "wounded healers," these guiding images of ministry will prompt them to emphasize certain tasks of ministry and to minimize others. They will speak and act in the ways demanded by those images. Woven into these organizing metaphors of ministry are not only convictions about the nature of the ministry but also key understandings of the mission of the church, the character of the world, the nature of the human situation, and the content of the gospel.

The same is true, in a more particular sense, about preaching. When a preacher delivers a sermon, that act is embedded in some larger framework of ministerial self-understanding. In other words, preachers have at least tacit images of the preacher's role, primary metaphors that not only describe the nature of the preacher but also embrace by implication all the other crucial aspects of the preaching event. In recent years homiletical scholars have identified many of these controlling images, but the vast majority of these pictures of the preacher can be clustered around three "master" metaphors: the *herald*, the *pastor*, and the *storyteller/poet*. At some points these three images share values about the ministry of preaching, but at other places they are rivals, embodying quite different and competing views of who a preacher is and what a preacher should do. If we explore each of these images, we can begin to grasp some of the possibilities they contain for a larger understanding of preaching, and we can also make some assessment of their respective strengths and weaknesses.

The Herald

The herald image was the most prevalent metaphor advanced by homileticians in the middle of the twentieth century when they sought to describe what they believed the role of the preacher ought to be, though it has probably not been the most influential one for the actual practice of preaching. In the image of the herald, the emphasis falls on the content of the sermon, on the message proclaimed by the preacher. The image is a biblical one, derived from one of the several Greek terms used in the New Testament to describe preaching (*kerusso*). The herald metaphor received its modern homiletical impetus not merely because it is a biblical term but also because of the prominence given to it by the early-twentieth-century theological movement that came to be called "neo-orthodoxy," especially among those who sought to be followers of Karl Barth. Barth himself employed this image in his definition of "proclamation," a term that is larger than preaching, but which includes it:

> Proclamation is human language in and through which God Himself speaks, *like a king through the mouth of his herald*, which moreover is meant to be heard and apprehended . . . in faith as the divine decision upon life and death, as the divine judgment and the divine acquittal, the eternal law and the eternal gospel both together.[8]

Obviously, the herald image contains a very high theological view of preaching since it emphasizes quite strongly the connection between preaching and the direct address of God. The preacher is the one who speaks the words of the sermon, but God actually does the proclaiming. The purpose of preaching, therefore, is not to provide a forum for the preacher to give moral advice, to express opinions on important topics, or to lay out religious "principles for living" but rather to be the occasion for the hearing of a voice beyond the preacher's voice: the very word of the living God. Preaching is not about the preacher; it is about the voice of God.

Built into the herald image, then, is the conviction that preaching is far more than it appears on the surface. If preaching involves an interplay between human action and divine action, the herald image so strongly emphasizes the divine role that the human side of the ledger threatens almost to disappear. Suppose two professors, a rhetorician and a homiletician (who happened to be committed to the herald perspective on preaching), were to hear the same sermon. The rhetorician would probably have some advice to give the preacher on how to improve the sermon. Maybe the structure could be a little tighter or the language a bit more colorful or the illustrations more cogent or the preacher more animated in the delivery. Our herald homiletician, however, would be wary about all of this rhetorical fiddling with the sermon and would be far more concerned about how well the sermon reflected the message of the Bible. The preacher's job, this homiletician would say, is to go to the Scriptures, to listen there for the dynamic event of God's word, and then to speak this word faithfully and truly and let the chips fall where they may. Fussing around trying to make the sermon more colorful or more engaging comes perilously close to a mistrust of the divine message, an arrogant assumption that we humans can improve on the speech of God.

For the rhetorician, then, preaching is a human language act, and we can think up ways to make it even better. For our homiletician, though, the important thing about the sermon is that it was the vehicle for the word of God, and this conviction places a strict limit on all talk about making the sermon "more effective." It would be a strange, even a blasphemous, idea to think that the preacher could rearrange a few words in the sermon and thereby enable God to speak more clearly. Better, then, to talk about the sermon being more "faithful" rather than more "effective." Herald preachers do not strive to create more beautiful and more excellent sermons but seek to be more responsive and obedient to the message they receive in Scripture. They do not aspire to be poets; they aspire to be mouthpieces of God, servants of the word.

How does a preacher do this? Let us explore this question by examining three additional facets of the herald image.

1. In the first place, what becomes truly important about preaching, viewed as an act of ministry, is the message, the news the herald proclaims. A herald has but two responsibilities: to get the message straight and to speak it plainly. The sovereign tells the herald what to proclaim, and the herald is obedient only to the extent that the sovereign's word is delivered faithfully and without alteration.

In the case of Christian preaching, the message is the gospel, the good news of Jesus Christ as entrusted to the herald through the Scripture, and the task of the preacher is to announce this news to those to whom the herald is sent. We must make a careful distinction here between the words of Scripture and sermon, on the one hand, and the dynamic word of God, on the other. The herald image does not rest on the claim that the preacher, by repeating or explicating the words of the Bible, actually speaks God's word. God's word is not a set of words; it is an event, the very presence of God in Christ addressing the hearers. The herald image underscores the promise of God to be present as we faithfully proclaim the Scripture in preaching. The herald preacher does not possess the word of God; the herald preacher possesses a command to preach the Scripture and the promise that as the Scriptures are faithfully preached, God will speak through Scripture and sermon.

So the herald preacher has one clear task with two parts: to attend to the message of the Bible and to proclaim it plainly. The preacher does not invent this message, nor should the preacher attempt to add anything to it. The preacher is not sent to evaluate the message, to try to make it more palatable, or to debate its relative merits—only to announce it faithfully. Preaching, wrote D. W. Cleverley Ford, "is not to be confused with lecturing, nor with diagnosing a situation, nor with providing homiletical advice. Preaching is being a herald because what it proclaims is the word of God which in itself is dynamic."[9]

It should come as no surprise, then, that herald preachers spend most of their time with the Bible and less of their time trying to figure out how to forge connections with the hearers. As Barth once said of his own preaching,

> I have the impression that my sermons reach and "interest" my audience most when I least rely on anything to "correspond" to the Word of God already "being there," when I least rely on the

"possibility" of proclaiming this Word, when I least rely on my ability to "reach" people by my rhetoric, when on the contrary *I* allow my language to be formed and shaped and adapted as much as possible by what the text seems to be saying.[10]

Dietrich Ritschl, a firm advocate of the herald model of preaching, is even more adamant on this point:

The lack of trust in the absolute priority and dependability of the Word is the main reason for the increasing interest of the Churches and their "experts" in the techniques of speech, communication, illustration, and rhetoric. . . . It is not the business of the preacher to try to force [the sermon's] result or even to speculate about it.[11]

That is strong medicine indeed. According to Ritschl, herald preachers are not supposed even to speculate about how their sermons were received by the hearers. Were they listening? Were they challenged? Were they moved? These are not proper questions for the herald. Heralds do not attempt to defend Christian doctrine or to persuade people that what they are preaching is true. They only speak the message. They do not say things to themselves like, "Now my hearers will resist this idea, so I must give reasons for it to soften their resistance." To do that would be to mistrust the message, to try to add some power to it because they fear it is weak.

2. If the herald image emphasizes the importance of the message, it correspondingly de-emphasizes the personality of the preacher. Heralding is a derivative activity. The task of the herald is not to *be* somebody, but to *do* something on another's behalf and under another's authority. A herald preacher, for example, would probably be hesitant to relate a personal experience in a sermon, lest attention be drawn to the preacher and away from the message. The preacher's dynamic personality, personal opinions, family stories, religious experiences, or colorful anecdotes are not truly important. Only the message is important, and once the message is spoken, the herald is thoroughly dispensable.

3. The herald preacher is both an outsider and an insider and bears, therefore, a paradoxical relationship to the congregation, the church. On the one hand, a herald always comes to the people with news from

the outside. A herald comes to the village saying, "Hear ye, hear ye!" and announces news of a victory or a royal marriage or a new law. Likewise, the preacher who is a herald brings news from the outside, news from beyond, God's news. On the other hand, unlike a herald who comes to town, announces a royal proclamation, and then leaves, the herald preacher stays, lives as a part of the congregation, and announces the gospel every time the people gather for worship. God not only sends preachers to the church; God also entrusts the church with the ongoing ministry of preaching. So preaching is an event that comes from the outside, but it is partly an inside activity, too. The church provides for regular preaching, nourishes the ministry of preaching, and calls preachers to their ministry. But the church expects preachers not just to say what the church already knows, to express only what the church already is; it expects news from the outside, news from God. So the herald preacher paradoxically comes both *from* inside the church and *to* the church with news from the outside. Again, as D. W. Cleverley Ford put it,

> [w]isdom counsels that the word of God as the Bible, the word of God as preaching, and the Church be seen as belonging together in a relationship which if broken can only distort the true nature of each of the separate parts. So preaching is proclaiming Christ from the scriptures, a ministry of the word specifically entrusted to the Church and which operates for the wholeness of the Church itself, but is also an instrument for the furtherance of God's will to reconcile [the world] to himself.[12]

What we have here is the idea that the Bible is the church's book, preaching is the church's ministry, and the preacher is the church's servant, but that something happens in biblical preaching that is not of the church's own making or doing. Within the reciprocal relationships among Bible, preacher, and church, an event occurs in which God freely speaks. Thus the herald metaphor underscores the conviction that the primary movement of preaching *is from* God *through* the herald *to* the hearers.

There is clearly considerable strength in the herald image. Its mandate for the preacher to remain close to the scriptural message means that herald preachers have something to say, news of vital importance to announce. It reinforces preaching that possesses a vigorous biblical and theological character, over against the thin gruel of moralisms, popular wisdom, bits and pieces of advice for creative living, and encouragements to positive thinking derived from the culture, which are found in all too many sermons. In a time when many church worship spaces have taken on the look of television studios, when worship services are rated for their entertainment value, and when preachers are prized for charm and charisma, the herald preacher recognizes this for what it is, a distrust of the power of the gospel itself and a famine of the authentic word, and says *No!*

The herald image also provides a strong basis for prophetic preaching, preaching that announces the reign of God over against the powers and principalities that seem to hold sway in the culture. Prophetic preaching does not necessarily imply that the preacher assumes the role of Jeremiah or Amos, but that the preacher remains faithful to the prophetic dimensions of biblical texts. If the word comes from God in the biblical text, the preacher remains true to that word, regardless of the reaction or the cost. As James Harris says in *Preaching Liberation*, his book on the prophetic mode in preaching, "Preaching liberation means capturing the spirit of protest in the words of scripture and particularly in the message of Jesus and sharing that spirit with those who are oppressed as well as the oppressors."[13]

The main value of the herald image, though, lies in its insistence upon the transcendent dimension of preaching. If the power of preaching is limited to the preacher's strength, if the truthfulness of preaching is restricted to the preacher's wisdom, it is ultimately too little to stake our lives on. "After all," we have heard Moltmann say, "the . . . community does not want to listen to itself and project its own image of itself; it wants to hear Christ's voice."[14]

But there are also weaknesses in the herald image. To begin with, its disdain for matters of rhetorical form and communication runs counter to what we now know, through literary biblical interpretation, about the Scripture itself. The biblical writers consistently employed rhetorical forms and techniques and were attentive to what biblical scholar Robert Tannehill has called the "forceful and imaginative language" of the Scripture.[15] Much of the Scripture was written explicitly to be read aloud and to create an impact in the ear, and the biblical writers were quite concerned not only with what they were saying but also with how they were saying it. It makes little sense to tell preachers that they should stick to biblical texts alone and forget matters of language, communication, and rhetoric when it is clear that those very texts attend to matters of language, communication, and rhetoric.

Moreover, for the better part of a century many biblical scholars have shown that the rhetorical dimensions of the Bible were not mere ornaments designed to make the message more pleasing and attractive; they were language forms called forth by the very experience of God witnessed to by the text. New Testament scholar Amos Wilder claimed that "the coming of the Christian Gospel was in one aspect a renewal and liberation of language. It was a 'speech-event,' the occasion for a new utterance and new forms of utterance."[16] In *The Poetics of Biblical Narrative*, Meir Sternberg has argued that the Bible's unusual literary style, one marked by a combination of real-life descriptions, discontinuities, gaps, and non sequiturs, calls on readers not simply to read the words on the page but instead to move through the twists and turns of coming to faith in an uncertain world. Reading the Bible, he says,

> . . . we are surrounded by ambiguities, baffled and misled by appearances, reduced to piecing fragments together by trial and error, often left in the dark about essentials to the very end. . . . [The] reading turns into a drama of understanding— conflict between inferences, seesawing, reversal, discovery, and all. The only knowledge perfectly acquired is the knowledge of our limitations. It is by a sustained effort alone that the reader can attain at the end to something of the vision that God has possessed all along: to make sense of the discourse is to gain a sense of being human.[17]

In sum, the biblical writers were about the business of creating effects with words, but they were not employing language as ornament or merely to create interest but as the inevitable result of having come to faithful awareness.

Pushing the same theme a bit farther, the herald image, taken alone, not only downplays what the preacher can do in the areas of language and form but, ironically, tends to undermine almost all serious theological thinking about the practical aspects of creating sermons. Sermons don't get created with a wave of a wand, and preachers must make decisions about sermon structure, illustrations, delivery, and the like. But how can those be good and thoughtful decisions when those matters are supposedly off-limits? The herald image so stresses that preaching is something that God alone does, insists so firmly that preaching is divine activity rather than human effort, that the role of the preacher is almost driven from sight. Another remark of D. W. Cleverley Ford shows how advocates of the herald image, in their zeal to defend divine action in preaching, can sometimes trip over their own logic: "The preacher cannot control the word of God, he cannot even forecast what his preaching of it will accomplish. . . . [I]n a sense he is not responsible for his preaching."[18]

To say that preachers are "not responsible" for their preaching is a dangerous overstatement. A preacher cannot, of course, control God, but a preacher can control what is actually said in the sermon and is responsible for the quality of that control. Moreover, it is plainly true that what a preacher decides to say and how the preacher decides to say it enormously influence the impact of the sermon. It is surely good theology not to equate God's activity and the preacher's actions, but it is bad theology to disconnect them so completely that they do not even touch and the preacher loses any sense of responsibility for the sermon.

Some homileticians have charged that the herald image does not take sufficient account of the doctrine of the incarnation. The herald is always bringing news from the *outside*, as if the good news were utterly separate from human life, but the incarnation affirms that God's word comes not only from outside and above but also from inside and below. God's word is born in our midst and is God-with-us. Catholic theologian Karl Rahner, clearly with his eye on Barth, claims,

> Only a Protestant and a theologian of the most extreme dialectical obscurity could maintain that the divine grace, redemption, and our new freedom, light and the love of God remain so much in the beyond that one can experience nothing at all of them in this world; that on the contrary all human discourse witness to the word and to the reality of God only by its character of absolute paradox.[19]

Rather than coming in like a herald with news from the outside, Rahner's view is that preachers uncover what is already there, hidden, on the inside. "Preaching," he says, "is the awakening and making explicit what is already there in the depths . . . , not by nature but by grace."[20] Finally, the herald image fails to take adequate account of the context of preaching. Preaching does not occur in thin air but always happens on a specific occasion and with particular people in a given cultural setting. These circumstances necessarily affect both the content and style of preaching, but if we think of preaching as announcing some rarefied biblical message untouched by the situation at hand, we risk preaching in ways that simply cannot be heard.[21]

The advocates of the herald do not want to factor into the equation such matters of context as the perceived moral character of the preacher and the relationship between the preacher and the hearers, but these factors are much more important in preaching than the task-oriented herald image would envision. Whether or not the congregation believes and trusts the preacher, whether or not the preacher is perceived to have integrity, undeniably affects to some degree the receptivity of the hearers. These circumstances shape the event of preaching, and the herald image, with its accent upon the unilateral movement from God to the hearers, along with its emphasis on the purity and the integrity of the message, can give the impression of preaching as an anonymous message dropped into a box.

Another way to say this is that the herald image downplays not only the role of the preacher but also the role of the congregation as well. The herald is encouraged to deliver the biblical word as is, somewhat oblivious to whether the hearers are rich or poor, Korean or African American, agricultural workers or corporate CEOs, residents of a nursing home or youth on a retreat. Once again, though, the Scriptures themselves are always words on target, words spoken to a specific people in a particular context, and attempting to "deliver the word" without taking the hearers into account runs contrary to the nature of the biblical word itself.

In their book *Preaching to Every Pew: Cross-Cultural Strategies*, James R. Nieman and Thomas G. Rogers point out that when St. Augustine wrote about preaching, he, like the herald preachers, focused on the task of biblical interpretation and "spent most of his energy showing how to read a book rather than how to appeal to crowds."[22] But Augustine also knew that the proper way to interpret Scripture was according to the central principle of love. "Whoever, therefore, supposes, to understand the divine scriptures . . . so that it does not build up the double love of God and of the neighbor does not understand it at all."[23] Good preaching, then, is preaching that leads to love of God, but also to the love of neighbor, and, for the preacher, the congregation is full of very specific and diverse neighbors. As Nieman and Rogers point out, increasing the love of neighbor in the multicultural North African congregation to which Augustine preached was no easy task:

> Preaching truly served Christ to the degree that it evoked love between Donatists and Catholics, patricians and slaves, Italians and Punics, and all the other culturally diverse neighbors in Hippo. Anything else would be a misuse of scripture, because anything else would lead away from God.[24]

One observer, Heinz Zahrnt, commented that, although Barth's idea of the preacher as herald invigorated the pulpit, his lack of attention to context in preaching ended up damaging preaching in his day: "On the one hand, without [Barth's theology] present-day preaching would not be so pure, so biblical, and so concerned with central issues, but on the other hand, it would also not be so alarmingly correct, boringly precise, and remote from the world." And again: "Not sufficient account is taken, in this theology of the word, of the fact that the situation to which the word of God has to speak possesses theological relevance, and that, as Martin Buber once expressed it, 'situations have a word to add as well.' "[25]

The image of the herald, then, can take us far, but it cannot finally take us home. In many ways, a thoroughgoing theology of the preacher as a pure herald was always something of an exaggeration, a corrective to preaching that had turned away from the Scripture and accommodated itself to cultural norms. Even Barth himself, when he actually preached, was a master of rhetoric and was vitally aware of the ways in which the context of his preaching and the needs of his hearers shaped the development of his sermons. Indeed, when he gave informal and practical advice on sermon construction, the herald metaphor tended to diminish, and a much more dialogical process emerged:

> One should . . . make every effort to ensure that one's sermon
> is not simply a monologue, magnificent perhaps, but not neces-
> sarily helpful to the congregation. Those to whom he is going to
> speak must constantly be present in the mind of the preacher
> while he is preparing his sermon. What he knows about them
> will suggest unexpected ideas and associations which *will* be
> with him as he studies his text and will provide the element
> of actuality, the application of his text to the contemporary
> situation.[26]

Most of the excesses of the herald image cannot, in fact, be attrib-
uted to Barth but rather to his overzealous disciples in the homiletical
field. But even the most enthusiastic advocates of the herald image
would acknowledge that proclaiming the word is not all there is to
preaching. "Faith comes through hearing," Paul said, and sermons
are ultimately to be heard and, as Barth said, to be "helpful to the
congregation."

However, if the aim of being helpful to the congregation becomes
the main goal of preaching and is allowed to govern the practice of
preaching, we have moved out of the world of the herald and into
another world and another ruling metaphor. It is to this other world
and image that we now turn.

The Pastor

The second image employed to describe the identity of the preacher is
that of the pastor. If the herald image focused on the biblical word, on
being faithful to God's message, then the pastor image moves all the
way to the other end of the preaching spectrum and focuses on the listener, on the impact of the sermon on the hearer. Built into the pastor
image is the idea, as J. Randall Nichols puts it, that preaching "deliberately sets out to touch and involve people's personal concerns."[27]
Sometimes other terms have been used to describe this understanding of preaching: "dialogical," "therapeutic," or even more broadly,
"educational" or "conversational." In all these terms, the underlying
assumption about the purpose of preaching remains the same: preaching should intentionally seek a beneficial change in the hearers, should
help people make sense of their lives, and should strive to be a catalyst

for more responsible and ethical living on the part of those who hear. In short, the pastor aims the sermon toward the listener, expressly shaping the sermon so that something good will happen to and for the hearers.

For the pastoral preacher, then, being aware of and responding to the needs of the hearers (not necessarily their wants) takes on much more prominence than it does for the herald. The preacher discerns these needs, we may even say *diagnoses* these needs, and then strives to be of help by intervening with the gospel, by speaking a word that clarifies and restores. "Preaching," maintains James A. Wallace, "is a call to feed the people of God."[28] He goes on to say, "God's word . . . weighs in as nourishment that can build up the body of believers, feeding their deepest hunger. It has the capacity to respond to the existential condition captured in the words of a contemporary troubadour, Bruce Springsteen, who has reminded us: 'Everybody's got a hungry heart.'"[29] Clement Welsh both implicitly criticizes the herald image and elaborates on the pastoral image in *Preaching in a New Key*:

> The preacher, standing in his special place . . . asks the complex question: "What shall I do to help [the hearer] grow? How shall I enable him to perceive, to understand, and to act: to do the human thing with the aid of those who have been most human before him?" . . . [The preacher's] function is partly therapeutic, partly educational. He does not drop a "message" into a box ready made for it. He hopes to adjust, delicately, some elements of [the hearer's] receiving mechanism to help it function more adequately.[30]

We quickly discover that with the image of "pastor" comes a whole ground-shift in the understanding of the preacher's responsibility. The herald has one job, remaining faithful to the message, but the pastoral preacher must think about what parts of that message hearers need at this moment and what aspects of the gospel they can receive amid the pain and clutter of their lives. Pastoral preachers, then, are charged with the additional responsibility of developing a communicational strategy designed to provoke change in the hearers. In sum, the pastoral preacher must know more than a set of messages; the pastoral preacher must also know people and how they listen to messages. The pastor in the pulpit must always be asking, "What is it like to hear?"[31]

The image of the preacher as pastor is not new. G. Lee Ramsey Jr. has traced the concept of pastoral preaching from the New Testament forward, pointing to figures throughout the church's history such as Paul, Origen, Augustine, Gregory the Great, Richard Baxter, and Catherine Mumford Booth as key examples of those who gave attention to the pastoral dimensions of preaching.[32] But the image of the preacher as pastor gained powerful momentum in the last few decades as society has become increasingly attuned to psychology and the language of therapy.

The one preacher who perhaps did more than anyone else to popularize the pastoral approach to preaching in the American context was Harry Emerson Fosdick. An enormously popular preacher in the mid-twentieth century, Fosdick was known for his ability to speak to a congregation of hundreds but to enable each hearer to feel that he or she was being addressed personally. People flocked to hear his sermons, and many other clergy imitated his style. Fosdick attacked the dull, Bible-lesson style of preaching in vogue in his day, and countered with a concept of preaching that helped people resolve personal dilemmas. He said,

> Every sermon should have for its main business the solving of some problem—a vital, important problem, puzzling minds, burdening consciences, distracting lives—and any sermon which does tackle a real problem, throw even a little light on it, and help some individuals practically to find their way through it cannot be altogether uninteresting.[33]

Edmund Linn, whose book on Fosdick's method is titled *Preaching as Counseling*, describes Fosdick's aim as follows:

> The supreme purpose of a sermon, [Fosdick] decided, is to create in the listener no less than the thing which is being spoken. A sermon on joy must rise above a mere dissertation on the subject of joy by producing a congregation which goes out with deeper joy than it had before. . . . The preacher's task is to create in the listener whatever he is preaching about.[34]

Historian Brooks Holifield indicates that Fosdick, perhaps more than any other person of his generation, "persuaded a large segment of the liberal Protestant clergy to refashion the sermon in the image of the counseling session. . . . Under his tutelage a generation of ministers constructed topical sermons on the mastery of depression, the conquest of fear, the overcoming of anxiety, and the joys of self-realization."[35]

We can clearly see here a 180-degree turn away from the understanding of pulpit communication that we found in the herald image. The herald disdains communicational concerns and strategies for changing the hearers; the pastor specializes in them. The herald starts with the Bible as source; the pastor starts with the human dilemma as experienced by the hearer and turns to the Bible as resource. For the pastor, the primary question is not "What shall I say?" but "What do I want to happen?"

Let us explore in more detail some of the implications of the pastor metaphor for the nature and practice of preaching:

1. If the herald preacher views the message as the most important element of preaching, for the pastoral preacher the crucial dimension of preaching is an event, something that happens inside the hearer. Whether this event is described using psychodynamic, ethical, or evangelistic language—in other words, whether the hearers get healed, get morally improved, or get saved—the sine qua non of pastoral preaching is that the hearers are different and better people at the end of the sermon than they were at the beginning.

2. If the herald image minimizes the personality of the preacher, the pastor image throws a spotlight on it. The preacher's personality, character, experience, and relationship to the hearers are crucial dimensions of the pastoral and therapeutic process. As a healer, counselor, and caretaker, the pastor must be seen by the hearers as competent, authoritative, compassionate, and trustworthy. Homiletical books that develop the pastoral theme, such as Gary D. Stratman's *Pastoral Preaching*,[36] typically spend much time and space discussing the personal virtues (e.g., sensitivity, vulnerability, empathy) and professional skills (e.g., diagnostic insight, ability to listen) required of the preacher. In other words, the pastor must be a certain kind of person in order to establish the sorts of relationships with hearers necessary to do the therapeutic pastoral task.

3. The pastoral image also carries with it a specific angle of vision regarding biblical interpretation. Pastoral preachers see sermons as healing words addressed to concrete situations of human need. Therefore, when pastoral preachers turn to the Scripture, they tend to focus on those aspects of texts that involve personal issues and healing possibilities. In the Bible, real people laugh, cry, steal, praise, lie, discover, wonder, repent, rebel, come to faith, commit adultery, and strive in hundreds of very particular ways to figure out who they are and what they are called to do in the light of God's claim on their lives. In short, the Bible describes people trying by the grace of God to be human, and the pastoral preacher views it as a resource for contemporary people attempting to do the same. "The human conflicts and dilemmas one encounters in the Bible and in the tradition of the church," states Nichols, "are already 'ours' in the sense that they are givens in the created order and human situation.[37]

A major strength, therefore, of the pastor image comes from the attention it gives to the healing power of the gospel and to the inner dynamics of the listeners. The pastor image carries a keen and immediate sense of the gospel as good news for us. Something *happens* in pastoral preaching; the needs, hungers, and torn seams in the hearers' experience are not irrelevant, nor are they simply distractions to the preaching of the gospel. They are, instead, the very places where the grace of God may be discovered.

Another strength of the pastoral image is that, in ways not open to the herald, it makes room for the preacher to think about sermons in practical terms. Pastoral preachers are invited, even compelled, to be concerned about communication, to experiment with language and structure, to analyze the specific personal and social contexts of the congregation, and to explore different approaches, styles, and tactics in order to make their sermons better at reaching hearers and speaking to their needs. Because pastoral preaching is measured by what happens in the lives of the listeners, boredom becomes a homiletical deadly sin. Pastoral preachers are not content with sermons that do not engage and enliven the hearers; they are constantly striving to preach the gospel in such a way that the hearers say, "This is good news for *me* . . . for us!"

There are, however, some weaknesses in the pastor image as well. To think of the preacher as pastor almost inevitably views the hearers as a collection of discrete individuals who have personal problems and needs rather than as a congregation, as a church, as a community with a mission. The public, corporate, and systemic dimensions of the gospel are often downplayed in favor of more personalistic themes. Pastoral preaching can end up downsizing the gospel, giving aid to the narcissistic notion that the purpose of the Christian faith is to make us happy and comfortable, reinforcing selfishness and undermining the call of the gospel to move out of ourselves and toward others in service. When preachers proclaim self-help nostrums or snare listeners with promises of the so-called "prosperity gospel," they are nothing more than pastoral preachers gone to seed. As G. Lee Ramsey Jr. notes, "[S]ermons that consistently counsel individuals over the hardships of life fragment Christian community and may lead to religious consumerism. If the sermon does not speak to 'my' needs, what is the use of listening?"[38]

Moreover, pastorally oriented sermons tend to focus upon situations in human life where people are hurting and need help. What can be forgotten in all this is that people bring their strengths as well as their weaknesses to church. To use the popular phrase, a church is "a hospital for sinners," but that is not all it is. A church is also a community of faith where people come to offer their commitment, energy, and intelligence for the mission of Jesus Christ. The gospel beckons, "Come to me all you that are weary and carrying heavy burdens," but it also says that disciples of Jesus are called to "take up their cross and follow me." Pastoral preaching, to be sure, is not by definition compelled to ignore people's strengths, but as a matter of practice it usually does. As Joseph Sittler stated:

> It has recently been remarked that whereas we have a gospel for the alienated, the hurt, the depressed, the defeated, we have not a gospel for the well, the effective, the joyous, busy, engaged [people] of this world. And while, to be sure, a gospel that has no word to desolation is no gospel at all, it is more and more widely true that a gospel whose scope does not address [people] in [their] joyous, creative, constructive, and effectual operations is unchallenging because uninteresting.[39]

A related difficulty with the pastor image is its tendency toward utilitarianism and an overworked notion of relevance. Because the pastoral preacher desires to speak to the immediate felt needs of the hearers, the gospel may end up being reduced to what seems useful and what "works" in the present moment. Yes, the gospel speaks to the situation at hand, but the gospel is also larger than the questions, issues, and needs contained in any particular moment. The gospel has a past tense and a future tense, not just a present tense, and preaching must do more than help people cope successfully with the challenges of the here and now. Preaching refreshes the memory of the people of God and announces the promise of God's future. Preaching insists that the Christian community not curl up on the pew to rest, but continue on the journey of discipleship. The pastoral preacher's query, "How can I help people with the problems of this day?" is a powerful and important question, but sometimes it may simply be too small.

This is an important theological point for preaching. Whenever preaching spends all of its time solving problems, the inevitable conclusion is that the Christian faith is a completed set of answers to life's dilemmas. All that is left to do is to apply it to our lives. The truth, however, is that the Christian faith is not yet finished, and the promised victory of God is not yet fully present or realized. Some tragic human suffering is for the time being unintelligible and meaningless to us. Some conflicts are for the moment beyond resolution. Some illnesses have no available cure, some problems contain no ready answer. There are, to be sure, places in our experience where healing does take place, where the dividing walls of hostility are broken down, where justice emerges out of oppression, but these are "signs and wonders" pointing toward the as-yet-to-be-realized triumph of God. The faithful preacher cannot always speak a pastoral word that makes life healthier and more manageable but may only declare the trustworthiness of Christ, celebrate the signs and wonders in the present, and point to the future, which belongs to God.

Ironically, the pastor image of the preacher, which is intended to focus on the hearers and their needs, may well end up overemphasizing the preacher by placing the preacher in the powerful position of healer and therapist. If, as Clement Welsh suggests, the pastoral preacher is supposed to stand in a special place and ask, "What shall

I do to help the hearer grow?" this assumes that the preacher is in a position of superiority and knows what is best for the hearers.

Recently, several homileticians, quite alarmed about any view of the preacher as elevated above the congregation (which they smoke out not only in the prevailing pastoral image of the preacher but in almost all traditional models of preaching) have proposed what they call the "roundtable pulpit," an idea that starts with the pastoral emphasis upon the hearers and moves it to its logical conclusion. For example, in his book *The Round-Table Pulpit*, John S. McClure decries what he calls (adapting a phrase from Bernard Swain) "sovereign preaching," namely, preaching that places the preacher hierarchically above the listeners, that puts the hearers in a position of submission and dependence, and that encourages listeners to receive obediently the word proclaimed by the preacher.[40] Such preaching, McClure claims, is "potentially, if not inherently authoritarian" and fails adequately to express "the servant charisma, hospitality, and mutuality that are fundamental to an empowering Christian ministry."[41]

As a remedy to the sovereign style, McClure advocates what he calls "collaborative preaching" that calls on the preacher to host a "sermon roundtable," a group of members of the congregation who serve as a sermon brainstorming group thrashing out the issues and themes of upcoming sermons. These roundtable conversations are communal events in which there are no privileged voices, and the resultant sermons "must both describe and imitate in the pulpit the collaborating process of sermon brainstorming that took place during the sermon roundtable."[42]

Similarly, but perhaps more radically, Lucy Rose suggests a version of roundtable preaching that she calls "conversational preaching," in which virtually all distinctions between preacher and hearer have been erased. She writes:

> In conversational preaching, the preacher and the congregation are colleagues, exploring together the mystery of the Word for their own lives, as well as the life of the congregation, the larger church, and the world. The preacher and the congregation gather symbolically at a round table without head or foot, where labels like clergy and laity disappear and where believing or wanting to believe is all that matters. Here the preacher is

neither the expert in scriptural interpretation nor the answer-person in matters of faith. Here the preacher is simply the one responsible for putting the text and the sermon into the midst of the community.[43]

Approaches such as those proposed by McClure and Rose are helpful to the extent that they remind us, as did Moltmann, that the preacher comes from the congregation, from the gathered assembly, to preach. This means that McClure and Rose are right to insist, as a magnification of the pastor image, that preaching emerge from an ongoing congregational conversation, and are right to remind preachers that they speak from within the church and not from on high. But we must be cautious not to let collaborative and peership models of preaching (which are by no means a new idea in homiletical thought) obscure Moltmann's other claim, namely, that the church finally "does not want to listen to itself and project its own image of itself; it wants to hear Christ's voice." The preacher will be wise to sit at the roundtable for a long time, hearing the voices, concerns, and opinions of the congregation.

But if the preacher, even the pastor, is set apart, called to be the one who must get up from the roundtable, stand in the preaching spot, and prayerfully say, "Let the words of my mouth be acceptable in thy sight, O God. Hear now the word of God," then to see this action as inherently authoritarian or as a de facto abuse of power is to confuse collaboration with charisma, illegitimate hierarchical power with a legitimate division of labor in the church, the practice of preaching with other forms of testimony, and the servant of the Word with the power of the Word.[44]

A final problem with the pastoral image is that it runs the risk of reducing theology to anthropology by presenting the gospel merely as a resource for human emotional growth. If the herald image created a one-directional model of preaching, from the Bible nonstop to the hearers, the pastoral image threatens simply to reverse the flow by moving from the experience of the hearer toward the gospel, with a resulting constriction of the gospel agenda. The gospel is true even when we are unable or unwilling to believe it, trust it, and live it out in our experience, and the adequacy of preaching cannot be fully measured by how much immediate change it effects in the hearers.

All this calls into question the way in which pastoral preaching typically uses the Bible. The critical question is whether preachers are supposed to help people "find their stories in the Bible" or are supposed to call the hearers, as George Lindbeck has suggested, to "make the story of the Bible their story."[45] This is a helpful distinction (even if it is possibly too sharply stated) because it highlights two quite different ways of connecting the Bible and contemporary human life. The pastoral preacher, as we have noted, assumes that the people in the pages of the Bible were, in important ways, much like the people now in the pews. We can begin, then, with some circumstance in contemporary life, explore it at some depth, and go to the Bible to see what insight is available to help us. What we understand about life thus becomes the key used to unlock the claims of Scripture.

The second approach moves down the same highway, but in precisely the opposite direction. In this view, the people in the Bible may be seen as people like ourselves, but what makes them critically different is that their lives became absorbed into the narration of God's action in the world. They have become, in other words, characters in a larger story that is not primarily about them but about God. If this is so, we do not go to the Scripture to gain more information about life as we know it, but rather to have our fundamental understandings of life altered. The task of preaching is not to set out some reality in life and then to go to the Bible to find extra wisdom. It is instead to tell the story of the Bible so clearly that it calls into question and ultimately redefines what we think we know of reality and what we call wisdom in the first place. The Bible becomes the key to unlock the true nature of life, not vice versa. "It is the text, so to speak," writes Lindbeck, "which absorbs the world, rather than the world the text."[46]

Telling the story of the Bible clearly requires, of course, narrative skills and poetic gifts, and the exercise of these talents governs the third major image of preaching, the storyteller/poet, to which we now turn.

The Storyteller/Poet

This image differs from the previous two in that it tells us *who* the preacher is by describing the *literary and artistic character* of the preacher's sermons: preaching marked by storytelling and poetically expressive language. Several times in the history of the church, storytelling and artful expression have emerged as important emphases in homiletics, but the storyteller/poet image of the preacher gained new prominence in recent years as homileticians became fascinated with theories of poetics, narrative, and the communicational potential of stories. If the "herald" image emphasizes the sermon's fidelity, and the "pastor" image emphasizes its therapeutic value, then the "storyteller/ poet" image emphasizes the rhetorical beauty and artfulness of the sermon. As Jana Childers says of the recent history of preaching in her book *Performing the Word: Preaching as Theatre,*

> [P]reaching had been going through its own changes. The kerygmatic preaching of the sixties gave way in the seventies to an interest in inductive preaching. The eighties brought an emphasis on narrative and imagination. By the nineties few people were shocked when preaching was referred to as an art.[47]

In recent years, the interest in storytelling in sermons has widened to include the use of poetic and imaginative language more broadly. Biblical scholar and homiletician Elizabeth Achtemeier emphasizes the linguistic skills of the preacher when she maintains that "in the art of preaching . . . language is framed in such a way that the congregation is allowed to enter into a new experience."[48] Nora Tubbs Tisdale has employed the nice phrase "folk art" to describe preaching. "The preacher," she says, "is . . . a 'folk artist'—searching for the expression of local theology through symbols, forms, and movements that are capable of capturing and transforming the imaginations of a particular local community of faith."[49]

Another homiletician who has developed the storyteller/poet image is Charles L. Rice, who argues in his *The Embodied Word: Preaching as Art and Liturgy* that the gifts of the poet and the artist are not ornamental but essential to preaching and liturgy:

> Successfully bringing art to the pulpit is not simply a matter of shaping an artistic idiom to express theology that we could just as well state in clear propositions, as if theology were not itself dependent upon imagination. Nor is it a matter of more

thoroughly scrutinizing art in order to find better sermon illustrations, although the pulpit seems always short at that point. Rather, it is the genuine affinity between the church at worship and the arts that makes for the effective appropriation of specific works of art to liturgy and sermon. What the church does on Sunday morning is, at its best, artful, and once we see it as such the doors swing wide to drama, literature, and the visual arts.[50]

Rice goes on to say that of all the poetic and artistic expressions needed in worship and preaching, "Storytelling is a particularly important form of art."[51] Indeed, Rice was one of the authors of *Preaching the Story*, a popular preaching textbook published in 1980 that focused on preaching as storytelling:

> We are trying to find that formative image that could both articulate what preaching is and free people to do it. Is there an image adequate to shape the form, content, and style of preaching? If we had to say, in a word or two, or in a picture, what preaching is and how it is done well, what would that phrase or picture be? . . . Let us consider the storyteller. . . . If we were pressed to say what Christian faith and life are, we could hardly do better than *hearing, telling, and living a story*. And if asked for a short definition of preaching, could we do better than *shared story*? . . . Perhaps the image of storyteller can move us toward . . . a holistic theory of preaching.[52]

Can we do better at defining preaching, these authors ask, than "shared story"? Herald preachers and pastoral preachers might well respond, "Yes, we certainly can!" For the herald, the picture of a preacher gathering people around for a time of story sharing would be far too soft, too immanent, too focused on the preacher's skill, too anthropologically oriented, too conversational. As a sociologist of religion Peter Berger once said, "Ages of faith are not marked by dialogue, but by proclamation."[53] Pastoral preachers would perhaps find a bit more value in the storytelling image, but even for them a sermon dominated by stories would probably lack the surgically sharp purposiveness usually associated with pastoral intervention.

Proponents of this image, however, would counter that the story-teller/poet preacher actually blends the best traits of both the herald and the pastor without bringing along their most serious faults. To begin with, the storyteller/poet can be just as focused on the Bible as is the herald. It is not an arbitrary choice for the storyteller/poet to speak in narratives and imaginative language. These are the language forms of the Bible and the essential language forms of the Christian faith itself. The gospel itself is basically a narrative, often told in poetic language and with evocative images, and one must finally respond to the question "What is the Christian faith?" by telling a story. "I believe in God," we say. Which God? "Well, the one who made heaven and earth, the God we meet in Jesus Christ, who was born of the Virgin Mary, suffered under Pontius Pilate . . . ," and off we go narrating the essential story of the faith.

The Bible, when taken as a whole, can also be described as a story, "a vast, loosely structured, non-fiction novel."[54] But what about those parts of the Bible that are clearly not narrative—epistles, proverbs, poems, doctrinal argumentation, and the like? Not only do these biblical genres employ imaginative language and poetic constructions; these materials also fit, the argument goes, into the larger and primary narrative framework of the Bible. In fact, the nonnarrative material grows out of the larger biblical narrative and makes little sense apart from the overarching biblical story that frames it. When Paul, for instance, is discussing the question of whether Christians should be free to eat meat previously used in pagan religious ceremonies (1 Cor. 8), he does not tell stories to score his points, but the narrative of the life of Jesus stands in the background of his argument. His case grows out of this story, appeals to this story, and is unintelligible apart from the narrative framework of the story of Jesus.

Even biblical proverbs, which seem to be utterly nonnarrative, are connected to stories. As biblical scholar William Beardslee has claimed,

> it is somewhat misleading to speak of the proverb as a statement of general truth. It is a statement about a particular kind of occurrence or situation, an orderly tract of experience which can be repeated. In this sense, though it is not a narrative, the proverb implies a story, something that happens, that moves through a sequence in a way which can be known.[55]

So advocates of the storyteller/poet image would say that they pay just as much attention to the Scripture as the herald preachers do— perhaps even more since they take the specific literary character of the Bible into account. They would also claim to be at least as alert to the hearers' needs as the pastoral preachers because they recognize the kind of communication listeners want and need. What do listeners want and need in sermons? Stories and images. Not only do we like stories; we live our lives out of them. We remember in stories, dream in stories, shape our values through stories. And we see the world through evocative images. Long after the rest of a sermon is forgotten, many hearers can still recall the stories told and remember the images. It is no accident that it is said of Jesus that "he did not speak to them except in parables," a story built on a metaphor (Mark 4:34). "Given the power of narration," writes David Buttrick, "is it surprising that through most of the Christian centuries preaching has been discursive, [that is to say] best described as storytelling?"[56]

So a persuasive case can be made for the preacher as a storyteller/ poet, but what, exactly, do homileticians mean when they call for this image to govern preaching? Many things, it seems:

Some advocates of the storyteller/poet image, for example, are simply after a more critical and effective use of what has been traditionally called sermon "illustrations." Preachers should tell stories and employ metaphors and images in their sermons about human experience, not merely to make their sermons clearer or more interesting but also because such stories show how the Christian faith can be embodied in the actual circumstances of life. The gospel, they argue, is not a set of abstract concepts or principles to which we give assent but a total way of being in the world, a way that only narrative can embrace.

If the preacher, for example, simply announces, "We can trust the goodness of God even in the midst of tragedy," the hearers may understand this idea—indeed, they may even believe it—but it may remain nonetheless remote from their experience. If, on the other hand, the preacher relates the story of a family that struggled with the meaning of God's love in the midst of the death of a child, the hearers participate vicariously in that struggle and have new possibilities opened up for their own lives.

Other advocates of this image move beyond the notion of stories and illustrations in sermons to the more expansive concept of shaping the whole sermon in a storylike way. Sermons are not just lists of ideas placed one after the other like beads on a string. They are shaped according to some logical pattern. The typical speech is arranged around a major idea, or thesis, with subpoints serving this main thought—one, two, three, and so on. What if it is true, though, that people listen and learn most deeply not when the ideas come at them in one-two-three fashion but when the ideas flow along like the episodes of a narrative? Sermons, then, would be most powerful when shaped according to such patterns. This is, in fact, the claim of some homileticians. Sermons, they argue, may or may not contain actual stories, but they should be designed to move in the listeners' consciousness like stories. Sermons should have plots rather than points, and they should flow along according to the logic of narrative rather than the more linear logic of a philosophical argument.[57]

Still others have been attracted to the "open-endedness" of stories, the fact that the best stories, the ones most faithful to real experience, have enough ambiguity built into them to force the hearer to make a decision about the story's meaning and application. The idea is that a story listener cannot be passive but must participate with the narrator in creating the world of the story. This emphasis upon the activity and responsibility of the listener is clearly quite appealing, since it undergirds a dynamic and interactive understanding of Christian preaching. What these advocates of storytelling preaching are after is a sermon that is open-ended: that is to say, not quite finished. The listeners have to roll up their sleeves and get involved in the project of making meaning in the sermon.

Some of the storyteller/poet advocates have been less interested in story per se and more interested in poetic, imaginative experiences through language. Barbara Brown Taylor describes the process of creating a sermon as follows:

> Once I have done all my homework and have a decent idea what the text means, I give it a rest. Understanding is not enough. I do not want to pass on knowledge from the pulpit; I want to take part in an experience of God's living word, and that calls for a different kind of research. It is time to tuck the text into the pocket of my heart and walk around with it inside of me. It is time to turn its words and images loose on the events of my

everyday life and see how they mix. It is time to daydream, whittle, whistle, pray. This is the gestation period of a sermon, and it cannot be rushed. It is a time of patient and impatient waiting for the stirring of the Holy Spirit, that bright bird upon whose brooding the sermon depends. Over and over again I check the nest of my notes and outlines, searching through them for some sign of life. I scan the text one more time and all of a sudden there is an egg in plain view, something where there had been nothing just a moment before, and the sermon is born.

. . . It is as hard for a preacher to say how this is done as it is for a painter to say how a tree takes shape on a canvas. Do the leaves come first or the branches? What combination of yellow and blue makes such a bright green? How do you make it look so real? All the parts of preaching can be taught: exegesis, language, metaphor, development, delivery. What is hard to teach is how to put them all together, so that what is true is also beautiful, and evocative, and alive.[58]

Finally, there are a few homileticians who are interested in narrative not as an artistic expression of the preacher but as an essential biblical and theological category. As Charles L. Campbell says,

[N]arrative is important neither because it provides a "homiletical plot" for sermons nor because preaching should consist of telling stories. Rather, narrative is important because it is the vehicle through which the gospels render the identity of Jesus of Nazareth who has been raised from the dead and seeks today to form a people who follow his way. . . . The story of Jesus, not the particulars of human experience, is the fundamental reality and starting point. . . . Faithful preaching thus enacts on behalf of the entire church an interpretive performance of the story of Jesus.[59]

In some ways Campbell is arguing more for something like the herald image of the preacher than the storyteller/poet, but Campbell's herald is one who has found that the biblical message comes as a narrative.

So, people mean different things by the picture of the preacher as a storyteller/poet, and they present varied reasons in defense of this image, but there are commonalities as well in these positions. We can spell these out more clearly by examining some additional implications of the storyteller image for preaching.

1. Like the herald, the storyteller/poet metaphor stresses the message of preaching but with an important difference. The herald seeks to discover the content of the gospel. The storyteller/poet does so as well but refuses to divorce that content from the rhetorical forms in which it is found. The storytelling image, as we have seen, grows out of a conviction that the fundamental literary form of the gospel is narrative. "I am convinced," claims Stanley Hauerwas, "that the most appropriate image . . . for characterizing scripture, for the use of the church as well as morally, is that of a narrative or a story."[60]

2. For the storyteller/poet, then, narrative is not merely *one* way to proclaim the gospel, it is the *normative* way. The gospel is essentially narrative in shape and, consequently, so is the expression of the church's faith in that gospel. As theologian H. Richard Niebuhr stated, "The church's compulsion [to confess its faith] arises out of its need—since it is a living church—to say truly what it stands for and out of its inability to do so otherwise than by telling the story of its life."[61]

3. Like the pastor, the storyteller/poet is deeply concerned about communication and the listening process. The pastor wants to know, "What is it like to hear?" The storyteller/poet wants to know, "What is the *process* of hearing?" and is persuaded that the dynamics of listening are narrative-like or fueled by poetic language to some degree. Stories that are well told both enable and demand a high level of involvement on the part of those who hear them. Stories "create a world" and invite the listeners to enter into that world and participate in it. In a sense, the storytelling image establishes a middle ground and a meeting ground between the concerns of the herald and the pastor, since the storyteller can both honor the integrity of the gospel message and take full cognizance of the life situation of the hearer. Preaching does not move unidirectionally but from both the gospel and the context toward the center. Those who advocate this image speak of the goal of preaching as creating, in

the sermon, an intersection between the gospel story (or God's story) and the hearer's story.

4. The storyteller/poet image places an emphasis upon the person of the preacher, not as pastoral expert but as one skilled in the narrative arts. Good preaching demands good storytelling. Moreover, while the herald would be reluctant to employ a personal anecdote in a sermon, the storyteller is convinced that the preacher's own life story is an indispensable resource for preaching. The preacher does not stand outside the community of hearers but in the middle of it—indeed, as a member of it. The story of the preacher's own experience of the gospel (in both positive and negative ways) can be participated in by the hearers and, to some degree, be recognized as like their own experiences.

5. The storyteller/poet image, like that of the pastor, places a premium upon the experiential dimensions of the faith. The goal of the storyteller/poet is for something eventful to happen to the hearer in a sermon, and the storyteller/poet seeks to find just the right language to stimulate the hearer's imagination. The pastor hopes for healing and transformation, but the storyteller has an even broader range of experiential goals. The listeners may see life and themselves in a new way, identify with a character in a biblical story, feel the presence of God, or understand more fully the intersection between faith and routine experience.

The storyteller/poet image thus possesses many strengths. It balances the concern for the objective truth of the gospel with a passion for religious experience. By weaving the stories of human experience into the biblical narrative, and by naming the theological dimension of those experiences, the storyteller/poet announces, "Today this Scripture has been fulfilled in your hearing." In addition, the storyteller/poet image is attentive to the rhetorical craft of preaching without forcing the gospel into an alien rhetorical mold. The concern for narrative and picturesque speech is not developed apart from the character of the gospel but rather on the basis of the gospel's own linguistic shape.

The capacity of narrative and metaphor to create a common world of experience allows the storyteller/poet to go a long way toward overcoming the dichotomy between individual and community in preaching. In listening to stories and participating in images we are willing, to an extent, to suspend our own concerns in favor of the experience we are having together. Moreover, there is a vigorous view of the church implied by the storyteller/poet image. The church is not only gathered by the story; it participates actively in the telling and finishing of the story. Finally, the effective storyteller/poet creates sermons that are popular in the best sense of that word. Good stories demand our attention, receive our interest, generate our involvement, and remain in our active memories.

As strong as this storytelling image is, though, it is not without weaknesses.

1. First of all, it tends to underplay the nonnarrative dimensions of Scripture and to narrow to a single method the communicational range of preaching. Despite the value of claiming that the gospel is essentially narrative and that every scriptural text fits somehow into the overarching biblical story, the fact of the matter is that there are nonnarrative texts, and for good reason. The biblical writers do not always tell stories, because the communication of some aspects of the faith is best done in a poetic or didactic or proverbial voice and not always through narrative. Even if the basic narrative shape of the gospel is always standing in the background, there comes a time when preaching must speak in another voice, drawing out concepts, singing songs, speaking of the logical character of belief, talking about practical ethics, and so on. These tasks of preaching may rest upon a narrative base, but a narrative form is not necessarily the best means to accomplish them.

2. The same warning sounded about the experiential dimension of the pastoral image applies to the storyteller/poet as well. There is a deep theological danger in measuring preaching by its capacity to generate religious experience. Theologian Hendrikus Berkhof has reminded us that, in the Old Testament, one of the reasons that Israel was continually abandoning Yahweh for Baal was that Baal was always more available, more visible, providing blessings that were more predictable.[62] One could always count on Baal for a religious experience, but not so Yahweh. Yahweh tended, on many occasions, to have a hidden face, to be absent in those times when the people yearned for a more readily available God. In sum, God does not always move us when we desire to be moved, and everything that moves us deeply is not God.

The herald image places an emphasis upon the biblical message or, to use the language of narrative, upon "God's story" as disclosed in Scripture. The storytelling preacher, on the other hand, recounts both

God's story and our stories, seeking to weave our stories, the narratives of contemporary life, into the framework of God's story. The result can be a powerful interplay between the Bible and life, but we must admit that it can also produce simply a confusion of stories. People have many ways of narrating the story of their lives. They can tell the "Christian story" of their lives, but they can also relate their family story, their national story, their racial story, their vocational story, the story of their psychosocial growth, and so on. Ideally, the Christian story serves as the normative center of this narrative universe, critically informing all lesser stories. The danger, of course, is that this process gets reversed, and the lesser story erodes or replaces the gospel story.

3. A third danger of the storyteller/poet image is that an attempt to produce an artful sermon can end up crafting a sermon that is merely "arty." When the legendary theologian Reinhold Niebuhr was a young pastor in the Hell's Kitchen section of New York City, he wrote in his journal, "I swear that I will never aspire to be a preacher of pretty sermons. I'll keep them rough just to escape the temptation of degenerating into being an elocutionist."[63] What Niebuhr meant by "pretty sermons" were sermons that are finally distracting because they draw more attention to their own linguistic beauty than to the gospel. A woman once complained, about many of the sermons she heard, that they sounded like "National Public Radio essays," lovely and interesting, but without urgency or claim.

Herald, pastor, storyteller/poet—these master images depict the ways in which the preacher has been described in the recent literature of homiletics. As you have read about them, you may have been comparing and contrasting these pictures with your own understanding of preaching, finding aspects of each to admire and forming your own criticisms of them. Most of us, I suspect, resist being tagged with any of these three labels, preferring to see ourselves as a creative blend of them all. We can imagine circumstances in which it would be better to be a herald than a pastor or a storyteller/poet, but we can probably also think of situations when the opposite would be so.

I want to suggest yet another image for the preacher. I do this not simply to add one more figure to an already crowded landscape, but because I believe this additional image is more suited than any of the others to disclose the true character of Christian preaching. Indeed, this image gathers up the virtues of the others and holds their strongest traits in creative tension. Also, this picture of the preacher, and the implications for preaching it contains, expresses the convictions about preaching that will guide our discussion throughout the remainder of this book. I refer to the image of the Christian preacher as witness.

Preaching as Bearing Witness

Seeing the preacher as a witness is not a new idea. It has deep roots in the Bible, appearing in such passages as Acts 20:24, where Paul is reported to have said, "But I do not count my life of any value to myself, if only I may finish my course and the ministry that I received from the Lord Jesus, to testify [that is, to bear witness] to the good news of God's grace." The New Testament concept of witness grows out of Old Testament precedents. Consider the following passage from Isaiah 43:8–13 (emphasis added):

> Bring forth the people who are blind, yet have eyes, who are deaf, yet have ears! Let all the nations gather together, and let the peoples assemble. Who among them declared this, and fore-told to us the former things? Let them bring their witnesses to justify them, and let them hear and say, "It is true." **You are my witnesses, says the LORD, and my servant whom I have chosen, so that you may know and believe me and under-stand that I am he.** Before me no god was formed, nor shall there be any after me. I, I am the LORD, and besides me there is no savior. I declared and saved and proclaimed, when there was no strange god among you; and you are my witnesses, says the LORD. I am God, and also henceforth I am He; there is no one who can deliver from my hand; I work and who can hinder it?

Commenting on this passage in an important essay, Paul Ricoeur identified four claims about the witness made by this text:[64]

1. The witness is not a volunteer, not just anyone who comes for-ward to give testimony, but only the one who is *sent* to testify.
2. The testimony of the witness is not about the global meaning of human experience but about God's claim upon life. It is Yahweh who is witnessed to in the testimony.

3. The purpose of the testimony is proclamation to all peoples. It is on behalf of the people, for their belief and understanding, that the testimony is made.
4. The testimony is not merely one of words but rather demands a total engagement of speech and action. The whole life of the witness is bound up in the testimony.

One can quickly see the relationship between preaching and the idea of witness, and in this light it may seem curious that the witness image has not been more prominent in homiletical literature. There are reasons for this, however. To begin with, the terms "witnessing" and "giving a testimony" have often been associated with some of the more aggressive forms of evangelism. Homileticians have sniffed the odor of manipulation around these words and thus have stayed far away from them. As such, "witness" is a good word that has gotten into some trouble through no fault of its own.

More significantly, homileticians have not been greatly attracted to the witness image because it seems out of place. Witness is a legal term; a witness appears in the courtroom as part of a trial. An aura of law and judgment surrounds the witness idea, and this appears to be at odds with the grace and freedom associated with preaching the gospel. It is important to keep in mind, though, that the image implies that the preacher is the one bearing witness, not the lawmaker, the police officer, or the judge, and in that light it is precisely the law court origin of the witness metaphor that gives it power as an image for the preacher.

Consider what happens in a court trial. The trial is conducted in a public place because what happens is a public matter. A trial is designed to get at the truth, and the people have a vested interest in the truth. In order to get at the truth, a witness is brought to the stand to testify. Now this witness is in every way one of the people, but she is placed on the stand because of two credentials: the witness has seen something, and the witness is willing to tell the truth about it—the whole truth and nothing but the truth. In one sense, the personal characteristics of the witness do not matter. The court is interested in the truth and in justice, not in the witness per se. In another sense, however, the character of the witness is crucial. If the witness lies—bears false witness—the ability of the people to discover the truth will suffer a grievous blow. "False testimony," writes Ricoeur, "is a lie in the heart of the witness.

This perverse intention is so fatal to the exercise of justice and to the entire order of discourse that all codes of morality place it very high in the scale of vices."[65]

The court has access to the truth only through the witness. It seeks the truth, but it must look for it in testimony of the witness. The very life of the witness, then, is bound up into the testimony. The witness cannot claim to be removed, objectively pointing to the evidence. What the witness believes to be true is a part of the evidence, and when the truth told by the witness is despised by the people, the witness may suffer, or even be killed, as a result of the testimony. It is no coincidence that the New Testament word for witness is *martyr*.[66]

What happens to our understanding of preaching when this image of witness is taken as a guide?

1. The witness image emphasizes the authority of the preacher in a different way. The preacher as witness is not authoritative because of rank or power but rather because of what the preacher has seen and heard. When the preacher prepares a sermon by wrestling with a biblical text, the preacher is not merely gathering information about that text. The preacher is listening for a voice, looking for a presence, hoping for the claim of God to be encountered through the text. Until this happens, there is nothing for the preacher to say. When it happens, the preacher becomes a witness to what has been seen and heard through the Scripture, and the preacher's authority grows out of this seeing and hearing.

Does this mean that the preacher is authoritative because the preacher has more Christian experience than the people in the pews? No, of course not. There may well be many in the congregation whose faith is richer, more mature, and more tested than the preacher's. In addition, there will probably be people in the congregation who have more education or more common sense, who have a firmer grasp of human nature, or maybe even know more Bible and theology than does the preacher. To call the preacher an authority does not mean that the preacher is wiser than others. What it does mean is that the preacher is the one whom the congregation sends on their behalf, week after week, to the Scripture. The church knows that its life depends upon hearing the truth of God's promise and claim through the Scripture, and it has set the preacher apart for the crucial activity of going to the Scripture to listen for that truth. The authority of the preacher, then, is the authority of ordination, the authority of being identified by the faithful community as the one called to preach and the one who has been prayerfully set apart for this ministry, the authority that comes from being "sworn in" as a witness.

Accordingly, the church prepares and trains its ministers, including sending them to seminaries and other places of instruction, not because ministers are better or smarter than other Christians, but because the church needs workers equipped to help the church to know the truth and to live in its light. If the preacher is to be the one sent to listen for God's truth in the Bible, the preacher not only must be willing to listen to the Bible but also must know how to listen. If the preacher is to be sent on behalf of the congregation, the preacher must also know how to listen to *them.* These activities require a right spirit, but they also require special preparation. Seminary training equips one to be not a professor in the church but, rather, a trustworthy witness. An unreliable witness does not make the truth any less true, but the community's quest to encounter the truth is undeniably damaged by false or unreliable witnesses.

2. The witness image embodies a way of approaching the Bible. Witnesses testify to events, and the event to which the preacher testifies is the encounter between God and ourselves. This event is the same one proclaimed in Isaiah, "that you may know and believe me and understand that I am [God]." One of the essential ways that we come to "know" God is through the Scripture, not because the Bible speculates about the nature of God in a metaphysical sense but because the Bible is itself the faithful witness to the interactions of God with the whole creation. We come to know God as the central "character" in the story, as a "Person" in relationship with human beings, as One who creates, judges, saves, loves, destroys, builds, forgives, and renews. "The primary focus [of the Bible] is not on God's being in itself," claims Lindbeck, "for that is not what the text is about, but on how life is to be lived and reality construed in the light of God's character as an agent as this is depicted in the stories of Israel and of Jesus."[67]

We go to Scripture, then, not to glean a set of facts about God or the faith that can then be announced whenever and wherever, but to encounter a Presence, to hear God's voice speaking to us ever anew, calling us in the midst of the situations in which we find ourselves to be God's faithful people. The picture of the preacher sitting alone in the study, working with a biblical text in preparation for the sermon, is misleading. It is not the preacher who goes to the Scripture; it is the church that goes to the Scripture by means of the preacher. The preacher is a member of the community, set apart by them and sent to the Scripture to search, to study, and to listen obediently on their behalf.

So, the preacher goes to the Scripture, but not alone. The preacher goes on behalf of the faithful community and, in a sense, on behalf of the world. Their questions and needs are in the preacher's mind and heart. The preacher explores the Scripture, faithfully expecting to discover the truth of God's claim there and always willing to be surprised by it. Those who have sent the preacher have questions and concerns, and sometimes the text will speak directly to those questions. The text may, however, call those questions into question. The truth found there may resolve a problem, and then again it may deepen that problem. The truth found there may generate a religious experience, but it may also create the experience of God's absence. Whatever needs of church and world have been brought to the text by the preacher, when the claims of God through the Scripture are seen and heard, the preacher turns back toward those who wait—and tells the truth.

3. The witness image carries with it guidance about the rhetorical form of preaching. The witness is not called upon to testify in the abstract but to find just those words and patterns that can convey the event the witness has heard and seen. One can even say that the truth to which the witness testifies seeks its own verbal form, and the responsibility of the witness is to allow that form to emerge. Most often the witness is invited to "tell your story"; thus the prominence given to narrative in the storytelling image is also implied in the image of witness. On other occasions, though, the truth will demand another form. Preaching, in other words, will assume a variety of rhetorical styles, not as ornaments but as governed by the truth to which they correspond. The shape of the witness's sermon should fit the character of the testimony. As biblical scholar Sandra Schneiders says, "[I]n articulating the testimony, the witness must embody it in some literary genre. Most often this is narrative, but it might also be direct proclamation, aphorism, or saying, poetry, prayer, or doxology."[68]

4. The witness is not a neutral observer. The truth is larger than the witness's own experience of it, and the witness is always testifying to a gospel larger than the preacher's personal faith, but the witness

preacher has experienced it at some depth and is thereby involved in it. This is especially true of the New Testament concept of witness, in which witnessing takes on an acted as well as a verbal form. The witness often testifies to hard truths, unpopular truths, and sometimes at great risk. As Paul Ricoeur has commented, "This profession [of a witness] implies a total engagement not only of words but of acts, and, in the extreme, in the sacrifice of a life."[69]

The witness is also not a neutral observer in the sense that where one stands influences what one sees. The location of the witness, in other words, is critical, and the preacher as witness is one who stands in and with a particular community of faith, deeply involved in the concrete struggles of that community to find meaning, to seek justice, and to be faithful to the gospel. Whether the community of faith to which the witness belongs and from which the witness comes is urban or rural, black or Asian, rich or poor, powerless or powerful, these circumstances firmly shape the character of the preaching. We have recognized, through the work of liberation and feminist theologians among others, that a "disinterested" reading of the gospel is neither possible nor desirable. Effective preaching has an invested local flavor because the preacher as witness participates in the mission of a specific community of faith, goes to the Scripture on behalf of that community, and hears a particular word for them on this day and in this place.

5. The witness image also underscores the ecclesiastical and liturgical setting of preaching. Though it is not always apparent, the worship of the church is a dramatic enactment of a great and cosmic trial in which the justice of God is poised against all the powers that spoil creation and enslave human life. In this trial Christ is the one true and faithful witness. "For this I was born, and for this I have come into the world, to bear witness to the truth" (John 18:37). All human testimony is authentic only to the extent that it remains faithful to the witness of Christ. "You also are witnesses, because you have been with me from the beginning" (John 15:27).

"It is only with the day of the Lord," writes Richard Fenn, "that all accusation ends, and the trial is over." He goes on: "It is for that reason on the Lord's Day that the people of God celebrate a mock trial, in which the law is read, confession and testimony obtained, and the verdict once again given as it was once before all time."[70]

"I give thanks to my God always for you," wrote Paul to the Corinthians, speaking of the relationship between witness and the life of the Christian community, "because of the grace of God that has been given you in Christ Jesus, for in every way you have been enriched in him, in speech and knowledge of every kind—just as the testimony of Christ has been strengthened among you" (1 Cor. 1:4–5).

6. The witness image also embraces those preachers who have stood outside the official structures of authority to proclaim their experience of the gospel. In her study of early American women preachers, Anna Carter Florence found that many of these preachers did not claim to be preaching but instead to be offering "testimony."[71] This allowed them to avoid the criticism, or even the censure, involved in presuming to do what only authorized male clergy were permitted to do. But Carter-Florence goes on to say that this testimony, this witness, "was viewed by supporters and opponents alike as *preaching,* no matter what the women themselves called it." Because it happened outside the approved channels, though, it was "open to all believers," and "it was seen as something new and powerful and dangerous."[72]

Preaching and Worship

Christian preaching bears witness to Christ both in the church and through the church to the world. Preaching occurs in the context of the Christian community gathered for worship, but it also takes place "out there" in the world—on street corners, in prisons and hospitals, on campuses, and in public assemblies. Preaching in the church and preaching in the world are not fundamentally different kinds of preaching but different settings for the same activity of bearing witness to Christ. Preaching, as David Buttrick has observed, continues "the work of Christ who gathered a people to himself and, by death and resurrection, set them free for new life in the world."[73]

Preaching and the community of faith, then, are reciprocal realities. Those who hear and believe the witness to Christ in preaching are thus gathered into the community of faith that continues to tell, to teach, and to celebrate that witness. "The proclamation of the gospel," Moltmann maintains, "always belongs within a community, for every language lives in a community or creates one."[74] And it is this very community that continues to bear witness to Christ in and for the world through every aspect of its life, including preaching.

For most of us, the majority of our preaching will occur in the context of the community of faith at worship. This means, in part, that preaching becomes woven into the dramatic structure of the larger service of worship, which itself is a witness to the gospel. This has many practical implications, of course, regarding the relationship between the sermon and the other parts of worship. More basically, however, it indicates that preaching is not merely a deed performed by an individual preacher but rather the faithful action of the whole church.

2

The Biblical Witness in Preaching

During my first pastorate . . . one of the deacons would ask me the same question every Sunday morning. . . . "Reverend, is there any word from the Lord?" . . . The voice that people want to hear is not really the voice of the preacher. The voice that people really need to hear is not that of the preacher. The message the people have assembled to receive is not whatever wit or wisdom may be on our mind on any given Sunday. After all the intervening years, I can still hear the voice of that deacon haunting me as I write my sermons and then stand to deliver them: "Reverend, is there any word from the Lord?"

—Marvin A. McMickle, *Living Water for Thirsty Souls*

All sorts of surprises can occur when the preacher takes the Bible seriously.

—Leander E. Keck, *The Bible in the Pulpit*

Bearing witness to the gospel means engaging in serious and responsible biblical preaching. Preachers who bear witness to the gospel do not merely spout their own opinions about the issues of the day but instead listen to Scripture before they speak. Preaching is genuinely biblical whenever the preacher allows a text from the Bible to serve as the leading force in shaping the content and purpose of the sermon. More dynamically, biblical preaching involves telling the truth about—bearing witness to—what happens when a biblical text intersects some aspect of our life and exerts a claim upon us. Biblical preaching does not mean merely talking about the Bible, using the Bible to bolster doctrinal arguments, or applying biblical "principles" to everyday life. Biblical preaching happens when a preacher prayerfully goes to listen to the Bible on behalf of the people and then speaks on Christ's behalf what the preacher hears there. Biblical preaching has almost nothing to do with how many times the Bible is quoted in a sermon and everything to do with how faithfully the Bible is interpreted in relation to contemporary experience. "A sermon that begins in the Bible and ends in the Bible," the renowned preacher Edmund Steimle once observed, "is not necessarily a biblical sermon."

Biblical Preaching as Normative

Biblical preaching is the *normative* form of Christian preaching. That statement can be taken in two different ways. When we call a certain practice "normative," we may mean either that it is what is usually done (the normal, customary practice) or that it is the standard (the norm, the rule) by which all other ways of doing the practice are measured. When we say that biblical preaching is normative, we mean both.

Historically, biblical preaching has been normative in the first sense, namely, that it is the usual and most common practice. Here and there people have questioned the idea that a sermon should be based on a biblical text, but down through the centuries the bond between Scripture and sermon has remained firm. When the Lutheran scholar Yngve Brilioth surveyed the history of Christian preaching, he discovered that the connection between a sermon and a biblical text has been a consistent feature of Christian preaching from the very beginning. The Christian sermon, Brilioth pointed out, is patterned after synagogue preaching, and as such has "its roots in the exposition of a [biblical] text."[1] When Jesus preached in the synagogue at Nazareth (Luke 4), he spoke from a text, and for the most part Christian preachers ever since have done the same.

Biblical preaching is also normative in the second and more vigorous meaning of the norm. Preaching that involves significant engagement with a biblical text is the standard over against which all other types of preaching are measured. If we ask about a particular sermon, "Is that a Christian sermon?" we are really asking if it bears true and faithful witness to the God of Jesus Christ, and answering that question inevitably takes us to the biblical story through which we know and encounter the God of Jesus Christ. If someone preached a hateful sermon, say a blatantly racist sermon, or if someone preached a trivial sermon, say one on how to handle time pressure and manage a hectic social life, we would reject such sermons as sub-Christian not just because they make us angry or leave us wanting but mainly because they run counter to the depth and vision of the gospel as we hear it in the biblical witness.

If biblical preaching is the norm, the standard of measurement, does this mean, as Harvard preacher George Buttrick once claimed, that "there is no true preaching except biblical preaching"?[2] Not exactly. Over the years, many strong and faithful sermons have been preached that were surely gospel sermons even though they were not drawn explicitly from specific passages in the Bible. Sermons of this kind, often called "topical" sermons, usually appeal to general theological themes, doctrines, creeds, and the like, rather than to specific biblical texts. But even though these sermons do not follow the norm, they are usually only one step removed from a direct encounter with the Bible since the doctrinal sources to which they appeal are to some degree themselves the result of biblical interpretation.

Because the Bible always exerts force on the church's understanding of the gospel and its theology, strong topical sermons are based on creeds or theological themes that are themselves the product of prior encounters with Scripture. All gospel preaching, then, is in some sense biblical preaching. Biblical interpretation stands either in the foreground or in the background. As homiletician David Buttrick says,

> [O]f course, we must be quick to admit that preaching from the Bible does *not* make a sermon more or less godly. There are "biblical" sermons that are tedious, trivial, or even badly heretical. . . . Likewise there are sermons that never mention Scripture but are truly "biblical" in spirit and content. Yet, down through the ages, more often than not, preachers have had recourse to the Bible when preaching within Jewish and Christian communities.[3]

So, we are claiming that biblical preaching is "normative" in both ways. Faithful engagement with Scripture is a standard by which preaching should be measured, and the normal week-in, week-out practice of preaching should consist of sermons drawn from specific biblical texts. Biblical preaching in this strict sense should be the rule and not the exception.

Why should this be so? Biblical preaching—the kind of preaching that involves sermons that engage particular texts in the Bible—is normative first of all because it reenacts the epistemology of the church, or to put it more simply, it models the primary way in which the church comes to know God's will. When the church seeks to discover God's presence and will, it looks in many places—its own life and worship, the world, theology, the workings of culture, and beyond—but primarily and essentially it looks to Scripture. Week after week, biblical preaching reenacts that search. If we were to play a video of a typical worship service with the sound turned down, at some point we would see someone pray and then open a Bible to read one or more texts. Then we would see someone, perhaps the same person who read the Scripture, begin to speak. Even though we could not hear the sound, just this threefold action—praying, reading the Bible, and speaking—would tell us a great deal because it is a ritual reenactment of how the church comes to know who it is, who God is, and what God calls it to be. How does the church find guidance from God? It prayerfully goes to Scripture and then wrestles with the meaning of what it finds there. Biblical preaching models this way of knowing.

Biblical preaching is also normative because the church has found that through such preaching the church is formed according to the pattern of Christ. The doctrine of the inspiration of Scripture has a history of divisive controversy and marked disagreements, but even though theological parties may disagree about what the Bible is and what it means to call it "inspired," there is a surprising consensus about what the Bible *does*. Throughout its history, the church has discovered that when it goes to the Scripture in openness and trust, it finds itself uniquely addressed there by God and its identity as the people of God shaped by that encounter. A biblical sermon, in its very form, models this primal and radical action of discernment, and therefore, when it is responsibly done, it is the basic and paradigmatic form of Christian preaching.

To put this another way, the church listens to Scripture because it recognizes that it is addressed there by Christ. This does not imply that the Bible itself is perfect, inerrant, completely consistent, or historically precise, or that the words of the Bible were somehow dictated by

God. What it does mean is that the church has discovered that when it goes to the Scripture in faith, it finds itself encountered by Christ in ways that serve as the keys for understanding its encounters with Christ everywhere else. "Christian faith," writes James Barr, "is not faith in the Bible, not primarily: it is faith in Christ as the one through whom one comes to God, and faith that through the Bible we meet him, he communicates with us."[4] When the church goes to the Scripture, it finds that there, unlike anywhere else, its life is nurtured and empowered by Christ and its identity is re-formed.[5]

So there are good reasons that Christian preaching should be called normative. So wed is the sermon to the biblical source that biblical scholar Walter Brueggemann argues that preachers today should consider themselves to be something like what the Bible calls "scribes," those who are entrusted with texts. This may take some adjusting on our part since scribes are often portrayed in the New Testament as the enemies of Jesus. But not always. In fact, Jesus calls on his disciples to be like scribes "trained for the kingdom of heaven" (Matt. 13:52), and it is this kind of scribe that Brueggemann means, stewards of texts who are "equipped for God's new reign."[6]

Sometimes we preachers like to fancy ourselves as prophets and heroes, like Nathan confronting the king or Moses taking on Pharaoh. But our true role, Brueggemann says, is to be people of the text. "Scribes, after all, do not try to *be* Moses before Pharaoh," he says. "Their job is to keep that confrontation between truth and power alive and available to the community through acts of textual interpretation and imagination." Indeed, it is the scribe, Brueggemann goes on to say, who can remind the community that the great biblical texts do not actually feature Moses and Jeremiah and Elijah in the starring roles. These texts, the scribe knows and insists, are really about God. These biblical texts are truly and finally about who God is and what God does. It is God, not Moses or the prophets, says Brueggemann, "who promises and delivers and commands," and the scribe is confident that this same God will act again "through the scribe's re-performance of the text."[7]

Why biblical texts? Because biblical texts have the power to release what Brueggemann calls a "counter-imagination," a way of seeing the world that is an alternative to the consumerist, militaristic, death-obsessed imagination of the culture. Brueggemann writes,

This counter-imagination is the treasure of the scribes and of the kingdom. It happens *by* texts and bread and *texts* and wine and *texts* and *texts* and *texts*. The oldest stories become the newest songs. Stories from Moses and Nathan and Elijah and Daniel and a host of others' old stories let the church sing—free, dangerous, energized, filled with courage. So much depends on scribes who are trained for the kingdom.[8]

So, week after week, in sermon after sermon, this action of going in faith to the meeting ground of Scripture is enacted. The very dynamics of reading and preaching correspond to the way the church comes to know the gospel, and the prayerful hope of preacher and hearers alike is that they will be formed and re-formed according to the pattern of Christ.

Scripture, Theology, and Contemporary Experience

The preacher goes on behalf of the church to the Bible, but the preacher does not go with a blank tablet. The preacher comes from the community of faith, a community with its own theological traditions, social location, and prior understandings of the nature of both the Bible and the Christian gospel. Thus, the preacher goes to Scripture with a set of categories and expectations already in place. The actual encounter with Scripture may upset these expectations, confirm them, or both, but the preacher brings them nonetheless, and they are vital aspects of the process of interpretation.

It would be impossible to describe everything that a preacher brings to the interpretation of a text, but at least three of these important frames of understanding deserve our special attention.

A Critically Informed View of Scripture

We know that the Bible contains a set of writings produced by human beings caught up in the circumstances of particular times and places, people who wrote both with a faithful vision and a culturally conditioned mind-set. This means that the church must not only listen obediently to the words of the Bible; it must also interpret those words as the human products of their own age. As Barr states, "Our recognition that the Bible provides an essential and God-given meeting-ground for our encounter with God in faith does not alter the fact that we have a right, and indeed a duty, to use the Bible critically."[9]

Christiaan Beker has described the aim of biblical interpretation as obtaining a "catalytic reading" of Scripture. What he means by this is that the goal of the interpreter is to hear the gospel as a kind of force at work in a biblical text cutting across two kinds of cultural static. First, there is the static that comes from the text's own cultural world. Every text is a product of a particular time and place and reflects cultural attitudes and assumptions that are not necessarily the gospel. The second kind of cultural static is our own culture, the culture of the interpreter, especially those aspects of our own culture that we may wish to force upon a text. Beker writes:

> A catalytic reading of Scripture intends to listen to the claim of the text on us, but it resists a literalistic and anachronistic transfer (as if, for instance, its culturally conditioned admonitions about submission of slaves and women to the rule of men and its prevalent androcentrism must directly apply to our time and culture). A catalytic reading of Scripture also resists modernist prejudices, as if [contemporary] perspectives can be imposed on [ancient] text. A catalytic claim of the biblical text, therefore, means that the text undergoes a necessary change in its transferral to our time and yet is not altered in its "substance." In other words, a catalytic view of a text's authority distinguishes between a variety of its components, especially between its abiding character (its coherence) and its time-conditioned interpretations (its contingency).[10]

It would be convenient, of course, if there were some method, some careful step-by-step process, by which we could separate the abiding gospel in a biblical text from the time-conditioned material, but no such procedure exists. Because the Bible is in human language, and the texts of the Bible were written both for and in social situations, everything about the Bible is culturally conditioned. Because the ultimate referent of biblical texts is God, everything about the Bible is infused with gospel.

Any preacher, for instance, who happened to preach a sermon on Ephesians 6:5ff. and simply repeated the text's message, "Slaves, be obedient to those who are your earthly masters," would be worthy of ridicule. This preacher would, at best, have presented the gospel as a foolish, obsolete word and, what is more, as a hateful, oppressive word. It is tempting, then, to write off a text like that one as "culturally conditioned" and to move on to other texts that seem free of social bias, like Ephesians 2:8: "For by grace you have been saved through faith, and this is not your own doing; it is the gift of God." It is not that simple, however. A careful and attentive reading of the passage from Ephesians 6 will yield much cultural material that must finally be emphatically rejected by Christians today, but it will also disclose another spirit at work in the text. Breathing through that passage is an underlying claim about the freedom from worldly structures found in one's relationship to God in Christ, who shows no partiality. In Ephesians this claim modifies the institution of slavery, and eventually the truth of this claim destroys that institution. Moreover, Ephesians 2:8, which seems so universal and timeless, actually contains concepts, such as "grace," "saved," and "faith," that are not ideas dropped from heaven. They are rather concepts with a long and varied cultural and theological heritage.

The point is, texts that scream cultural bias are also gospel texts, and texts that shout the gospel are also culturally conditioned. There is no surgical procedure for dividing the tissues, no guaranteed way to separate the wheat from the chaff. Hearing the claim of God in and through a biblical text demands an act of faithful imagination, a refusing to let a text go until it has blessed us. Ultimately, hearing the gospel in and through culturally conditioned biblical texts involves not only learned and critical study of those texts, but also hearing them as people of faith who live and move and worship in the community of faith. This is why a key Catholic biblical commission said, "Exegesis produces its best results when it is carried out in the context of the living faith of the Christian community, which is directed toward the salvation of the entire world."[11] That is also why many biblical scholars and teachers of preaching recommend that biblical interpretation take place not only in conversation with the best and most critical scholarship available, but also in the context of prayer and spiritual expectation.[12]

A Theological Heritage

Preachers go to the Scripture not only with a critically informed understanding of the Bible but also with prior understandings of the Christian faith embodied in rich and culturally specific theological traditions. What is a theological tradition? It is a complex, often ambiguous, but somewhat systematic way that a certain group sees the Christian faith as a whole, built up slowly over time and deeply influenced by the social circumstances of the people who participated in its formation.

Brazilian Pentecostals, for example, have different ways of describing the Christian faith, and therefore a different theological tradition, than do Scottish Presbyterians, African Methodist Episcopalians in Georgia, Roman Catholics in Quebec, Pennsylvania Quakers, Wisconsin Lutherans, members of a "mega-church" in Charlotte, or Mennonites gathered in a circle for worship in Toronto. These differing theological traditions affect not only large matters, such as creeds and liturgies, but also show up in less prominent places, like the organizational structure of hymnbooks. For example, one denomination, which tends to place prime value on systematic theological thought, arranges its hymnbook accordingly. The hymns are categorized according to a classical systematic doctrinal scheme: hymns about God followed by hymns about Christ, then hymns about the Holy Spirit, hymns about the church, and so on. The hymnbook of another more liturgically oriented denomination, however, arranges the hymns according to the worship life of the church, especially the seasons and festivals of the church year: Advent, Christmas, Epiphany, Lent, and so on. Yet another hymnal, that of a denomination with a more personal and experiential theological tradition, is ordered around stages in the experience of the Christian believer. Congregations that do not use printed hymnbooks but instead project a variety of praise songs, spirituals, and other selections onto screens reflect in this very spontaneity and mixture a kind of counter-tradition. A hymnbook, or the lack of a hymnbook, is an expression of a theological tradition, and the different organizational patterns reflect important differences in these traditions.

Even within denominational groups, there is considerable theological diversity. All Christians recite, confess, sing, and preach the same gospel story, but with their own characteristic styles and places of emphasis. They all share a basic commitment to the Christian faith, but they have different patterns for "seeing it whole," of understanding what aspects of the faith form the centers around which all else is organized. In their book *Claiming Theology in the Pulpit*, John McClure and Burton Cooper say, "A sermon is not simply a witness to the passions of one's faith; it also involves rational and critical reflection upon that faith. . . . [T]he simplest statement of faith can imply a vast theology and, at minimum, invites a theological discussion."[13]

Preachers go to the Bible, then, not as "universal Christians" (there is no such thing) but with a particular theological heritage and viewpoint. We may wish that we were free of these theological presuppositions so that we could go to a biblical text with a completely fresh and open mind, but not only is this not realistic; it is actually not desirable. Knowing that we come to Scripture from and within a theological tradition reminds us that entirely new ground is not being broken. The church has been to this text before—many times—and a theological tradition is, in part, the church's memory of past encounters with this and other biblical texts. A theologically informed interpreter of Scripture enters the text guided by a map drawn and refined by those who have come to this place before. Coming to a text from a theological tradition, the interpreter arrives not as a disoriented stranger but as a pilgrim returning to a familiar land, recognizing old landmarks and thereby alert for new and previously unseen wonders.

A theologically informed interpreter is also steered away from the distortions of the gospel that can result when a single text is heard in isolation from all others. Since a theological tradition is a way of seeing the Christian faith whole, it provides a means for placing the word of one text into the larger pattern of the witness of the whole Bible. Some New Testament passages, for example, refer to the Jews in ways that could lead to a harsh anti-Semitism, were these texts not seen in the brighter light of the whole of the Christian faith, with its affirmation of the God who keeps promises and who, as Paul wrote, has by no means rejected Israel.

To put it bluntly, a theological tradition gives us permission not only to receive what texts have to say to us but sometimes to argue with texts, to engage in what biblical scholar and homiletician David Bartlett has described as "a lover's quarrel" with particular texts.[14] The Bible itself invites such quarrels, Bartlett says, because there are disagreements in the Bible itself. Take Paul's not-always-consistent views on women. "We read 1 Corinthians," says Bartlett, "and discover that the Paul who says that 'in Christ there is neither male nor female' sometimes says other things that seem contradictory. As preachers, how are we faithful to a Bible that sometimes argues with itself? Sometimes when we preach 'the Bible says,' that is the end of the matter. Sometimes it is just the beginning."[15]

Theologian Majorie Hewitt Suchocki describes this process of arguing with a text:

> So when you disagree with the theology in a text, whether that theology be implicit or explicit, pick up the challenge and figure out on what basis you disagree. Where does this text push you in terms of the continually transforming Christian tradition? Don't ignore the text! Quarrel with it; struggle with it; probe it for the thinking the text forces you into. Perhaps your struggle will lead you to acquiescence, or perhaps your struggle will lead you to some adaptation, or perhaps your struggle will lead you to outright rejection, which is itself a form of faithful transformation.[16]

Theological traditions, then, are good things, guiding us in the conversation with Scripture. But there is a shadow side as well, and theological traditions can mislead us, too. We need a vantage point to be able to see something, but we cannot see everything from a single perspective. Theological traditions serve as means for the church to remember, organize, and comprehend what has been discerned of the gospel over time. They are, as we have said, ways of seeing the gospel whole, but they do not see the whole gospel. This is why ecumenical conversation, dialogue among the various traditions in the larger church, is so crucial. Church unity is at stake in these discussions, but so is the fullness of the gospel. As preachers, we are called to humility about what we can see and know of the gospel. We can see, and we do know, but we must be content to see and know only in part, for, as Paul said, "we know only in part, and we prophesy only in part" (1 Cor. 13:9).

Theological traditions can also become hard-of-hearing, fixed systems no longer open to listening to any new claims of Scripture. Whenever a church or a preacher hears in Scripture only that which has been heard before, finds there only a confirmation of what is already known and believed, be assured that the theological tradition has ossified and is being employed not as a means for hearing the living word of Scripture but as a replacement for it.

It is important for preachers to go to Scripture illumined by a theological tradition larger than their own personal creeds, more comprehensive than their private theological opinions. All of us are changing and growing in regard to our own theological views. We do not believe the same things in the same ways when we are fifty years old that we did when we were sixteen or thirty-six, and our theological traditions are being stretched by encounters with other traditions and by new experiences in our lives. For example, David Bartlett once described how, when he was a young scholar, he made a confident presentation to a group of preachers on how to preach the difficult text found in Genesis 22, Abraham's near-sacrifice of his son Isaac. But as he became older, Bartlett's experiences and perspectives changed, and, taking a different view of the text, he wondered if maybe the best sermon on this passage would be one that candidly admitted that this is a difficult text to preach:

> My life has changed. When I made [that earlier] presentation I had no children of my own; now I have two. "Take your son . . . whom you love" has existential bite as it did not in the days of my youth. My Christology has changed. Not that far out of graduate school, I was not only impressed with, I was enamored of some of the claims of the substitutionary doctrines of the atonement. God spared us at the expense of his own son. Now I wonder whether a doctrine of the atonement, a doctrine that runs the risk of making God sound like an abusive parent, is congruent with the gospel. My ease with the text is not helped by my dis-ease with instances of child abuse—sometimes religiously driven child abuse—so evident in our society. What about a sermon on Genesis 22 that raises questions without jumping to premature answers?[17]

The preacher's own faith and beliefs are important for preaching, of course, but if they are living, they are always changing. Also, the church's theological heritage is always larger, more enduring, and less privatistic than anyone's set of personal convictions. As we prepare to preach, we go to Scripture not just as individual believers but as practicing theologians on the front lines of the church, seeking to hear the gospel today in conversation with the shifting realities of our own lives and in continuity with the living theological memory of the whole church.

How can preachers become acquainted with their theological traditions? This is really a complex and lifelong task, since theological traditions are not lists of beliefs but comprehensive ways of living, worshiping, serving, and believing. A good and simple way to begin is to make a list of every important feature you can think of that characterizes your theological tradition. What would you include? My own theological heritage is the Reformed tradition, and among other things I would write down such convictions as "a profound trust in the goodness and kindness of God," "a radical understanding of salvation by grace," "an understanding of the church as a covenant community," "a clear distinction between the Creator and the creation," and "a respect for order in church life and worship." What would you list? Would you name "a focus upon the sacramental life" or "an emphasis upon the new birth of the Christian believer" or "a seeking after the gifts of the Spirit" or "a firm peace ethic"?

McClure and Cooper help preachers to define their "theological profiles" and begin to unpack the complex, "vast theology" that a preacher may bring to the pulpit by describing what they call "the four basic theological modes," characteristic ways that various preachers approach theology, the world, the congregation, and virtually everything else, including, of course, the interpretation of Scripture. Some preachers, they say, customarily assume the *existential mode*. These preachers almost always start with human brokenness, with the negative and painful aspects of life such as anxiety, meaninglessness, or guilt, and then look to God (and to Scripture) for the answers to human despair. Other preachers start with the *transcendent mode*, that is, they begin not with the human condition but with the God question, with God's self-revelation, and they seek to bring life into harmony with the character of God as disclosed in Scripture. Other preachers assume the *ethical political mode*, that is, they focus on the struggle for justice as the arena for knowing and serving God, and thus would concentrate on the social-ethical dimensions of Scripture. Finally, some preachers assume the *relational mode*, looking for theological meaning in the web of relationships—personal, social, environmental—that define life and in the dynamic processes that underlie change and growth. Scripture is seen as one element in a constellation of relationships, a force spurring and energizing development.[18] One can imagine finding all four modes among a group of Methodist preachers, or Presbyterians, or Catholics. Whatever we may claim as central to our theological worldviews, once we have named them, the next step is for us to consider every emphasis we have named to be a slogan, a formula, even a cliché, and to push deeper. Only when we have dug underneath the mottoes of our tradition and grasped the historical and theological forces that gave them birth can we claim to know our own heritage. Only when we perceive what was—and is—at stake in these affirmations, only when we know what is gained and what is lost by making them, do we begin to have a working understanding of our theological tradition.

An Awareness of the Circumstances of the Hearers

The biblical word does not come as a disembodied word, speaking timeless verities to all people everywhere. The Bible speaks to particular people in the concrete circumstances of their lives. It speaks "a word on target," illumining our situation from within. The word of God we encounter in the Scripture does not attack idolatry in general; it dethrones *our* idols, severs the bonds of our old and crippling loyalties. It is not the word of God in the abstract but of God who is for us, of God who is against us in order to be truly for us. The living word that comes to us in the Bible does not hum generically about concepts like "salvation" and "hope"; rather, it divides the seas that churn around us, saves our lives, and beckons us to follow toward a new and hopeful land. When preachers go to the Scripture, then, they must take the people with them, since what will be heard there is a word for them. How does the preacher do this? In part, we do this by heightening the awareness of our own struggle to be faithful. The more honest we are with ourselves about our own lives—the places of strength and trust, the crevices of doubt, the moments of kindness, the hidden cruelties—the more we find ourselves on common ground with the others who will hear the sermon. Eventually we will be the preacher of the sermon, but we must not forget that we will also be one of its hearers as well. When we go to the Scripture seeking not what "the people ought to hear" but hungering ourselves for a gospel word, we will hear a word for them too.

It is not enough, though, to go to the Bible only with our own lives in view. We must self-consciously embody the needs and situations of others, especially those who are different from ourselves. Some preach-ers find it helpful, as a part of the process of interpreting the Scripture, to visualize the congregation that will be present when the sermon is preached. They survey the congregation in their mind's eye, seeing there the familiar faces and the lives behind them. They see the adults and the children, the families and those who are single, those who par-ticipate actively in the church's mission and those who stand cautiously on the edges of the church's life. They see those for whom life is full and good and those for whom life is composed of jagged pieces. They see the regulars sitting in their customary places, and they see the stranger, the newcomer, the visitor, hesitating and wondering if there is a place for them. They see the people who are there, and they see the people who cannot be there, or who choose not to be there. When preachers turn to the Scripture, all these people go with them.

Other preachers invite members of the congregation actually to participate with them in exploring the biblical text, gathering a small group early in the sermon development process to listen to the text, to study it together, to raise questions about it, and to name the concerns it evokes. This may be a general group, or it may be a group of people who have a special relationship to the issues in the text. Suppose, for example, a preacher—in this case, a man—is preparing a sermon on the passage in John 16 that includes these words of Jesus:

> You will be sorrowful, but your sorrow *will* turn into joy. When a woman is in travail she has sorrow, because her hour has come; but when she is delivered of the child, she no longer remembers the anguish, for joy that a child is born into the world. So you have sorrow now, *but I will* see you again and your hearts *will* rejoice, and no one *will* take your joy from you. (John 16:20–22, emphasis added)

Now, the preacher, as a man, can certainly understand the birthing image in this passage, but there are obvious limits to his ability to know its full depths. Time spent exploring this text with women who have experienced childbirth, who know from their own experience its fear-ful anguish and its even more intense joy, would almost surely open up the richness of the image and disclose connections with human experi-ence that otherwise would simply not be available to him.

Many other methods can similarly bring the questions, needs, and insights of the congregation into the preacher's awareness as the text is encountered. In *Preaching as Local Theology and Folk Art*, homiletician Leonora Tubbs Tisdale has even suggested that "preachers need to become amateur ethnographers—skilled in observing and thickly describing the subcultural signs and symbols of the congregations they serve."[19] She has developed an elaborate and very helpful set of questions and categories for preachers, as "participant-observers," to explore the worldviews and deep concerns of their congregations.[20]

Basically, though, when a preacher interprets Scripture deeply mindful of the lives and needs of the hearers, this is more than some strategy or a technique. This is not so much "exegeting the congregation," as if the people were strange, remote, and difficult to understand; rather it is a way of being open to them, paying attention to them and to the constraints and possibilities of their lives. In other words, bringing the hearers into the event of biblical interpretation is simply a matter of good ministry. As Tisdale maintains, it involves "a new way of seeing and perceiving that which already happens in the ordinary course of ministry."[21] Going to the Bible on behalf of the people is a priestly act. As an exercise of the priestly office, the preacher represents the people before the text as a way of representing them before God. Leander Keck has aptly compared this priestly view of biblical interpretation to the pastoral prayer in worship. "To pray on their behalf," he says, "one must enter into their lives to the point that one begins to feel what they feel, yet without losing one's identity as a pastor."[22] What is brought to expression in the pastoral prayer? The urgent pleas of the congregation? Yes, but not only the cries of the faithful. The pastor prays on behalf of the world too, seeking to speak the words that the world would speak to God if it could find them and if it could feel the unfailing embrace of God's love.

Just so, the preacher goes to the biblical text as a priest, carrying the questions, needs, and concerns of congregation and world, not as an agenda to be met but as an offering to be made. And then the preacher listens to the text. The word heard there may be one of comfort, but it may also be one that judges. It may answer our questions, but it may call our questions into question. It may be a word that brings us joyfully home, or it may call us deeper into the wilderness. Whatever that word may be, the preacher must tell the truth about it. The priest must now become the witness.

In the Beginning

At first glance it would appear that the study of the biblical text ought always to be the starting place for a biblical sermon, and most of the time this is so. Preachers usually begin developing sermons by first going to biblical texts. When we do this, we do not yet know what the sermon will be "about." We only know that the sermon will be based on a passage from Genesis or Isaiah or John or Romans, and beyond this we look to the text to form the focus of the sermon. Theological traditions and the life situations of the hearers are, as we have said, already present as we go to the Scripture, but the text initiates the conversation and names its topics.

On other occasions, however, biblical sermons begin with a concern generated outside the Bible. Sometimes the starting point will be a line from a creed, like "I believe in the holy catholic church"; a historic doctrine, such as the Trinity; a question from a catechism; a theological and ethical issue, like abortion or ecology; or a theological theme, such as "grace" or "discipleship." At other times an event in the community (a wedding, a funeral, the dedication of a church building, the closing of a plant, the start of a war) or a concern among the people (grief, family life, conflict, work) initiates the discussion.

When the sermon originates outside the text, we know from the beginning what the sermon will be about, but if it is truly to be a biblical sermon, we must not decide in advance what the sermon will say. The text must be allowed to surprise us, even to violate our expectations. Suppose, for example, that a preacher finds that the issue of personal self-esteem has become a concern of some people in the congregation. Pastoral conversations often come around to this topic, paperback books on self-esteem are being read and discussed, television talk shows on the issue are watched with interest, and the time has come to address the matter from the pulpit. The preacher who goes to the Bible digging around for material for a sermon on "Christian self-esteem" will be disappointed. Self-esteem, as defined by the paperbacks and the talk shows, is a psychological phenomenon peculiar to modern culture and unknown to the biblical world. The preacher can, of course, force the Bible to march to the cultural drumbeat, but then the sermon will only be a word from the culture to itself.

Underlying the contemporary quest for self-esteem, however, is a more basic hunger to know what it means to be human, and about this the Scripture and theology have much to say. The preacher begins, then, with the cultural issues and questions but goes in a theologically informed manner to the text, prepared for those issues to be redefined and for those questions to be both answered and overturned. The preacher not only has a critical understanding of the Bible but also gains a critical understanding of the culture. The resulting sermon will be about self-esteem, but the engagement with the biblical text will provide a new way of seeing what is truly at stake in that concern.

Regardless of the sermon's starting point, then, preaching is biblical when the text serves as the leading force in shaping the content and purpose of the sermon.

The Exegetical Habit

Responsible biblical preaching does not come easily. It requires time, study, and hard work. The time required for the study of Scripture is not spent apart from ministry; it is not even done in preparation for ministry. It is ministry, and as such it should be cherished and protected. There are ways to use study time wisely and efficiently. There are even shortcuts we can take in the process of biblical interpretation, but there are no short circuits.

Presented in the next chapter is a description of a brief exegetical process for biblical preaching. Every responsible preacher engages in a process something like this one, but no two preachers do it exactly the same way. In whatever way we perform the task of biblical study toward preaching, though, it must become a habit, a routine carved so deeply into our schedule and our way of doing ministry that it becomes second nature.

3

Biblical Exegesis for Preaching

> When your head droops at night, let a page of Scripture pillow it.
> —St. Jerome, *Letter 22*

> The text sits beside us like a conversation partner on the bus. Will
> we be open to a new hearing? . . . This particular conversation has
> never happened before: this text speaking to these people in this
> time and place. Through such Spirit-born conversation, God is at
> work transforming memory into presence.
> —Barbara K. Lundblad, *Transforming the Stone*

B roadly speaking, exegesis is a systematic plan for listening to and seeking to understand a biblical text.[1]
Any good exegetical plan involves tools, such as con-
cordances and Bible dictionaries, and methods, such as historical
and literary analysis, but it is important to remember that discerning meanings in a biblical text is more a matter of faithful listening
than it is precise research. It is more like getting to know another
person than it is doing a forensic analysis of a crime scene. As is true
of developing human relationships, getting to know a biblical text
takes time, requires patience, and involves a willingness to attend
to the other, even when the other seems strange or even unconge-
nial. In fact, overconfidence in objective exegetical methods can
end up muting the voice of Scripture, turning biblical interpretation into an autopsy of a dead text rather than a hearing of the lively
and active word of Scripture. As historian and missiologist Lamin
Sanneh, a native of Gambia, has observed about overly scientific
and detached methods of biblical interpretation, "The tradition of
exegesis that has been practiced in the West seems to have run its

course. . . . The standard exegesis spins faith into just so much cultural filibuster."[2]

The brief, step-by-step process outlined in this chapter is designed to be a mixture of precise method and freestyle art. In some ways it is a condensed, less technical version of the sort of exegetical scheme typically encountered in a seminary course in biblical studies. In other ways, however, it is distinctly a preacher's exegetical procedure. When we interpret a biblical passage for preaching, it changes not just what we do with the results of the exegesis, but also the way we go about the exegesis in the first place.

For example, the exegetical plan in this chapter involves, as we might expect, consulting the best scholarly biblical commentaries but, significantly, it delays bringing in those commentaries until late in the process in order not to stifle the creative interactions that can and should occur between the preacher and the text. Preachers need to get to know these texts and to view them from every possible angle before allowing the voices of "authoritative scholars" to narrow the range of interpretive possibilities.

Also, despite much talk in biblical scholarship about the "social location" of the interpreter, there is still one aspect of social location that the preacher knows well but is mostly lacking in biblical scholarship, namely that the preacher is not interpreting texts in general but always on behalf of those who will hear the sermons.[3] A Pauline scholar working on the syntax of a passage in Galatians, for instance, would probably go about business in the same manner regardless of whether or not the local auto plant was out on strike or whether a couple in the congregation was contemplating getting a divorce. Preachers, though, cannot—should not—filter out such local circumstances from the interpretation of Scripture. The whole aim of a preacher's study of a biblical text is to hear in that text a specific word for us, and who "we" happen to be at this moment makes a considerable difference in how the preacher approaches the text. If families in the congregation are in crisis, if some who will hear the sermon are unemployed, these circumstances bring new questions and concerns to the encounter with Scripture.

Moreover, preachers usually have to weave sermon preparation into a pressure-filled schedule of other responsibilities. So the exegetical process outlined here is designed to be thorough enough to provide a solid engagement with the text but brief enough to become a regular part of a pastor's weekly schedule. Warning: the first time a preacher tries out this process, it may take many hours to complete. Each step is explored here in some detail, and consequently the procedure may appear hopelessly protracted for the busy pastor. But once the process becomes familiar, the process goes faster, and it can be accomplished in a reasonable length of time. For some, this will mean setting aside (and guarding) a single undisturbed block of time for textual study and sermon preparation. Most preachers, however, will divide the process into smaller strands, weaving them into the weekly mix of constant tasks and unexpected demands that compose a minister's life.

Even though the process is presented as an A-B-C list of steps, in actual practice it operates more like a spiral. Each step turns back around to the earlier steps, allowing us to see more and more about each step the farther along we travel. The goal of this process is to hear the text speaking to our current context, and this can happen at almost any point along the way, in step A, in step K, or somewhere in the middle.

Finally, this exegetical process is like an off-the-rack dress or sport jacket. It will almost surely need to be tailored to fit each preacher just right. Preachers who employ this process a few times will find that they will want to adjust and edit it around their own sensibilities and also around different texts. Indeed, we are beginning with a recommended step-by-step process, but the ultimate goal should be eventually to move beyond the notion of biblical interpretation as a sequence of steps and toward an instinctive way of dwelling critically, attentively, and faithfully with the text. "A method will be most fruitful," claims Fred Craddock, "when it has become as comfortable as an old sweater."[4]

Outline of a Brief Exegetical Method for Preaching

    I. Getting the Text in View
        A. Select the text
        B. Reconsider where the text begins and ends
        C. Establish a reliable translation of the text

    II. Getting Introduced to the Text
        D. Read the text for basic understanding
        E. Place the text in its larger context

III. Attending to the Text
   F. Listen attentively to the text

IV. Testing What Is Heard in the Text
   G. Explore the text historically
   H. Explore the literary character of the text
   I.   Explore the text theologically
   J.   Check the text in the commentaries

V. Moving toward the Sermon
   K. State the claim of the text upon the hearers (including the preacher)

A Brief Exegetical Method for Preaching

I. Getting the Text in View

The goal of this exegetical process is not to find "the meaning of the text" hidden inside, like the peanut in a chocolate-covered M&M. The assumption we have about biblical interpretation is that biblical texts are living realities, that their possible meanings are many, that they are not merely jars with one correct idea inside. The Scripture speaks ever afresh to each new situation. Therefore, biblical interpretation is dynamic, and the goal of this process is to put ourselves in a position to hear when the text freely speaks.

When and where such hearing takes place is unpredictable. It can occur at any place along the way in this process, or it can occur outside this process, when we are taking a shower, pouring a cup of tea, in prayer, dreaming in our sleep, or having a conversation with friends. Sometimes, we must admit, it does not happen at all. As hard as we may work to study the text and to prepare the sermon, the Spirit seems not to speak. On those occasions, we are compelled to go to the place of preaching and simply speak what we know about the scriptural passage, praying like mad that the Spirit, so silent in the study, will nevertheless speak in the moment of proclamation.

We best put ourselves in the position to hear the voice of the Spirit, though, when we take the biblical text seriously and attend to it with all of our intelligence and imagination, and that is what this process is designed to allow. Most of the time, as we go through these steps, the voice we are yearning to hear will grow in volume. It may begin as a whisper somewhere early in the process and then build in intensity, so that when we reach the final step, we are convicted that this text has a new and compelling word for those who will hear the sermon.

But we must begin somewhere, and here, in this opening phase of the exegetical process, the preacher simply puts the chosen text on the table for viewing. This involves not only choosing a text for the sermon but also ensuring that the chosen text is indeed the right length and scope and that it is translated accurately.

A. Select the text

The first concrete step a preacher takes in beginning a biblical sermon is an obvious one: choosing the text on which the sermon will be based. There are four basic ways for a preacher to select the biblical text for a sermon.

1. *Lectio continua.*   The term means "continuous reading," and this ancient method of textual selection involves preaching through the Bible, book by book, text by text. Preachers of an earlier era would read as much Scripture as time would allow and then preach on what they had read, often blending the preaching and the reading into a single action. The ending spot would be marked, and the preacher would pick up at that point the next time the community gathered for worship.

Not much pure *lectio continua* preaching exists now. Sixteen weeks marching seriatim through the Levitical laws would be a desert experience for most congregations. The clear advantage of this approach, though, is that the congregation hears each book of the Bible as a unified whole. The hearers would not, for instance, receive just a snippet from Romans every now and then; they would get Romans.

In most settings, *lectio continua* preaching could best be an occasional exception to the normal pattern of text selection and would take the form of a series of sermons on a single book of the Bible. A preacher might wish to spend several weeks, for example, preaching through the cycle of David stories in 1 and 2 Samuel or through Ephesians.

2. A lectionary.   A lectionary (sometimes called *lectio selecta* to indicate that it includes selected, rather than continuous, readings) is a list of biblical passages assigned to the various days in the church calendar. Some lectionaries have readings only for Sundays, major festivals, and other holidays, while other lectionaries designate texts for every single day in the year. In the more liturgical traditions the use of a lectionary is already the established practice, but lectionary usage is increasing in many circles where a generation ago lectionaries were virtually unknown. This is especially true of Protestants who have adopted the Revised Common Lectionary (1992), an ecumenically produced revision of the 1969 Roman Catholic lectionary. In general, the use of a lectionary is a superb plan for obtaining sermon texts. The readings are set to the rhythm and seasons of the church year, which provides an opportunity for coordinated planning of the sermon, music, prayers, and other aspects of worship. The wide range of readings included in the major denominational lectionaries ensures that preachers and congregations will encounter the breadth of the biblical witness, and these lectionaries share enough common readings that many fine and relatively inexpensive lectionary-based preaching commentaries and sermon Internet websites have appeared. The recent growth in the use of lectionaries has encouraged groups of preachers, sometimes from several denominations, to study the Bible together as a part of sermon preparation.

Lectionaries have their limitations, however. A wide range of biblical texts is included in a good lectionary, but still many texts are omitted, including some entire books of the Bible. Moreover, since a particular set of readings always appears in relation to a certain time in the church calendar, the interpretational deck gets somewhat stacked. It makes sense, of course, for a text about the crucifixion normally to be preached on Good Friday, as the lectionary provides, and not, say, during the Christmas season. As a matter of fact, though, the crucifixion has much to speak to the Christmas season, and the story of Jesus' birth cannot really be understood apart from the account of his death. The story of the crucifixion belongs on Good Friday, but not only then. In addition, since lectionaries are designed, for the most part, around the texts from the four Gospels, there is a subtle built-in pressure to preach on those passages rather than from the Old Testament or the rest of the New Testament.[5] The result can be a practical constriction of the full canon of Scripture in the preaching of the church.

3. Local plan.   Sometimes those who are responsible for planning congregational worship create, in effect, a local church lectionary. They take into account the seasons of the Christian year, the denominational program of special days and emphases, the congregational calendar of events, and perhaps even the cultural calendar of holidays, and they blend these to produce a schedule to which biblical texts are matched. As long as a wide range of biblical texts is included, the advantages of this plan are the same as those of the regular lectionary, minus, of course, the large benefit of ecumenical support and resources.

4. Preacher's choice.   In this approach the preacher selects the texts based on the pressing needs of the moment, usually on a week-to-week basis. The only real advantage of this process is flexibility, which can also be a liability. Obviously, if the church burns down or a riot erupts in the town, no preacher will feel bound to a lectionary or any other prior program for selecting a text. Also, when sermons are intended to present doctrines, public issues, pastoral themes, and the like, the preacher will begin with the issue and search for an apt text (note the cautions about this discussed in chapter 2). To go on a search mission every week for a text, though, is not only time consuming, it also invites a haphazard and episodic relationship to the Bible. Flexibility can create serendipity, but it can also be mere randomness.

The preacher's choice method of selecting a text is the only one of the four that depends entirely on the personal preferences of the preacher. It is often claimed that a lectionary or other systematic plan of text selection is a superior method because it keeps a preacher from riding personal hobby horses. Actually, any preacher unwise enough to use the pulpit as a private forum can manage to throw a saddle over any text, no matter how it is selected. The personal-choice method, however, does tend to favor biblical passages that the preacher already knows well, and, when it is used, care must be taken to ensure that the preacher and the congregation encounter the richness present in less-familiar texts.

B. Reconsider where the text begins and ends

A preaching text taken from its setting in the Bible is an artifical creation. The Bible does not come to us in little bits and pieces, in individual texts and isolated pericopes. It comes as a canon, a set of documents that are themselves letters, legal writings, historical narratives, and so on. A preaching text taken from the Bible is like a small piece of wallpaper torn from a very large pattern. We have to tear a small-enough piece to handle in a single sermon, but when we do so we risk losing sight of the overall pattern. We should look, then, with a slightly suspicious eye at the way we—or the commentaries or the lectionaries—have cut our text. Examine what comes before the text, and what comes after it, to see if the surgical incision has been made at a responsible place.

In an often-preached story found in Mark 12:41–44, a poor widow enters the Temple, and, in contrast to the rich folk who make their offerings by raking a little off the top, puts into the treasury everything she has, two small copper coins. The temptation for the preacher, of course, is to turn this story into a simple, upbeat stewardship sermon about how wonderful and worthy is this woman's example of sacrificial giving and how we need the same sort of selfless, costly giving today. But if we pull the camera back a bit and look at this section of Mark with a wide-angle lens, we get a somewhat different picture. Immediately before this story of the woman's offering, Mark tells us that Jesus denounces the religious leaders of his day who, among other crimes, "devour widow's houses" (12:40). No sooner has he said this than a widow comes into a religious institution, where the rich are playing at religion, and she pours all she has, her whole "house," into the offering box. From this perspective, we can see that the woman is not only an example of sacrificial giving, but she is also the victim of a corrupt religious institution that sucks the blood out of poor widows.

This wider reading of the text pulls the carpet out from under any easy and chipper sermons on the widow's mite. Taken in larger context, this text now asks us to deal with matters like the seductions of the clergy, the hypocrisy and evil that lurk near the door of every religious institution, and the meaning of acts of great sacrifice performed in the context of corruption. It may even be that the widow's action will end up being less a model for our stewardship and more a christological sign pointing toward Jesus himself, who in the midst of a cynical, self-serving world also poured out all he had. If we keep on reading, the next thing that Jesus says in Mark is, "Do you see these great buildings? Not one stone will be left here upon another; all will be thrown down" (13:2). This now sounds both fearful and hopeful, a divine warning and a divine promise about justice in the house of God.

As another example of the need to be wary about where a text begins and ends, notice that the major Protestant and Catholic lectionaries divide John 20 into two sections, assigning the first part (20:1–9 or 20:1–18) to Easter and the second part (John 20:19–31) to the first Sunday after Easter. Given the length of John 20, this division makes some practical sense, but when we look at the unified literary character of the chapter, a problem surfaces. John 20 contains several resurrection appearance stories, and there is every indication that these stories are supposed to be read together to form a cluster or an ensemble. As biblical scholar Gail O'Day notes, "Each of the resurrection stories in John provides the Gospel reader with a different angle on what it means to meet the risen Jesus."[6] The implication is, if we want to understand John's complete vision of what it means to meet the risen Christ, we need to take John 20 in its entirety. So even if we decide to follow the lectionary and cut the chapter into two parts, we should be careful to interpret the individual parts of John 20 in light of the whole.

As yet another example, the Revised Common Lectionary includes as one of its texts Leviticus 19:1–2, 15–18. This is a passage about the call to God's people to be holy. The curious preacher, though, immediately wonders about those verses chopped out of the middle and discovers upon reading them that they are specific laws relating to the doing of justice in society. Without these verses, the passage could be read in an exclusively private and inward manner, but when they are included they give the notion of "holiness" some social bite.[7]

Sometimes a text itself will give us clues that it is explicitly connected to the material that surrounds it. Watch especially for connecting phrases such as "there were some present at that very time who . . ." (what time?) or "while he was still speaking . . ." (speaking what?). Such phrases are clear signals that the author intends the reader to connect the dots between one passage and another.

What we are trying to find in this step is not a completely self-contained text that can stand entirely alone. All texts are part of the overall flow of a document and are linked to their surroundings. Rather we are seeking a text that can stand as a reasonably coherent unit of thought. When we are fairly sure we have such a text, we can move to the next step. At this point in the exegetical process, though, we should make only a provisional decision about the limits of our text, since what we discover through the rest of the exegesis may cause us to change our minds.

C. Establish a reliable translation of the text

Given the number of fine translations of the Bible now available, why should preachers be concerned with translation issues? The reason is that every translation of a biblical text is already an interpretation of that text. The vocabulary and thought patterns of the biblical languages do not square up one-to-one with contemporary languages, so even the best translations involve hermeneutical decisions and approximations of meaning. The goal of this step is to take preachers behind the scenes so that they can see the translation process at work and test the choices that have been made in rendering a text into English.

The best way to do this, of course, is to work with the original language of the text, examining the textual variants, and comparing our own translation with well-established translated versions of the Bible. But even if we don't do a word-for-word translation, just reading through the text in the original language, perhaps even using an interlinear translation (one that shows both the original language and the English side by side) and a Greek or Hebrew dictionary to look up key terms, can give us much insight into the text.

If working in the original languages ourselves is not an option, the next-best process is to select two or three reliable English translations— such as the New Revised Standard Version, the New International Version, the Revised English Bible, the New Jerusalem Bible, and the Tanakh (Jewish Study Bible)—and then to compare the translations word for word. Since at this point our goal is reliability and accuracy more than readability, it is best to stay with the major scholarly translations, such as the New Revised Standard

Version (NRSV) and the New International Version (NIV), and away from paraphrase versions, such as the *New Living Translation* or *The Message*, and versions that intentionally use limited and simplified vocabularies, such as the *New Century Version,* the *Common English Bible,* and the *Good News Translation.* These more popularly aimed translations may be valuable to consult at a later point, but they can be misleading at this stage.

In comparing translations, whenever we find differences in wording that are more than merely stylistic, we should make note of them. For example, here are the different renderings of Psalm 46:10a in several translations:

New Revised Standard Version: "Be still, and know that I am God!"
New International Version: "Be still, and know that I am God!"
Revised English Bible: "Let be then; learn that I am God."
Tanakh (Jewish Study Bible): "Desist! Realize that I am God!"
Common English Bible: "That's enough! Now know that I am God!"

Look at the shades of possible meaning in just the opening phrase. The New Revised Standard Version and the New International Version both translate the phrase "Be still," which perhaps implies a kind of quiet, peaceful waiting, while the Revised English Bible's "Let be then" carries more of a connotation of yielding and letting go. The Tanakh, however, with its insistent "Desist!" seems like a command to stop doing something destructive and prideful, and the Common English Bible's "That's enough!" leaves no doubt that God is weary of this destructive activity.

How do we know which of these various renderings is the best? We can look at the rest of the text to see if any of the translations makes more sense than the others in context, but even if we don't have enough information to make a judgment at this point, we can still note the interesting differences and allow them to provoke our awareness of and curiosity about the text. Perhaps some other step in the exegesis will help us decide, or maybe the commentaries, which will be consulted later in the process, can be of help.

Also, don't overlook the footnotes given in each translation. These footnotes provide valuable details about the text, indicate traditional translations, or show renderings that were a close second choice to the one picked by the translators. For example, the New Revised Standard Version translates 1 Corinthians 3:16 "Do you not know that you are God's temple and that God's spirit dwells in you?" The footnote adds the potentially important information that the word "you" in this verse is *plural* in the Greek. In other words, the footnote discloses what could well be hidden in the English translation, that the text is talking about the whole community as the temple of the Spirit, that God's spirit dwells in the community of Christ and not just in discrete individuals. Or again, in Matthew 26:25, when Jesus warns the disciples that a betrayer is among them, Judas says, "Surely not I, Rabbi?" and, according to the New International Version, Jesus responds, "Yes, it is you." But the footnote gives a second, and a more literal, translation: "You yourself have said it." The footnote, then, adds some insight, namely that Judas's question was a kind of self-incrimination.

II. Getting Introduced to the Text

Now that we have chosen the text and placed it clearly on the table, we need to take the first steps in the complex process of getting to know our text well:

D. Read the text for basic understanding

There is nothing fancy about this step. We are not trying to pry loose hidden meanings or perform theological analysis at this point. We are simply trying to make sure that we understand the straightforward meaning of the words and syntax of the text. This is the time to look up any unfamiliar terms in the text, like "ephah" or "zealot" or "phylactery," in a Bible dictionary. The punctuation of the text can be a good guide to syntactical meaning, but we should be warned that punctuation marks are later additions to the text and are therefore already interpretations of a sort.

Suppose our text is Matthew 12:1–8:

> At that time Jesus went through the grainfields on the sabbath; his disciples were hungry, and they began to pluck heads of grain and to eat. When the Pharisees saw it, they said to him, "Look, your disciples are doing what is not lawful to do on the sabbath."

He said to them, "Have you not read what David did when he and his companions were hungry? He entered the house of God and ate the bread of the Presence, which it was not lawful for him or his companions to eat, but only for the priests. Or have you not read in the law that on the sabbath the priests in the temple break the sabbath and yet are guiltless? I tell you, something greater than the temple is here. But if you had known what this means, 'I desire mercy and not sacrifice,' you would not have condemned the guiltless. For the Son of Man is lord of the sabbath."

Here are some of the questions, most of them about simple facts, that, depending upon what we already know and don't know, we may want to look up in a Bible encyclopedia, a Bible dictionary, or the background section of a commentary just so we can understand the plain meaning of the text:

- What is the "sabbath"?
- What are "heads of grain"?
- What is a "Pharisee"?
- What did David do when he and his companions were hungry, and where is it written down? Is it in the Bible?
- What is the "bread of the Presence"?
- What is the law about eating this bread, and where is it written? Is it in the Bible, too?
- What is a priest?
- Where in the law is it written that "the priests in the temple break the sabbath and yet are guiltless"?
- What is the temple?
- What does the title "Son of Man" mean?

Obviously, any one of these questions could trail off into a lengthy research project, but that is not the goal here. We just want to make sure we understand the plain, surface meaning of the text, and that means finding some basic definitions of terms.

E. Place the text in its larger context

Earlier we pointed out that a biblical text is like a swatch of wallpaper torn from the wall. We have a text, but the larger pattern can get lost.

In this step, we are, just for a moment, going to put our "swatch" back on the wall so that we can see where it fits in the overall scheme of things. Suppose someone handed you a page from a mystery novel that contained a scene in which a corporate accountant is arrested in his office by the police and charged with embezzlement, and then the person asked you, "What does this scene mean?" You would not be able to give a good answer to that without asking more questions. Does this scene occur at the beginning of the novel, in the middle, or at the end? What else do we know from the novel that would help us interpret this scene? Do we know what the police don't seem to know, that the accountant is innocent of the crime? Or maybe we know that the accountant is guilty of embezzlement, all right, but that the accountant is also guilty of murder as well. Or perhaps we know that the "accountant" is actually an undercover informant employed by the police to gather information about the corporation, and therefore the arrest is part of the cover. In sum, in order to interpret this scene, we need see it in its place in the whole novel.

Just so, in order to understand a biblical text, we need to know how it fits into the whole, at least into the context of the biblical book in which it is found. How do we discover this? How do we paste the swatch back onto the wall? One place to start is to find (or create) an outline of the book in which our text is found and to locate our text in that outline. Most good biblical commentaries and reliable Bible encyclopedias include outlines of biblical books. By examining two or three of these outlines, we can begin to see possibilities for how our text fits into the larger structure and into the overall flow and development of the book.

Let us imagine, for example, that our text is the story of Jesus' encounter with the tax collector Zacchaeus, found in Luke 19:1–10. Here is how several significant commentaries situate that story:

- Alan Culpepper in *The New Interpreter's Bible* places this story in a large unit called "The Journey to Jerusalem" (9:51–19:27) but also sees it as a part of a smaller subunit called "Jesus' Gospel to the Rich and Poor" (18:1–19:27). This subunit includes such texts as the parable of the Persistent Widow, the parable of the Pharisee and the Tax Collector, and the story of the rich ruler who asked Jesus about eternal life.[8] Culpepper aims our vision on the text in a particular direction, then: How is our passage about the issue of wealth and poverty?

- Keith Nickle in *Preaching the Gospel of Luke* also places the Zacchaeus story in a large unit called "Journey to Jerusalem," but he has a different title for the subunit in which the text appears: "Hearing with Understanding and Seeing with Perception." Nickle, then, gives us another way to see our passage as a part of the whole of Luke. The theme of this section in Luke, Nickle indicates, is rightly perceiving that the reign of God has come near in Jesus. Who gets it right? Not the rich ruler (18:18–25), nor the disciples (18:26–35). Improbably it is a blind man who rightly sees (18:35–43) and a rich sinner who humbly submits (Zacchaeus).[9]

- Sharon Ringe in her commentary on Luke in *The Westminster Bible Companion* series places the Zacchaeus story in a long section she calls "Making the Path While Walking: The Road to Jerusalem" (9:51–19:28) and also in a smaller unit called "Following Jesus" (18:1–19:28). The emphasis, then, in Ringe's outline is on Jesus' journey toward Jerusalem as a metaphor for a certain way of life, a journey others are invited to share and a path of life that people are beckoned to follow.[10]

What can we learn about the Zacchaeus story by looking at these three outlines of Luke? We have found that this story is a small part of a grand Lukan narrative describing Jesus' journey to Jersualem. We have also gained three interesting and different angles of vision on the Zacchaeus part of this journey. Culpepper's outline encourages us to be attentive to issues of wealth and poverty, while Nickle alerts us to matters of discernment and perception, and Ringe calls our attention to the way of life that Jesus presents and to which Zacchaeus responds.

Some biblical texts, especially certain sections of the Gospels, appear in more than one place in the Bible. If a version of our text appears elsewhere, a careful comparison of the text with its parallels can reveal differences—sometimes small, sometimes large—that can serve as interpretive clues. Suppose that our text is Matthew 16:5–12, the conversation between Jesus and the disciples about bread, faith, and the teaching of the religious leaders. Some version of this appears also in Mark (which most scholars believe Matthew copied) and Luke. Here are the three parallel texts:

Matthew 16:5–12

5When the disciples reached the other side, they had forgotten to bring any bread. 6Jesus said to them, "Watch out, and beware of the yeast of the Pharisees and Sadducees." 7They said to one another, "It is because we have brought no bread." 8And becoming aware of it, Jesus said, "You of little faith, why are you talking about having no bread? 9Do you still not perceive? Do you not remember the five loaves for the five thousand, and how many baskets you gathered? 10Or the seven loaves for the four thousand, and how many baskets you gathered? 11How could you fail to perceive that I was not speaking about bread? Beware of the yeast of the Pharisees and Sadducees!" 12Then they understood that he had not told them to beware of the yeast of bread, but of the teaching of the Pharisees and Sadducees.

Mark 8:14–21

14Now the disciples had forgotten to bring any bread; and they had only one loaf with them in the boat. 15And he cautioned them, saying, "Watch out—beware of the yeast of the Pharisees and the yeast of Herod." 16They said to one another, "It is because we have no bread." 17And becoming aware of it, Jesus said to them, "Why are you talking about having no bread? Do you still not perceive or understand? Are your hearts hardened? 18Do you have eyes, and fail to see? Do you have ears, and fail to hear? And do you not remember? 19When I broke the five loaves for the five thousand, how many baskets full of broken pieces did you collect?" They said to him, "Twelve." 20"And the seven for the four thousand, how many baskets full of broken pieces did you collect?" And they said to him, "Seven." 21Then he said to them, "Do you not yet understand?"

Luke 12:1

Meanwhile, when the crowd gathered by the thousands, so that they trampled on one another, he began to speak first to his disciples, "Beware of the yeast of the Pharisees, that is, their hypocrisy."

We can see a number of differences among these three versions. For example, in Mark the story ends with Jesus exclaiming, "Do you not yet understand?" In other words, for Mark the spotlight falls on the disciples and their failure to understand what Jesus is talking about. In our Matthean text, however, the story ends quite differently. A light bulb goes on in the disciples' heads; they *do* understand what Jesus meant. This not only presents a different portrait of the disciples—they can and do understand Jesus—it also shifts the emphasis toward what Jesus is teaching them, namely, to beware of the religious leaders. When we look at Luke's version, his is much shorter. Mark says that Jesus and the disciples are on a boat trip across the sea, and Matthew implies they have just finished this journey, but Luke eliminates the travel story altogether and cuts right to the chase: the warning about the religious leaders. But notice, however, that according to Luke the problem with the religious leaders is *hypocrisy*, whereas in Matthew, Jesus warns the disciples about their *teaching*. In Luke, Jesus is concerned that the religious leaders talk one way but act another, but Matthew's Jesus doesn't even like the way they talk! There are several other variations among these three versions, but we can already see how comparing them makes visible some of the distinctive emphases of our text from Matthew.

Even at this early phase in the process, multiple strands of interpretation emerge. Having all these different possibilities on the table may seem confusing at this point, but it actually suggests the richness of any single biblical text. Here in the early going, the preacher probably will want to keep all of the options on the table, waiting for more information to make choices among them. Or it may be that, by exploring these various possibilities, the preacher is already beginning to hear one speaking more clearly and forcefully than the others. Even if this is the case, this early intuition about the text can be treated seriously, but there is no need to tighten down the bolts just yet. There is much more yet to learn about the passage.

III. Attending to the Text

Now that we have been introduced to our text, it is time to become even more deeply acquainted by engaging the text in vigorous conversation. This phase of the exegesis is playful and freewheeling, in its own way. We are trying to get to know the text in much the same way that we would get to know a new friend, by spending time with the text, asking it many questions, and experiencing the text in many different moods and contexts.

F. Listen attentively to the text

The art of biblical exegesis, put very simply, involves learning how to ask questions of a biblical text.[11] Two major problems can cause this to go awry: (1) We can ask "trick" questions, or (2) we can ask good questions but refuse to listen to the responses that the text gives. When we ask only questions to which we think we already know the answers, these are nothing but trick questions. When we dare to ask real and open questions but then resist being surprised or troubled by what the text replies, we have shut our ears to its voice.

At this step in the exegesis, the preacher begins the interrogation of the text by asking every potentially fruitful question that comes to mind. This is not the place to worry about whether our questions are theologically correct or reverent enough. This is instead the place to bombard the text with every honest query we can think up. This is the place to challenge the text, even argue with it. Sure, some of the questions we ask of a text will turn out to be trivial or misguided, but this is not the time for caution. What happens in the conversation between us and the text will be checked later. Indeed, most of the remaining steps in this exegetical process are designed to put the results of our interrogation to the test. So if we give ourselves at this point the freedom to attend to the text in all its gnarly complexities and to ask of it every question we are provoked to ask, the chances are increased that we will genuinely hear the text's voice and receive its claim upon us.

Where do our questions come from? Some of them will be generated by the theological tradition of the preacher, some by the emphases of the church year,[12] others by what is happening in the contemporary situation, and still others by puzzling or intriguing aspects of the text itself. Most of the time, though, the questions will emerge from the interaction among these conversational partners: that is, from the totality of our situation as we stand before the text.

Take, for example, the prophet Amos's word from the Lord denouncing the religious festivals of the people:

> I hate, I despise your festivals,
>   and I take no delight in your solemn assemblies.
> Even though you offer me your burnt offerings and grain offerings,
>   I will not accept them;
> And the offerings of well-being of your fatted animals
>   I will not look upon.
> Take away from me the noise of your songs;
>   I will not listen to the melody of your harps.
> But let justice roll down like waters,
>   and righteousness like an everflowing stream.
>
> (Amos 5:21–24)

The preacher may ask such questions as:

- What in the world does God have against festivals and songs? Is it that the people participating in them are sinful? But didn't the father of the prodigal son throw a noisy, merry party for his sinful son? Why not here?
- What is the "character" or personality of God in this text? Is God petulant or just deeply aggrieved? Is God always this offended, or has God simply had it with *these* people?
- I can understand God's anger in this text, but why does God explicitly refuse the people's offerings? What kind of God turns down offerings?
- God wants "justice" and "righteousness." Are these two different things or two ways of emphatically expressing the same thing?
- If Amos were to issue his prophetic word in our worship setting today, would he deliver the same message? Is our worship a "solemn assembly" that God despises and does not enjoy? If so, what is it about our worship that God hates? If it isn't, why are we different from Amos's audience?
- Or maybe Amos wouldn't even come to our worship setting today. Could his contemporary audience be the whole culture and not just the religious folk? Where are the festivals and solemn assemblies in society?
- Is there a way to make our festivals places of justice and righteousness? Can justice and worship be connected? If so, what would this look like?
- This text sounds grim, like really bad news. That's OK, but what about the people who come to church just barely hanging on by a thread? Would Amos deliver the same word to them? Or is there a possibility that what sounds like bad news is really the "good news"? Can it be bad news and good news at the same time? For the same people?

Or suppose the text is Mark 5:21–34, the story of the woman with a flow of blood who touched Jesus' cloak. Ronald J. Allen, who suggests a similar process for interrogating texts in his *Interpreting the Gospel: An Introduction to Preaching*, provides a list of questions preachers could ask of this text, including:[13]

- Is it significant that the main character (other than Jesus) is a woman?
- What is the role of women in Mark and of the woman in this passage?
- Why does this woman approach Jesus from behind?
- What is the role of touch as an agency of healing?
- What is Mark telling us about Jesus by emphasizing that Jesus felt power go out from him at the woman's touch?
- Why does he want to know who touched him?
- What is the significance of Jesus' address, "Daughter"?
- Is faith necessary for healing?
- Why does Jesus tell the woman at the end of the story to be healed of her disease when the narrative is already clear that she is healed?
- If Jesus had unlimited power to heal, why did he heal only a handful of the multitudinous sick and infirm in Palestine?

Many other questions could be asked of these texts. The temptation that must be resisted is simply to leap over this free-flowing time of questioning and go directly to the biblical commentaries, the books written by the expert interrogators of texts. Later on, it will be important to consult the biblical experts, but it is a mistake to do so too early. Commentaries can provide many valuable services, and they can check and guide our exegesis, but the one thing they cannot do is tell us what the text is saying this day, in this place, to the people who will hear our sermon. The preacher, not the author of the commentary, is the only person who has one foot firmly planted in the biblical text and the other foot firmly planted in the concrete circumstances of the hearers. The preacher, not the commentator, is the one sent by these people at this moment to this text, and, therefore, only the preacher truly knows the full range of questions to ask. The commentator's interrogation of the text can assist the preacher's exploration, but it cannot replace it. Commentaries were made to serve the preacher, and not the preacher to serve the commentaries.

Questioning a text is a creative, imaginative activity—something like brainstorming. The main difference is that we are not trying to expand the range of our own creativity; we are trying to knock the barnacles off our assumptions about the text so that it can speak to us anew. No one can prescribe or predict how such a free-form activity takes place, but here are some suggestions for getting a fresh look at the text. The preacher may want to engage all of these suggestions, but most of the time, the preacher will select the most promising possibilities:

1. A number of homileticians encourage the writing of a paraphrase of the text. If we attempt to rephrase every line of the text in contemporary language, questions of meaning are quickly brought to the surface. Another good approach to the paraphrase is to set the text completely aside at some point and then write the passage as you remember it, in your own words. Now, compare what you have written with the text itself. What, if anything, did you leave out? Were the omissions minor or major? Were elements left out because they are insignificant or because they are troublesome in some way? What, if anything, did you emphasize in your paraphrase? Was it underscored because it connects to some concern you brought to the text?

2. If the text is a narrative, stand in the shoes of each of the characters and experience the story from these varied perspectives. For instance, if the text is the story of the healing in the synagogue in Mark 3:1–6, move through the narrative taking the role of Jesus. Then go back through the story from the point of view of the man with the withered hand, as a member of the Sabbath congregation gathered for worship, and finally as one of the Pharisees present. As much as is possible, suspend judgment about who is the hero and who is the villain.

Identify with each character and take a sympathetic view of that character's understanding of the world. Try to experience, for instance, what is truly at stake for a loyal Pharisee as the action unfolds in the synagogue that Sabbath.

3. Explore the text looking for details that appear, at first glance, to be unusual or out of place. Why, for example, does Mark tell us that the grass was green out in the desert where the five thousand were fed by Jesus (Mark 6:39)? It seems to be a random bit of graphic detail in an otherwise straightforward description. Perhaps so, but it may also be that Mark is linking this story to Isaiah's vision of the desert in blossom. Or again, Mark has told us that the crowd that day was "like sheep without a shepherd" (Mark 6:34). The prophet Ezekiel employed the same image and went on to announce the promise of God: "I myself will search for my sheep, . . . and I will feed them on the mountains of Israel. . . . I will feed them with good pasture . . . ;

there they shall lie down in good grazing land" (Ezek. 34:11, 13, 14). Mark also told us that Jesus "ordered them . . . all . . . to sit down," on the green grass (Mark 6:39), and that command echoes the language of Psalm 23: "He makes me lie down in green pastures" (Ps. 23:2). Is Mark's "green grass" an Old Testament allusion? If so, what does this say about the feeding of the five thousand?

4. Ask if the text has a center of gravity—that is, a main thought around which all other thoughts are organized. To illustrate, I can remember hearing many sermons in my youth on the phrase "all have sinned and fall short of the glory of God" (Rom. 3:23). The thrust of these sermons was, of course, that everybody is a sinner and needs to repent. "All have sinned," the preacher would boom, his accusing finger roaming across the guilty congregation. Now the verse does say that, to be sure, and it is a truth that deserves to be proclaimed, but look at the whole passage in which this one verse is found:

> But now, apart from law, the righteousness of God has been disclosed, and is attested by the law and the prophets, the righteousness of God through faith in Jesus Christ for all who believe. For there is no distinction, since all have sinned and fall short of the glory of God; they are now justified by his grace as a gift, through the redemption that is in Christ Jesus, whom God put forward as a sacrifice of atonement by his blood, effective through faith. He did this to show his righteousness, because in his divine forbearance he had passed over the sins previously committed; it was to prove at the present time that he himself is righteous and that he justifies the one who has faith in Jesus. (Rom. 3:21–26)

Viewing this larger passage, we can quickly see that sin is not the main event here. This single phrase about human sin is spoken in the service of a more central theme, namely the righteousness of God. The whole passage is built like a folk dance, the phrases spinning out toward concepts like law and prophecy, sin and redemption, but always returning to circle the main theme of God's righteousness. Four times the text names God's righteousness, and the center of gravity of this passage is not you and me and our sin, but rather God who is mercifully righteous. When we preach this text, then, our fingers may point for a moment at ourselves and our sinfulness, but ultimately the magnetic north of the text will swing the compass toward the gracious and righteous God.

5. Look for conflict, either in the text or behind it. Human communication is a force that implies the presence of opposing forces. A command ("Clean up your room!") implies the presence of the counterforce of inaction or active resistance. A question ("Do you love me?") arises from the struggle between knowledge and the counterforce of uncertainty. A declaration ("Marilyn is a fine lawyer") implies other, less flattering possibilities and attempts to sweep them aside.

So we can look for the conflict implicit or explicit in a text. Sometimes conflict clearly occurs *in* a biblical text. "Get behind me, Satan! For you are setting your mind not on divine things," said Jesus to Peter (Mark 8:33), making the conflict plain. "You foolish Galatians! Who has bewitched you?" said Paul (Gal. 3:1), fanning the flames of the debate. In other texts, the conflict lies *behind* the text, and the passage stands as a response to the conflict hidden in the situational context.[14] Why would Psalm 150 urge that God be praised with crashing cymbals and blasting trumpets unless it were working over against lethargy, passivity, or, at the very least, a less celebrative view of worship?

Conflict can be simultaneously present both in the text and behind it. When Jesus said, "Give therefore to the emperor the things that are the emperor's, and to God the things that are God's" (Matt. 22:21), it was in the midst of conflict with the Pharisees, but it may well have been remembered and cherished by the early church because it also illumined a debate among them about conflicting loyalties with the power of the state.

6. Look for connections between the text and what comes before and after it. Mark 8:22–26, for example, relates the story of a blind man who is healed by Jesus. The story is quite unusual in that Jesus' first touching of the man's eyes brings only partial vision. It is only with a second touch that the man sees clearly. Notice, though, that this story of two touches is followed by the story of Jesus asking Peter, "But who do you say that I am?" Peter sees in part—"You are the Messiah"— but he misunderstands that messiahship means the cross. In other words, if Peter is going to see who Jesus truly is, he will need two touches as well. The story of the growing awareness of the disciples and that of the growing vision of the blind man serve as mutually interpreting narratives.

7. View the text through many different "eyes." How would this passage appear to a man? A woman? A child? To a rich person? A poor person? A homeless person? To a farmer? A city dweller? A prisoner? To a feminist? To an employer? A worker? An unemployed person? To a homosexual? To a parent? To a person outside the church? To a Jew or a Buddhist? To a person of a race different from our own?

Sometimes, as we noted earlier, exegesis takes place in a group setting, and the preacher can actually hear the reactions of a variety of people. Much of the time, though, preachers will need to imagine the presence of a diverse group. Preachers cannot, and should not, presume to know how all these people would respond and must therefore always be reading, studying, and listening to voices of people unlike themselves.

Here is the place for the preacher to survey the congregation in the imagination's eye. Picture the people who are likely to hear the sermon; call to mind what you know of their lives. Go to the text on behalf of the young family in the front row, the teenager in the back, the young woman just beginning a career, the man whose father has recently died, the eight-year-old girl sitting there with her mother and new stepfather. Ask the text questions they would ask. Ask, on their behalf, the questions they may not dare to ask. Be their pastor—their advocate—and then listen to the text, hoping for a word for them.

8. Think of the text, as J. Randall Nichols suggests, "as someone's attempt to reflect on the answer to some important question,"[15] and then try to discern what that question could be. Nichols cites as an example the text in the book of Esther where Mordecai challenges Esther to use her position as queen to speak a courageous (and illegal) word to the king on behalf of the Jews: "Who knows? Perhaps you have come to royal dignity for just such a time as this?" (Esth. 4:14):

> On the surface, it looks like an anguished, but provincial, issue largely unrelated to anything we might face these days. To try to find a point of contact on the surface of the text would be ludicrous—rather like saying that the text teaches us we ought to get out and vote for the reform candidate even at the risk of pneumonia on a bitter November day.[16]

When the text is explored beneath the surface, though, as a response to questions such as, When is it more critical to be faithful than to save one's own skin? or, Are we more defined by the circumstances we find ourselves in or by those things we are willing to die for? Then, claims Nichols, "there is a point of contact, several in fact, with the modern hearer."[17]

9. Ask, as Fred Craddock suggests, what the text is *doing*.[18] Is it commanding, singing, narrating, explaining, warning, debating, praying, reciting? The words "Praise the Lord!" mean one thing if they are the opening lyrics of an exuberant anthem, quite another if they come as a rebuke to inattentive worshipers. In each case we have the same words, but because they are sent out to perform different tasks, they mean quite different things.

One way to get at what a text is doing is to imagine that it is to be set to music. What sort of music would that be? Mark's announcement that "Jesus came to Galilee, proclaiming the good news of God" (Mark 1:14) may call for a bright trumpet flourish, while Lamentations's cry, "How lonely sits the city that once was full of people!" (Lam. 1:1) calls for a melancholy violin, and the thunderous hymns of the multitudes in Revelation will demand a full orchestra complete with throbbing timpani and crashing cymbals.

At this point in the exegetical process, curiosity and freewheeling inquisitiveness are virtues. The preacher floods the text with questions, even with bold challenges, and listens eagerly for responses, faith to faith. The preacher should fill a blank sheet with the resulting insights and ideas, no matter how far-fetched some of them may seem at the moment. Like the maidens in the famous parable, some of these insights will turn out to be foolish and some will be wise, but for the moment every possibility from the text should be preserved.

When this is done, the preacher begins the task of testing these insights by placing them into the crucible of scholarly and critical exegesis. Actually, the step of listening attentively to the text and the subsequent steps of critical testing form a repeating loop in exegesis. We listen, then we test, but the testing sharpens our ears to listen again. Both the open listening and the rigorous testing are important, since, ironically, critical exegesis is better at warning the preacher about what the text does *not* say than it is at telling the preacher what the text *does* say. So we listen to the Bible faithfully, but if we do so uncritically, we will often mistake the whispers of our own inner voices for the biblical word. If we only perform the critical analysis and not the attentive listening, we will gather data *about* the Bible rather than hear the living word that comes *through* the Bible.

IV. Testing What Is Heard in the Text

If all has gone well with the brainstorming, we should have a page or two filled with ideas and insights. Are they good ideas and insights? We will not know until we put them into the crucible of scholarly inquiry. As we said earlier, biblical scholarship done at a distance and contained in commentaries cannot tell what to say in a sermon, but it can help to burn away the stubble of glittering thoughts that finally have no standing in the text.

The preacher should now explore the text historically, literarily, and theologically. The best and fastest way to do this is to look at what responsible scholars have said in biblical surveys, such as:

Birch, Bruce C., et al. *A Theological Introduction to the Old Testament* (Nashville: Abingdon Press, 1999)

Blount, Brian K., et al. (editors). *True to Our Native Land: An African American New Testament Commentary* (Minneapolis: Fortress Press, 2007)

Boring, Eugene. *An Introduction to the New Testament: History, Literature, Theology* (Louisville, KY: Westminster John Knox Press, 2012)

Brown, Raymond. *Introduction to the New Testament* (New York: Doubleday, Anchor Bible, 1997)

Brueggemann, Walter. *An Introduction to the Old Testament: Canon and Christian Imagination* (Louisville, KY: Westminster John Knox Press, 2003)

Collins, John. *Introduction to the Hebrew Bible* (Minneapolis: Augsburg Fortress Press, 2004)

Gottwald, Norman. *The Hebrew Bible: A Socio-Literary Introduction* (Minneapolis: Augsburg Fortress Press, 2002)

Holladay, Carl. *A Critical Introduction to the New Testament: Interpreting the Message and Meaning of Jesus Christ* (Nashville: Abingdon Press, 2005)

Johnson, Luke Timothy. *The Writings of the New Testament: An Interpretation*, rev. ed. (Minneapolis: Fortress Press, 1999)

Newsom, Carol A., and Ringe, Sharon H., eds. *The Women's Bible Commentary*, exp. ed. (Louisville, KY: Westminster John Knox, 1998)

Page, Hugh R., et al., eds. *The Africana Bible: Reading Israel's Scriptures from Africa and the African Diaspora* (Minneapolis: Fortress, 2009)

G. Explore the text historically

To explore the text historically means looking at two levels of history at least. Biblical texts often speak of events in history, such as the reign of a king or the destruction of Jerusalem, but biblical texts also *have* a history, in the sense that they were written in particular moments in history and sometimes modified as they were passed along from generation to generation. It is possible, then, maintain John Hayes and Carl Holladay, to speak of both "the 'history *in* the text' and the 'history of the text.'"[19]

The book of Daniel, for example, describes events set as early as the sixth century BCE, but the best evidence indicates that the book itself was composed in the mid-second century BCE. The interpreter, therefore, needs to know about both the period depicted in the book and the period in which the book was written.[20]

Fred Craddock has noted that the interpreter of 1 Corinthians 10:1–5 needs to be aware of not just two levels of history, but several. In this passage Paul refers to a Jewish interpretation of the exodus, and at least four historical levels are implicitly present: (1) the exodus event itself, (2) the narrative description of this in the book of Exodus, (3) the later Jewish interpretation, and (4) Paul's use of the story in the context of the situation at Corinth.[21]

In *The Living and Active Word*, O. C. Edwards Jr. compared the historical levels in a biblical text to the architecture of an ancient cathedral:

> Perhaps you have had the experience of visiting an English cathedral that includes in its structure almost the entire history of English architecture. The crypt may be Saxon and the nave Norman, the choir Decorated and the sanctuary

Perpendicular, while the rood screen is Jacobite and the baptistry Victorian. The same kind of indications of period in a gospel story are obvious to a trained eye. One can detect which elements go back to the ministry of Jesus, which were added during the time the story was handed down by word of mouth, which came from the hand of Mark, and which from a later gospel writer.[22]

The goal of the preacher is to discover as much as possible about all the historical levels of the text. It would take a lifetime to do this thoroughly, of course, but much can be learned about a text's authorship, date of composition, social setting, and so on in Old and New Testament introductory textbooks, or in the opening sections of a good commentary. More recent reference works are especially helpful because they are likely to include sociological and political perspectives on the text's history often missing from older historical analyses.[23] The historical environments in which biblical texts were created were as highly charged politically as our own, and as Walter Brueggemann insists, no biblical text is socially "innocent or disinterested."[24]

A preacher gathers historical information not simply to garner data but to test the results of the brainstorming, "listen attentively to the text" phase of the exegesis (step "F"). How might the preacher test the exegesis historically? Suppose that the preacher is working on Galatians 6:11–18:

> See what large letters I make when I am writing in my own hand! It is those who want to make a good showing in the flesh that try to compel you to be circumcised—only that they may not be persecuted for the cross of Christ. Even the circumcised do not themselves obey the law, but they want you to be circumcised so that they may boast about your flesh. May I never boast of anything except the cross of our Lord Jesus Christ, by which the world has been crucified to me, and I to the world. For neither circumcision nor uncircumcision is anything; but a new creation is everything! As for those who will follow this rule—peace be upon them, and mercy, and upon the Israel of God.

From now on, let no one make trouble for me; for I carry the marks of Jesus branded on my body.

May the grace of our Lord Jesus Christ be with your spirit, brothers and sisters. Amen.

In the brainstorming phase of the exegesis, the preacher made some notes about key phrases in the text:

- *See what large letters I make when I am writing in my own hand!* This is obviously so important to Paul that he is personally invested. What about the faith today summons our personal investment?
- *"those who want to make a good showing in the flesh"*: Is this text saying something about the tendency to show off with religion, to make a public display of religion to earn brownie points with others? Like having a "God Is My Co-Pilot" bumper sticker on your car?
- *"compel you to be circumcised"*: Is this about power plays in the church, like compelling people to believe something or do something to count as real Christians?
- *"that they may not be persecuted for the cross of Christ"*: What is this about avoiding persecution? Is someone trying to make Christianity safe from cultural rejection?
- *"they want you to be circumcised so that they may boast"*: Why would somebody else's circumcision be grounds for boasting? Is this about legalism or pride? Is it about making other Christians do what you want so you will look good?
- *"As for those who will follow this rule—peace be upon them"*: Is this text a case of Paul's rules versus his opponents' rules? Are some rules better in the faith than others? Is the rule of the "new creation" really a rule? or is it a vision that goes beyond all rules?

Not all of these ideas and hunches are good, of course, and the purpose of this phase of the exegesis is to put these brainstorms to the test. When this preacher read Luke Timothy Johnson's *The Writings of the New Testament*, one comment on the historical background of this text jumped out:

What stake did community members have in circumcision? According to Paul, it made them appear to be normal members of Israel rather than candidates for persecution that was brought about precisely because the crucified Messiah was a stumbling block to those who saw Torah as the ultimate form of righteousness (3:13)—a point illustrated by Paul's own past experience (1:13–14). While it may be difficult to contextualize these statements in the life of the Galatian church—since we know so little about their experience— it is clear that, in Paul's eyes, the choice of circumcision was both cowardly and a rejection of the experience of God through the preaching of the crucified Messiah (3:1).[25]

What Johnson says highlights a couple of the preacher's hunches about the text, but adds deeper meaning to them. Johnson connects circumcision in this text with the desire to appear "to be normal" and not to be "candidates for persecution." In other words, the key issue here is not mechanical legalism but fear. Paul's opponents advocate circumcision so that they will look harmless to the outside world, just normal religious people and not people whose religion is dangerously countercultural. Now the preacher has an angle on the claim of the text. The text challenges all attempts by Christians to get out of harm's way by sanding away the rough edges of the Christian faith so that we will come across as "normal folks," and not weird countercultural people who eat and drink with sinners, who do not believe that the nation is God, who work for reconciliation and peace, and who call into question the voracious appetites of a consumer culture.

H. Explore the literary character of the text

Here the preacher examines the text to determine both its literary character and function. A laundry list is different from a short story, a poem, or a political essay. A psalm is different from a proverb or a parable. Each of these types of literature has its own stylistic features and pattern of construction. A letter in our mailbox and a letter to the editor in the newspaper are both letters, but they serve quite different functions.

Suppose that the preacher is working on Mark 10:35–45:

> James and John, the sons of Zebedee, came forward to him and said to him, "Teacher, we want you to do for us whatever we ask of you." And he said to them, "What is it you want me to do for you?" And they said to him, "Grant us to sit, one at your right hand and one at your left, in your glory." But Jesus said to them, "You do not know what you are asking. Are you able to drink the cup that I drink, or be baptized with the baptism that I am baptized with?" They replied, "We are able." Then Jesus said to them, "The cup that I drink you will drink; and with the baptism with which I am baptized, you will be baptized; but to sit at my right hand or at my left is not mine to grant, but it is for those for whom it has been prepared."
>
> When the ten heard this, they began to be angry with James and John. So Jesus called them and said to them, "You know that among the Gentiles those whom they recognize as their rulers lord it over them, and their great ones are tyrants over them. But it is not so among you; but whoever wishes to become great among you must be your servant, and whoever wishes to be first among you must be slave of all. For the Son of Man came not to be served but to serve, and to give his life a ransom for many."

During the brainstorming phase, the preacher has come up with dozens of ideas about this text. Now, in order to explore the literary character of the text and because this text is obviously a narrative, the preacher decides to read Robert C. Tannehill's article "The Gospels and Narrative Literature" in *The New Interpreter's Bible*.[26] There the preacher finds that the text is not just a garden-variety story but a particular kind of narrative called a "pronouncement story." In pronouncement stories, Tannehill says, "Jesus responds to a person or situation, and this response is the main point of the narrative." In fact, Tannehill identifies this story even more sharply as a "correction story," a type of pronouncement story in which Jesus' word corrects the views of someone else. The effect of these correction stories is to shift the reader from one view to another.[27]

So the preacher learns that (1) the main emphasis of this text, the thing everything else turns upon, is the statement of Jesus at the end,

"Whoever wishes to become great among you must be your servant, and whoever wishes to be first among you must be slave of all. For the Son of Man came not to be served but to serve, and to give his life a ransom for many," and (2) this statement of Jesus is a correction of a rival view, namely, the disciples' attitude of ambition. As a pronouncement story, everything about this text is colored by this conflict of views, servanthood versus ambition, so the preacher reviews the results of the brainstorming, weeding out all the ideas that are not reflective of this tension in the text.

I. Explore the text theologically

Critical theological exploration of the text involves pulling out of the textual fabric a single thread already glimpsed, through historical analysis, as a part of the pattern. We are trying to discover what specific assumptions and claims are present in the text regarding God-in-relation-to-humanity. J. Randall Nichols reminds us that we are not trying "to shoehorn a text into a theological mold or to lay an interpretive template over it." Rather, we are attempting "to connect the narrative or poetic or historical content of a text with the ways of thinking the Christian tradition has used to make sense of itself."[28]

The introductory historical background material recommended in step "G" will help in naming major theological themes and issues present in each book of the Bible. Another key factor is the theological vocabulary employed in the text. Words like "faith," "grace," "Lord," "covenant," "flesh," "glory," and "savior" are powerful and rich theological concepts that vibrate with memory and meaning wherever they are used. When Paul uses the word "law," he means both the same thing and something different than the psalmist does in Psalm 1. The preacher must maintain the tension between understanding a theological word in a text as a musical chord with harmonies throughout the Bible and grasping the explicit meaning of that same word as it is used in this text. The preacher can often find help in theological wordbooks and in commentaries that include discussions of a book's significant theological vocabulary.

The biblical surveys recommended on pp. 101–2 will also help the preacher test the exegetical brainstormings theologically. Suppose the text being considered is the Song of Miriam and Moses in Exodus 15, which is sung as a response to the exodus, to God's saving of the people at the Red Sea. It begins,

> Then Moses and the Israelites sang this song to the LORD:
> "I will sing to the LORD, for he has triumphed gloriously;
>   horse and rider he has thrown into the sea.
> The LORD is my strength and my might,
>   and he has become my salvation;
> this is my God, and I will praise him,
>   my father's God, and I will exalt him.
> The LORD is a warrior;
>   the LORD is his name."
>
>   (vv. 1–3)

At first, the preacher is so offended by the warrior images and the seeming triumphalism in this passage that little of value can be seen. It sounds to the preacher like a "We won and you lost!" cheer. But gradually the preacher notices other things about this text—that it is a *song*, for one thing, that it is a kind of ecstatic praise, and that the song is not so much about the people's victory as it is about something triumphant God has done. This doesn't eliminate all of the problems, but it does open up another angle of vision.

Then the preacher, in order to test the exegesis theologically, turns to the discussion of this text in *A Theological Introduction to the Old Testament*, by Bruce C. Birch and others.[29] There the preacher finds the idea that this song actually encapsulates what the authors call "the pattern of Exodus faith . . . a paradigm for understanding the experience of God's grace."[30] This pattern is "Situation of Distress → Unexpected Deliverance → Response in Community."[31] Further, the preacher learns that the song springs from a liberated group of oppressed people whose first response to being freed is ecstatic praise. "The initial response of liberated Israel is *doxological*. The joy of Israel in their new freedom spontaneously bursts forth in praise."[32] These discoveries underscore the insights of the preacher about ecstasy and praise.

J. Check the text in the commentaries

Now that we have done our own exegetical work, the time has come to explore the text in biblical commentaries. "Why should one turn to a commentary, anyway?" asks Old Testament scholar Bernhard W. Anderson. "Reaching for a commentary is not the first step in interpreting a text," he acknowledges, and, indeed, "one should turn to a commentary only as a last resort." Nevertheless, commentaries are important resources for the preacher, and "in the final analysis," Anderson claims, "one ought to turn to a commentary." The reason? He puts it this way: "The reason is that we do not, or anyway should not, interpret the text individualistically but within a larger circle of interpretation, a community of discrimination where private views are checked, enriched, corrected, deepened."[33]

What is implied in Anderson's statement is that consulting commentaries is a way for the preacher to create a community of interpretation, a scholarly seminar on the biblical text. Here is yet another way to avoid the perils of doing biblical interpretation in an isolation ward. The preacher, now acquainted with the text, can summon a tableful of experts and scholars to assist in understanding the text and testing the preacher's hunches and insights. In the exchange of ideas and viewpoints, the preacher's understanding of the text is both challenged and enhanced. If the preacher consulted the commentaries too early, before engaging in the earlier steps, the temptation would be for the preacher to be quiet while the experts did all the talking. But we have waited until now to consult these commentaries—that is, until we have done our own homework on the text—and now we are prepared to moderate the discussion, to hear the experts as colleagues and consultants, and to contribute to the conversation ourselves.

Obviously, the greater the number of responsible voices we can gather at the table, the richer and more interesting the conversation will be. Recent commentaries will bring us the latest word in critical textual interpretation, but older, precritical commentaries should not be neglected, because they are in touch with textual issues filtered out by the refracting lenses of modern criticism. Some modern commentaries also include discussions of how the text has been interpreted throughout the church's history. Ancient interpreters, precisely because they are not products of our time, can often help us discover treasures in the text otherwise hidden to our modern eyes.

Moreover, as biblical scholar Elisabeth Schüssler Fiorenza warns, preachers ought not depend entirely upon the "established" biblical scholars at this point. Only by listening to scholarship that springs from less traditional perspectives—liberationist, feminist, ethnic, poetic, psychoanalytic, and so on—can the "vested interests" of all interpretation be exposed (even that which falsely presents itself as "neutral" and "objective"),[34] our own unstated presuppositions be challenged, and the fullness of the text be explored.

Most good commentaries will cover the same historical, literary, and theological ground we have traversed, and they can refine and challenge our findings at each point along the way. The commentators are not the ones, though, who bear the responsibility of preaching, and eventually we must leave the seminar and cross the bridge ourselves from the text to the place where our congregation waits to hear the sermon. The commentators can, at best, go only halfway across with us. Most of them, in fact, bid farewell much sooner, and we must go without them to the final step of the exegesis.

V. Moving toward the Sermon

Up to this point, we have engaged in a variety of exegetical activities, all in the hopes that the text would speak anew to our circumstances. We have looked carefully at the text. We have playfully and artfully engaged the text. We have consulted with the best scholars who have studied this text. Now the critical moment has come. Exegesis can go on forever. There is always more to learn about a biblical text, more facts to gather, more commentaries to consult. Preachers never get the sense that they are finished with exegesis, but, even with many loose ends dangling, the time for preaching fast approaches and we get to the point where, admitting we don't know everything we would like to know, our attention must nevertheless turn toward the sermon.

K. State the claim of the text upon the hearers (including the preacher)

Good exegesis can point us in the right direction, and it can eliminate wrongheaded interpretations of the text. It can provide essential information about the text, and it can uncover issues in the text we would never have seen at first glance. Exegesis can help us in many ways, but it finally cannot do what is most important: tell us what this text wishes to say on this occasion to our congregation. The preacher must decide this, and it is a risky and exciting decision.

As we have said, getting to know a biblical text is much like getting to know another person in a profound way. It takes time and energy to get to know someone else well. We must be with them long enough, and attend to them carefully enough, to know not only who they are at the moment but also who they have been in the past and the vision toward which they are moving. We must ask them questions and tell them of our own life, but we must not do all the talking. We must listen to them unselfishly, cherishing their word even when it does not connect immediately to our own desires and interests. We must observe them in many different situations, learning about their values and commitments as we see them in action. We must discover the patterns, customs, and even the habits around which they organize their lives. If we look at them and see only our own reflection, we do not know them. If we look at them and see only an "other," an object of our scrutiny, we do not know them. Only when we know who they are with us can we claim really to know them. An exegetical process introduces us to the text. It provides some crucial biographical information, and it even discloses some of the text's secrets. It is up to the preacher, then, to bring the life of the congregation into the text's presence, to dwell there long and prayerfully, and to discern the reality of this text as it is with us.

This is eventful. Something happens between text and people: a claim is made, a voice is heard, a textual will is exerted, and the sermon will be a bearing witness to this event. As the final step in the exegetical process, the preacher throws the first cord across the gap between text and sermon by describing the text's claim upon the hearers, including the preacher. We are ready to move on to the creation of the sermon itself only when we can finish the following sentence:

> **"In relation to those who will hear the sermon,
> what this text wants to say and do is . . ."**

Even though this "claim" step may seem simple, it is not. Preachers are tempted here merely to state ideas from the text, such as "All human beings are created in the image of God." True as that statement may be, it is not yet a *claim*. A claim is more like personal address.

It speaks to real people, and it wants a response. In fact, a good test of whether a statement is a claim or not is to address it to some real person who will hear the sermon, like DeShaun or Barbara, and to ask, "Does this statement call for any change in their lives?" Consider this statement: "DeShaun, Barbara, you and all other human beings are created in the image of God." This is not a claim, because it is simply a flat statement of theological truth. No response is called for; it is merely the announcement of an idea. But now consider this statement: "DeShaun, Barbara, despite those times when you may consider yourself to be of little value, you can be assured that you are, in fact, beloved by God, created in God's own image." Note how this does call for a response, a change of perspective, and it counts as a claim. The way this is stated, it is clear that the hearers (as represented here by DeShaun and Barbara) are being summoned to see themselves in a different light, to think about themselves in a different way. To state the claim of the text is to find that aspect of the biblical passage that speaks beyond the ancient page and into the contemporary context, addressing the hearers with the good news of God, news that calls for a change of mind, of heart, and of action—or a combination of these.

4

The Focus and Function of the Sermon

> Someone recently gave my son a compass. I see it almost
> everywhere around the house amid the rest of the clutter.
> Nothing in our house seems to stay in the same place, not even
> that compass. But the compass always seems to know where it is.
> Every time I see it, it is pointing in the same direction. This is the
> impressive thing about Christian witness.
>
> —Carl Michalson, "Communicating the Gospel"
> in *Theology Today*

> If you see something, say something.
> —U.S. Department of Homeland Security

The verb "to witness" has two main meanings: to see and to tell. Initially, witnessing is an act of seeing. If I say, "I witnessed the third game of the World Series" or "I witnessed the efforts of the fire company battling to save the school," I mean that I was there at the event and saw and experienced for myself what happened. To witness means in the first place to behold, to be present and active as an observer, to "take something in."

The other meaning of "to witness," however, faces in the opposite direction. Rather than "taking something in," witnessing involves "giving something out." Rather than seeing something, it means saying something. Rather than becoming aware of some event, it means making others aware of that event. "Witness" in the first sense means to *perceive*; in the second sense it means to *testify*. As Anna Carter Florence says, witness in the form of testimony "is both a narration of events and a confession of belief: we tell what we have seen and heard, and we confess what we believe about it."[1]

113

An unbreakable bond exists, of course, between these two meanings. One cannot witness in the second sense unless one has witnessed in the first sense. We can give testimony only about that which we have experienced. This does not imply that we have to understand everything before we can bear witness. Sometimes we testify to events we have experienced but don't yet comprehend, and sometimes our testimony is about things that remain partially hidden to us, as in, "I saw what happened, but I could tell there was more going on than I could see." But if we have seen and experienced nothing at all, we cannot be a witness. "I want to testify to the fact that the fire company fought the school fire bravely and put out the flames in less than an hour" is valid and reliable testimony only when said by one who experienced the firefighting firsthand.

When the preacher makes the turn from the exegesis of the biblical text toward the sermon itself, the preacher moves from being the first kind of witness to the second kind. We have been sent to the Scripture on behalf of the people, and having encountered and listened to the text, we have experienced firsthand the claim of the text. Now we turn toward the sermon, toward the pulpit, toward the people to tell the truth about this claim. The move from text to sermon is a move from beholding to attesting, from seeing to saying, from listening to telling, from perceiving to testifying, from *being* a witness to *bearing* witness.

From Text to Sermon: The Debates

This move from text to sermon is a decisive moment. Remember, the last step in the process of exegesis, the goal of the process really, was to try to say in a single sentence the text's claim upon us, to describe concisely the force of the text as it moves across our contemporary context, what the text wants to say and to do among us.

Stating the claim of the text is obviously a judgment call, a decision based on everything we have seen and experienced in the exegetical encounter, a decision that demands that we make some choices. Even the smallest biblical text is larger than any one sermon. A biblical text can potentially yield many meanings, many different sermons, and the next time we go to the same biblical text we may well hear a very different claim than we heard this time. The claim of the text is quite occasion specific; it is what we hear on *this day*, from *this text*, for *these people*, in *these circumstances*, at *this juncture* in their lives. Is there a word from the Lord *today?*

But now that we have used our best judgment to state the claim of the biblical text, we turn from the text to the task of crafting the sermon. This involves, among other things, a shift of genre, from the genres of biblical texts (parable, proverb, epistle, miracle story, and so on) to the different literary genre of the sermon or homily. How do we travel across the bridge from the "claim of the text" to the sermon itself? A claim, after all, is a single concise sentence. How do we unfold this claim into the larger and more expansive sermon?

Teachers of preaching are not in agreement about this most critical moment in sermon development. Two matters are especially up for debate. First, some homileticians advise that once the preacher has exegeted the biblical text the next step is to perform a similar "exegesis of the congregation" or "exegesis of the contemporary context." I believe this is somewhat misleading advice because it implies that the preacher is standing out in empty space with the biblical text on one side and the congregation on the other. But the preacher is not in midair at all. As we have been saying, the preacher rises from the assembly of God's people, is a member of the community, is a part of the congregation, and, in fact, is sent by them to the text. Therefore, when the preacher is exegeting the biblical text, the congregation is already there, sometimes literally in the form of a textual study group, and always in the preacher's mind, imagination, and heart.

Preachers do not leave the congregation and their world behind to go into the sterile laboratory of biblical exegesis. They couldn't even if they wanted to. The preacher has stood at gravesides with these people, wept with them when trouble comes, laughed and rejoiced with them in seasons of blessing. The congregation is not a strange and alien community. The preacher goes to the biblical text *from* these people, *on behalf of* them, and in important ways, *with* them. The congregation's struggle to be human and faithful to Christ in the contemporary world is also the preacher's own struggle. Their common life has been the very context in which the interpretation of the text has taken place.

The second issue of debate among homileticians about how to move between claim and sermon involves the traditional opinion that the preacher should boil the claim down to some central idea or sermon thesis. In many preaching manuals, especially of an earlier generation, the Bible was understood to be a repository of theological ideas, or truths, and the purpose of exegesis was to reach into the text and pluck out the main theological nugget. Once the preacher had grasped this key biblical idea, the text itself could be left behind, and the preacher could break this idea down into its various components to create the "points" of the sermon.

Beginning in the middle of the twentieth century, though, many homileticians (with the help of biblical scholars) gradually became suspicious and critical of this "main idea" approach to biblical preaching. In the first place, they claimed, it is a distortion of the Bible itself, which is not merely a box of ideas. No one who reads a rousing novel or sees a powerful play or views a provocative movie would be tempted to squeeze those rich experiences into only one main idea. Engaging a biblical text is at least as multifaceted as any of those encounters, and while ideas are surely uncovered in biblical interpretation, there are also moods, movements, conflicts, epiphanies, and other experiences that cannot be pressed into a strictly ideational mold. Sermons should be faithful to the full range of a text's power, and those preachers who carry away only main ideas, it was alleged, are traveling too light.

In the second place, homileticians realized that sermons organized only around ideas and points tend to plod dully along. They march according to the measured beat of strictly linear logic, and while people *can* listen in linear fashion, they do not often find it very interesting to do so. Moreover, idea-centered sermons are prone to communicate, over time, that the Christian faith itself can be boiled down to a set of concepts, doctrinal bullet points, to which people are supposed to give assent. The gospel thus gets presented as a list of propositions, and sermons become didactic devices for explaining these truths and how each of them logically connects to the others.

So for the past half century, a good many homileticians have been aiming their cannons at the idea-centered approach to moving from text to sermon. After a few warning shots in the 1950s and early 1960s, two direct hits on idea-based preaching occurred within two years of each other. The first was David James Randolph's *The Renewal of Preaching*, first published in 1969, and the second was Fred Craddock's *As One without Authority*, first published in 1971.

Randolph had studied the new linguistic and philosophical movement then gathering force in Europe known as the "new hermeneutic," which emphasized the power of language, biblical language in particular, to generate events to be experienced rather than merely thoughts to be learned and applied. An oft-quoted slogan of the new hermeneutic was, "We don't interpret texts; they interpret us." In other words, biblical texts are not inert objects to be analyzed and dissected but instead active forces that confront the interpreter through language and precipitate crises of self-understanding. Randolph immediately saw the value of this for preaching. Instead of conceiving of preaching as messages from the Bible, "preaching," insisted Randolph, "must be understood as an event."[2] Indeed, "Preaching is the event in which the biblical text is interpreted in order that its meaning will come to expression in the concrete situation of the hearers." For Randolph, this new understanding of preaching meant that the important question was not what a sermon *is*, or even what a sermon *says*, but what a sermon *does* in the real lives of the hearers. Using lingo popular in the 1960s, Randolph called the sermon "a happening."[3]

However, it remained to homiletician and New Testament scholar Fred Craddock, who was also a student of the new hermeneutic, to present this eventful notion of preaching in a clear and systematic fashion, that is, in a way that could be learned as a method. His little book, *As One without Authority,* which represents an early phase in Craddock's homiletical thought, is a recasting of new hermeneutical thought into practical homiletics that still stands as one of the most important and influential books on preaching written in the contemporary period.

The problem that most caught Craddock's attention was the frustration that good and responsible preachers often feel when they try to squeeze the energy and excitement of biblical interpretation into an idea-oriented, propositional style of preaching. Sermons, Craddock claimed, are not primarily ideas processed in the brain. They are, instead, events that happen in the ear. "Faith comes by hearing."[4] For the preacher, said Craddock, exegesis of the text is a potentially thrilling process of discovery. Facing the biblical text, the preacher follows hunches, explores possible avenues of meaning, and puts together clues on the way toward interpreting the text. Exegesis is, in short, an exciting adventure that darts first this way, then that way, resisting all reduction to a process of linear logic. It proceeds, rather, according to the logic of induction, guesswork, and trial-and-error—moving from bits and pieces of information about the text to larger insights about textual meaning.

The problem with sermons, Craddock claimed, is that much of this excitement gets filtered out when the preacher turns from the exegesis to the sermon. A good preacher, Craddock would say later, spends enough time with the text to experience the "formative force" of the text and not just the "informative force."[5] A sermon, too, should embody the text's formative force, not merely its information. But an unfortunate shift in logic occurs, Craddock said, between exegesis and the sermon: The inductive, exploratory process of exegesis is replaced by the deductive exhortation of the sermon. On one side of the bridge the preacher has an exciting, freewheeling experience of discovering the text, but the preacher has been trained to leave the exegetical sleuthing in the study, to filter out the zest of that discovery, and to carry only processed propositions across to the other side. In other words, doing the creative work of exegesis allows the biblical text to become an event for the preacher, but the customary methods of sermon construction drain the power out of that event for the listeners. The joy of "Eureka!" becomes, in the sermon, the dull thud of "My thesis for this morning is . . .":

> The preacher cannot recapture his former enthusiasm as he breaks his theme into points, unless, of course, his image of himself is that of one who passes truth from the summit down to the people. The brief temptation to re-create in the pulpit his own process of discovering is warded off by the clear recollection of seminary warnings that the minister does not take his desk into the pulpit. What, then, is he to do? If he is a good preacher, he refuses to be dull. And so between the three or four "points" that mark the dull deductive trail he plants humor, anecdotes, illustrations, poetry, or perhaps even enlivening hints of heresy and threats of butchering sacred cows. But the perceptive preacher knows instinctively that something is wrong with his sermon: not its exegetical support, not its careful preparation, not its relevance; it is the movement that is wrong.[6]

Craddock's solution to this problem was that the sermon should re-create for the hearers the inductive adventure experienced by the preacher in exegesis. In short, the eventfulness of exegesis for the preacher must transfer to the eventfulness of the sermon for the listeners. Speaking of the preacher doing biblical exegesis, Craddock said, "It is, I said to myself, unfair to arrive at a conclusion in private and then announce the conclusion in public. Why not let the listeners arrive at a conclusion? It isn't fair in the race we call preparation of the sermon for the minister to have a ten-mile head start."[7]

When the preacher goes to the text to interpret it, Craddock thought, the preacher is a kind of pioneer, the first one to do what the whole congregation will eventually do in the sermon: discover the power and meaningfulness of the text. So the sermon, Craddock maintained, should be patterned inductively, not deductively, patterned in other words after the very discovery process the preacher goes through in exegesis, displaying the logic of induction, not deduction. In the sermon the preacher should invite the hearers to make a series of small discoveries about the biblical text building toward a larger "Aha! So that's what this passage is generating in us!" We have more to say about this proposal in the next chapter, on sermon form, but at this point it is important to note the way Craddock redesigned the bridge between text and sermon. Instead of ideas moving across the bridge from texts to sermons, he proposed an experiential bridge carrying the discovery process itself. Craddock wanted the eventfulness of exegesis to become the eventfulness of the sermon.

When it first appeared, Craddock's proposal was immediately felt as a breath of fresh air, a breakthrough in homiletical thinking, and he was joined by many other voices urging a general revolt against propositional preaching. Story preaching, image-rich preaching, sermons centered upon metaphors, sermons involving indirection, dialogue sermons, and other nondiscursive styles quickly became the homiletical fashion in the latter part of the twentieth century—in short, almost any sort of biblical preaching except "a thesis in three points." In many ways the climate of the times was ripe for a protest against the deductive preaching of biblical "ideas," since the reigning biblical theology movement, which emphasized biblical concepts and the quasi-systematic theological unity of the Bible, was at that time rapidly giving way to the "new hermeneutic" and other event-centered approaches to biblical interpretation.

Not everyone, however, was thrilled by this rebellion against propositional preaching. One teacher of preaching, Ronald Sleeth, was concerned that preachers who turned away from ideas and toward events would almost inevitably turn to storytelling and superficial autobiography in which preachers recounted narcissistic little "private parables in the name of self expression." Sleeth, swimming forcefully against the stream, argued for the traditional notion that texts do, in fact, yield "main ideas" and that sermons should be arranged to serve them. He wrote,

> Surprisingly, there is a great deal of negative reaction to the idea that a sermon should have a clear, main idea that controls the sermon. Some suggest that we live in a frenetic, kaleidoscopic world where persons do not think logically, and we apprehend material holistically through an all-at-onceness. . . . To these persons, a thesis suggests a rationalistic discourse. . . .
>
> Yet, many sermons fail, simply because they are not clear. People do not know what it is all about, and it becomes a mystery hour. What some take for creativity and expressive language may in reality be evidence of a fuzzy mind.[8]

African American homiletical scholar Cleophus LaRue remembers being taught Craddock's method in seminary, and he recalls how out of touch it seemed with the realities of the black church:

> So strong was Craddock's broadside against the deductive three-point sermon and a poem that when I arrived as a student at Princeton Theological Seminary in the 1980s, the perception that the three-point sermon was long-since history hung heavily in the air. That perception struck me as quite strange because I'd just heard a three-point sermon the day before in one of New York City's premier black churches. I immediately sensed a disconnect between what white homileticians were espousing and what was going on in the black church.[9]

There was also resistance to non-idea-centered sermons among many evangelical teachers of preaching. For example, Haddon Robinson, one of the most influential homileticians in the evangelical world, though certainly aware of and, to a degree, appreciative of Craddock's approach, nevertheless insisted, "Effective sermons major in biblical ideas brought into an overarching unity. . . . People shape their lives and settle into eternal destinies in reponse to ideas."[10]

Two Paths: Idea and Event

Underneath all this fuss about points, propositions, main ideas, eventfulness, and happenings about inductive, deductive, three-point, and narrative sermons was actually a fruitful argument about proper emphasis in biblical preaching. For the old so-called "mainline" churches, preaching had become remote and boring. "Three points and a poem" was an epigram standing for a dull, arid, and abstract sermon, full of bromides and theological maxims disconnected from lived experience. No wonder Randolph and Craddock struck a nerve with their promise of sermons that were energetic "happenings" instead of staid "messages," sermons that created events and generated experiential "ahas!" What was sometimes lost in the discussion, though, was that for both Randolph and Craddock these eventful sermons were still about truth and ideas and content. Even when the center of gravity fell on the side of eventfulness and lived experience, there was still a gospel with content being proclaimed.

In other traditions and settings, however, such as the black church that LaRue describes or many evangelical churches, preaching may have had many problems, but boredom was not at the top of the list. There was no reason, then, to doubt what was serving these traditions well, namely the tried and true way of organizing sermons around biblical ideas arranged into a series of two, three, or more points. They just needed to be *good* points, well-presented. But what was often hidden here was that these "point" sermons were never as propositional and abstract as they may have appeared on paper. A sermon might technically be arranged into three points but still be filled with drama, narrative, movement, poetic appeal, energy, and eventfulness. Points needn't be abstractions; they could instead be mileposts on a sermonic adventure. And when these homileticians urged preachers to look for biblical ideas, these ideas were never understood to be cold, rationalistic doctrines, but living and dynamic truths. So even when the center of gravity fell on the side of ideas, there was still an eventful gospel being proclaimed.

There are undeniable differences, of course, in these two approaches: event and idea. To go to a biblical text searching out the "main ideas" of the passage is a very different path of interpretation than asking about what is happening in a text, about what world of experience a text generates. To craft a sermon that logically presents the big ideas of the text to the hearers is not the same thing as designing a sermon as a piece of drama intended to precipitate a powerful and life-changing experience. But there is no reason to foreclose on one of these paths for the sake of the other. They can, instead, be seen as complementary, even overlapping. Yes, the gospel is a constellation of ideas, but they are not ideas like "it is 2,100 miles from Chicago to Los Angeles." The gospel is composed of ideas like, "Despite everything that has happened and despite all that has come between us, I love you." An idea, yes, but an idea that is in the form of personal address, an idea that generates an event.

So some preachers and teachers of preaching continued down the path of "idea preaching," but many others followed Randolph's and Craddock's lead. Eugene Lowry, for example, claimed that the Bible itself is largely "nonpropositional" and warned that, at its worst, propositional thought "distorts and even reforms the experiential meaning" of the gospel.[11] He called for sermons to be essentially narrative in character (by which he meant sermons shaped like narrative plots, not necessarily sermons filled with stories), since the narrative form best conveys the "aesthetic communication" found in the Bible.

Some sought to go even further than Craddock had gone, claiming in fact that he had not finished the job of getting rid of points and propositions, charging that what he had blocked at the front door—an idea-centered approach to preaching—he welcomed through the back door. True enough, in Craddock's scheme the preacher engages in an exciting inductive search through the text, but, when all is said and done, the goal of this adventure, the object of this quest, is an idea. The preacher romps through the text, looking under rocks and peering into hidden caves in a stimulating exegetical hide-and-seek, but what is finally discovered, albeit with energy and excitement, is a main idea from the text. Craddock said, in fact, that the goal of exegesis is to find *the point* the author sought to make,"[12] and, as for the sermon, "[t]here is a point, and the discipline of this one idea is creative in preparation, in delivery, and in reception of the message."[13]

So, upon closer examination, it turned out after all that ideas from the text do come across Craddock's bridge between text and sermon. What made his approach innovative is that these ideas do not come alone but always clothed in the garments of the inductive sleuthing process by which those ideas were discovered in the first place. In other words, Craddock managed successfully to travel both alternative paths, the event and the idea.

But some homileticians were not satisfied with Craddock's compromise and rejected the whole idea approach, no matter what kind of clothing it wore. They preferred what can be called an aesthetic approach to the text; that is, instead of reducing the text to rational ideas, they would let the text simply generate its total, experiential, and not-always-rational reaction. What happens, Richard L. Eslinger asked Craddock, when the preacher encounters a biblical text that will not reduce to a single idea?

> Either the preacher must impose a thematic on the text from outside, or be threatened with a collapse of sermonic unity. . . . [T]he "weak link" in [Craddock's] approach remains the assumption that the interpretive payoff of every text is a proposition which then becomes the homiletic payoff of every sermonic form. Viewed from this perspective, the distance between a homiletics of induction and that of deduction closes considerably. Both seem to be bound to a rationalist hermeneutic.[14]

Craddock's position turned out to be pivotal in the technical sense; that is, the homiletical world turned around him. He stood at the juncture between a deductive, idea-centered approach to preaching and an inductive, process-fueled, aesthetic approach, and he had one foot planted in each. The debate he precipitated about propositions, inductive movement, and rationalistic heremeneutics was compelling and intriguing, but it was also confusing to preachers and students, of course, and formed something of a standoff among homileticians themselves. Finally a shaft of light broke through the murkiness when homileticians (again aided by developments in biblical studies and hermeneutics) took a fresh look at the actual practices of working preachers, that is, at the sort of biblical interpretation that preachers really do when they are preaching faithfully and effectively.

From Event to Claim to Event

In real-life practice, a preacher who intends to preach to a congregation goes to a biblical text seeking to hear a word for the life of this congregation and, indeed, expects to hear such a word. The preacher, then, views the text as a living resource for the community of faith and not merely as a historical object. A pure historian may examine a biblical text looking for data, but a preacher performs exegesis expecting something to happen, expecting some eventful word that makes a critical difference for the life of the church. To use David Kelsey's terms, the preacher approaches the Bible not as a set of texts, in the technical sense, but as Scripture. "Part of what it means to call a text 'Christian scripture,'" he writes, "is that *it functions to shape persons' identities so decisively as to transform them . . . when it is used in the context of the common life of Christian community.*"[15]

So if biblical texts interpreted in the context of Christian community function to shape Christian identity, then the goal of the preacher's exegesis is neither the plucking of an abstract idea from the text nor some nonconceptual aesthetic experience but, rather, the event of the text's actively shaping self and communal understanding. Every aspect of a biblical text—its concepts, its language, its literary form, its social and historical placement—works in concert to exert a claim upon each new set of faithful readers. Scripture, again to use Kelsey's words, "is taken as *doing* something that decisively shapes the community's identity."[16] Biblical texts *say* things that *do* things, and the sermon is to say and do those things too.

How do biblical texts shape Christian identity? That depends on the text in question. Some texts form Christian identity through the transmission of doctrine, others render biblical characters powerfully "present" through narration, some evoke wonder or provoke memory, and still others issue ethical demands. The list could go on, of course, since texts are multifaceted, and every text possesses its own unique and complex set of intentionalities.

Texts do all these things through words, of course, which means that they *do* things by *saying* things in certain ways. And it is here—in the interplay between saying and doing—that we find the key to building the bridge between text and sermon. The bridge must be able to bear the traffic of both word and event. The preacher should bring to the sermon both what the text says and what the text does; or, to put it another way, what the text does by its saying. The main-idea crowd was right about this—texts say something, and therefore express ideas—but the event crowd was also right. Texts also make things happen, create events in the imagination and in the ear. Content and intention are bound together, and no expression of textual impact is complete without them both.

Advocates both for idea-centered preaching and for event-centered preaching could be forgiven for overstatement. Keen to make his case for aesthetics, for example, Eugene Lowry said, "Perhaps you went to church and were overwhelmed in the singing of 'Amazing Grace'—and not at all because of the particularities of the propositional content of the third stanza."[17] What Lowry probably meant by this is that the impact of singing "Amazing Grace" cannot be reduced to the content of the lyrics alone, and he is certainly right about that. It goes too far, however, to claim that this experience is *not at all* related to the propositional content of the hymn text. Yes, a person can get caught up in the emotion of a familiar hymn and not really be aware of the words, but this is because it is a familiar hymn and because at some previous point the ideas, claims, promises, and warnings of the text of the hymn shaped their identity. If a congregation had always sung other lyrics to the tune of "Amazing Grace," say, the words to "Mary Had a Little Lamb" or "Jamaica Farewell," that would have produced quite a different effect. What a text *says* clearly governs what it *does*.

This notion of biblical texts as both conceptual and eventful allows us to build a far more satisfactory bridge between text and sermon. As David Buttrick put it, "True 'biblical preaching' will want to be faithful not only to a message, but to an *intention*. The question, 'What is the passage trying to do?' may well mark the beginning of homiletical obedience."[18] O. C. Edwards Jr. stated the same truth when he reminded preachers that a sermon "is not just about a thought, but about a thought that makes a difference."[19] Interpreting a biblical text is much like listening to one end of someone else's telephone conversation. We hear the text saying something to someone else for some purpose. As we discussed in the last chapter, the larger task of the contemporary interpreter is not simply to grasp that historical act of communication but rather to experience that communication as a claim upon us *now*. Once upon a time, everything about the biblical text made a claim upon its first readers, and now everything about that text makes a new claim upon us. What we bring across the bridge from text to sermon is not just an idea, or even an idea wrapped in our own inductive process of discovery, but rather this claim upon the hearers. A text's claim involves both a message and an intention bound up in the text's own manner of embodying that message, both what the text wishes to say and what the text wishes to do through its saying.

For these reasons, the final step of the exegetical process calls on the preacher to complete this sentence:

> In relation to those who will hear the sermon, what this text wants to say and do is . . .

This is what the preacher should bring from text to sermon: the claim of the text, the intention of the text to say and do something to and with the hearers. The preacher is both kinds of witness, having witnessed in the exegesis what the text wishes to say and do and now bearing witness to that claim in the sermon. This process represents an arc from event to claim to event: the eventfulness of the text is expressed in the claim of the text, which then guides the eventfulness of the sermon.

Focus and Function

What the biblical text intends to say and do governs what the preacher hopes to say and do in the sermon, and the next step in sermon development is to name more explicitly just what it is that the preacher hopes to say and to do. When we stated the claim of the text in a single sentence, saying and doing were all bound and blended together, but now, for the sermon, we take tweezers and separate these two elements of saying and doing.

What the sermon aims to say can be called its "focus," and what the sermon aims to do can be called its "function." Since the whole sermon will be gathered around these two aims, the preacher needs to become clear about the sermon's focus and function as an initial step in the process of actually building the sermon. Most experienced preachers do not actually write down the focus and the function of a sermon; they have an intuitive grasp of what they hope the sermon will say and do. But beginning preachers are helped greatly by the discipline of writing out formal focus and function statements. Even experienced preachers, especially when they get stuck or lost in trying to develop a sermon, can often find their way through by stepping back and writing out the sermon's focus and function as an exercise in sharpening sermon intention.

> A *focus statement* is a concise description of the central, controlling, and unifying theme of the sermon. In short, this is what the whole sermon will be "about."
>
> A *function statement* is a description of what the preacher hopes the sermon will create or cause to happen for the hearers. Sermons make demands upon the hearers, which is another way of saying that they provoke change in the hearers (even if the change is a deepening of something already present). The function statement names the hoped-for change.

Stating the focus and the function of a sermon is not, of course, a rhetorical magic trick. Just because the preacher writes down what the sermon will say and do does not guarantee that people will hear what is said or be shaped by what is done. It would be silly and presumptuous to assume that the preacher can predict and control all that is heard and all that happens in a sermon. Focus and function statements are merely compass settings for the sermon journey. They guide the preacher in the creation of sermons that possess unity, clarity, and a firm connection to the biblical text. Without them, the sermon runs the danger of wandering aimlessly. But they obviously do not describe everything that may happen to the hearers on the trip.

If the focus and function statements are to be genuinely useful to the preacher in the development of the sermon, they should fulfill the following three principles.

1. The focus and function statements should grow directly from the exegesis of the biblical text.

Suppose the text for the sermon is Romans 8:28–39:

> We know that all things work together for good for those who love God, who are called according to his purpose. For those

whom he foreknew he also predestined to be conformed to the image of his Son, in order that he might be the firstborn within a large family. And those whom he predestined he also called; and those whom he called he also justified; and those whom he justified he also glorified.

What then are we to say about these things? If God is for us, who is against us? He who did not withhold his own Son, but gave him up for all of us, will he not with him also give us everything else? Who will bring any charge against God's elect? It is God who justifies. Who is to condemn? It is Christ Jesus, who died, yes, who was raised, who is at the right hand of God, who indeed intercedes for us. Who will separate us from the love of Christ? Will hardship, or distress, or persecution, or famine, or nakedness, or peril, or sword? As it is written,

> "For your sake we are being killed all day long;
> we are accounted as sheep to be slaughtered."

No, in all these things we are more than conquerors through him who loved us. For I am convinced that neither death, nor life, nor angels, nor rulers, nor things present, nor things to come, nor powers, nor height, nor depth, nor anything else in all creation, will be able to separate us from the love of God in Christ Jesus our Lord.

As is the case with all biblical exegesis for preaching, the claim of this text will depend in part on what the preacher brings to the text, upon the congregation's present circumstances. Suppose the preacher comes to the text from a congregation where all hell has been breaking loose, from a congregation wrestling with distress and trouble, illness and conflict, issues of life and death. In this context, the text speaks an empowering word of reassurance and hope. For a congregation facing conflict, the dissolution of families, poverty, cancer or other devastating illnesses, racial prejudice, death, persecution by the government, dwindling membership, hunger, or doubt, the hearers will surely find their own cry rising up from the text's key question, "Who shall separate us from the love of Christ? Shall tribulation, or distress, or persecution, or famine, or nakedness, or peril, or sword?" Then comes the response: "No, in all these things we are more than conquerors through him who loved us. . . . [Nothing] will be able to separate us from the love of God in Christ Jesus our Lord."

So, the preacher who listens to this text on behalf of a troubled and perplexed congregation may well state the claim of the text this way:

Claim of The God we have come to know in Jesus Christ will not
the Text: forsake us in distress, but will instead love and care for us even in the face of experiences that seem to deny this.

Moving toward the sermon, this preacher may turn this claim into the following focus and function statements:

Focus: Because we have seen in Jesus Christ that God is for us, we can be confident that God loves and cares for us even when our experience seems to deny it.
Function: To reassure and give hope to troubled hearers in the midst of their distress.

What this preacher now has are two tasks for the sermon drawn directly from the exegesis of the text. Note that the first task, the focus statement, is something that the sermon will say, and it is expressed as content, as an idea. Note also that the second task, the function statement, is something that the sermon will do, a deed to perform. Therefore, it is expressed with verbs: "to reassure," "to give hope." The sermon as a whole is to accomplish both of these tasks simultaneously. The preacher will try to design the total sermon around these two tasks—saying and doing—so that every aspect of the sermon will work toward their accomplishment. The goal is that, by the end of the sermon, the focus will have been said and the function will have been accomplished, and the entire sermon, therefore, will be an expression of, a witness to, this text's claim upon this congregation.

Is this the only claim and are these the only focus and function statements that could come from this text? No, this claim and these focus and function statements are for a sermon to a congregation in distress. Texts potentially make many claims, and a change in congregational situation would also alter the results of the exegesis and therefore the tasks of the sermon.

Suppose the preacher goes to the same text, but this time from a very different congregation with a very different set of circumstances. Imagine that this second congregation has among its members a strong "sunshine and success" view of the Christian faith. A big theme for many people in this congregation is a subtle but prevalent image of the gospel as "thinking positively" and turning problems quickly and easily into possibilities. Because this congregation emphasizes the upbeat and the cheerful, sometimes the deep and enduring fissures in human experience cannot be faced honestly, since the fear is that faith may collapse under the heavy weight of the tragic. While the text from Romans spoke a word of encouragement and cheer to the openly troubled and anxious church, the same text speaks a very different word to this "Smile, God loves you!" congregation. To this second congregation, trying desperately to remain at ease by carefully stepping over the threatening places in life and hewing to the smoothly cheerful path, this very same text generates a claim like this:

> Claim: Because God's care and presence can be counted on even in the deepest distress, we do not need to fear life's dark shadows and deep valleys.
>
> Focus: True faith does not mean pretending that life is always cheerful and positive, but trusting that God's love in Christ will be with us even in the midst of peril and distress.
>
> Function: To help the hearers be less afraid of life's dark valleys and to help them to move from a superficial "sunshine and success" understanding of the faith toward a willingness to trust God in the fullness of their experience.

These focus and function statements are quite different from the first set, but they are drawn just as firmly from the exegesis of the text. What makes them different, of course, is the changed congregational context, which evoked another claim from the text.

2. The focus and function statements should be related to each other.

What a sermon says should be intrinsically related to what that sermon does, and vice versa. The focus and function statements should reflect this connection and clearly express the mutuality of saying and doing. In other words, the focus and function statements should be a matched pair, one growing out of the other.

Suppose a preacher is developing a sermon from Luke 6:12–16, the text in which Jesus chooses the twelve apostles after a night of prayer. After interpreting the text, the preacher formulates the following focus and function statements:

> *Focus:*   Today, just as it was in the beginning, the leadership of the church and the shape of the church's mission grow out of the prayers of Christ.
>
> *Function:*   To encourage a spirit of greater openness in the church to many diverse people that Christ calls into leadership.

These are useful statements, but the problem with them is that they are not matched. They belong to two different sermons, and each statement requires a different partner. Sermon 1 could take our original focus statement and match it with a more suitable function:

Sermon 1

> *Focus:*   Today, just as it was in the beginning, the leadership of the church and the shape of the church's mission grow out of the prayers of Christ.
>
> *Function:*   To strengthen the confidence of those who lead and those who serve that they are participating in the very mission of Christ.

Sermon 2 would find a better focus statement partner for our original function:

Sermon 2

> *Focus:*   Just as Jesus' prayerful selection of the twelve embraced a surprising diversity of people, Christ's prayerful call continues to come to a wide variety of people.
>
> *Function:*   To encourage a spirit of greater openness in the church by enabling the hearers to see that Christ calls many different kinds of people into service.

3. The focus and function statements should be clear, unified, and relatively simple.

Whenever a preacher engages in responsible exegesis of a biblical text, the chances are good that many creative and engaging insights will occur. When a preacher dwells at length with a text, interrogating it with zest and open expectation, that text, which may have appeared at first to say little, or only one thing, often breaks open to reveal a richness of claims. The temptation facing the preacher is to attempt to bring everything heard and seen in the text into one sermon. If this temptation is not resisted, the sermon will almost inevitably end up accomplishing little because the preacher has tried to accomplish it all. Sermons should say and do one thing: that is, they should be unified around a single claim from the text. One of the purposes of creating focus and function statements is to allow the light from the text to be refracted into a single clear beam illuminating these hearers through this one sermon on this given day.

The practical implication of this principle is that we should review our focus and function statements to assure that each embraces a single unified task. If the focus and function statements require that we accomplish several different tasks, the resulting sermon will probably lurch off in many directions at once. It is possible, of course, to overdo this piece of advice and produce sermons that are simplistic rather than simple, but the essential wisdom obtains nonetheless: the focus and function statements should attempt to express a single claim from the text.

A similar problem occurs when the focus and function statements lack crispness and specificity. Focus statements like "God is love," "the birth of Jesus," or "God calls us to justice" are too vague to be helpful to the preacher. Likewise, such function statements as "to help the hearers show forgiveness," "to create joy," or "to enable service" also lack specific bite.

Imagine that a preacher is studying, in preparation for a sermon, John 5:1–18, the story of Jesus' Sabbath healing of the lame man beside the pool at Bethzatha. The preacher finds this a fascinating text, one that moves simultaneously in several directions. The preacher is intrigued, for example, by the final verse, which states that the religious authorities "were seeking all the more to kill [Jesus], because he was not only breaking the sabbath, but was also calling God his own Father, thereby making himself equal to God." This verse gives a theological reason for the plot to kill Jesus.

But this preacher is also attracted to the story of the healing in this text, an account that has its own power apart from the consequences for Jesus and his ultimate fate. In particular, the preacher is curious about Jesus' seemingly strange question to the sick man: "Do you want to be made well?" This man had been ill for a long time, thirty-eight years, and Jesus' question seems to imply that the man might *not* want to be healed, that he just might prefer his illness to health. The man's cry, "Sir, I have no one to put me into the pool . . ." (desperate need? whining?) is met by Jesus' firm command to health and action, "Stand up, take your mat and walk."

So, after wrestling with this text and finding several compelling angles of vision, the preacher makes a first attempt to compose focus and function statements:

Focus: Jesus was a controversial healer.
Function: To help the hearers understand the importance of this for their lives.

But this pair of focus and function statements will not work. They are obviously too broad to be genuinely helpful to the preacher. To be sure, the text discloses that Jesus was a controversial healer, but how was he controversial? And what does this controversy have to do with contemporary hearers? Also, what specifically is important about this for the hearers' lives? So the preacher tries again:

Focus: Jesus unsettles our comfortable illnesses (blindness to injustice, paralysis of love, deafness to the cry of the needy) with the disturbing question, "Do you really want to be healed?" When people are healed, in the power of Christ, of such illnesses, opposition comes, not from evil people but ironically from good people who mistake their religious traditions for the will of God.
Function: To enable hearers to become aware of Christ's continuing challenge to the sometimes comfortable complacency of our illnesses, and to enable hearers to perceive how our

> allegiance to religious traditions can sometimes stand in the
> way of the saving and healing work of God in our midst.

In terms of being specific, these statements are better, but because they are more specific, we can clearly see another problem. They are too long and too complex. The preacher was intrigued by two different aspects of this healing story and is now trying to include both of them into this one sermon. Most of the time (not always) this is a sign that the preacher has bitten off more than can be chewed in a single sermon. At least two claims from the text are competing here for time and attention, and while it is not impossible to imagine a sermon fulfilling all that these statements embrace, the odds are that the sermon will end up being either jumbled or a series of brief and independent "sermonettes" that happen coincidentally to share the same root text.

Realizing that the first set of focus and function statements was way too vague and the second set was too ambitious, divided, and jumbled, the preacher tries again to create focus and function statements that are clear, unified, and simple, and this time comes up with two possibilities:

Focus: Jesus unsettles our comfortable and complacent illnesses with the disturbing question, "Do you want to be made well?"

Function: To challenge the hearers to leave their comfortable "mats" and to live out the health Jesus offers.

And:

Focus: Sometimes, the healing power of Christ is opposed not by evil people but ironically by good people who mistake their religious traditions for the will of God.

Function: To provoke the hearers to question if our own allegiance to religious traditions sometimes stands in the way of the saving and healing work of God.

These two sets of focus and function statements hit the mark: they are clear and simple, and they display the unity that comes from not trying to accomplish everything in one sermon. There are other possibilities for good focus and function statements from this text, of course, but the point is that the preacher has arrived at crisp and concise descriptions of what this sermon will say and do.

It is important to realize that a good set of focus and function statements indicates where a sermon is headed; they are a description of the sermon's overall destination. When they are formulated well, the preacher has a clear idea where the sermon is going and can begin to make coherent plans for how the sermon will get there. In other words, when we have crafted serviceable focus and function statements, we can anticipate and begin to create the sermon structure that will get us from here to there. The focus and function of a sermon seek an appropriate form, and this issue of suitable sermon form is our concern in chapters 5 and 6.

5

The Basic Form of the Sermon

> One could speak of the basic musicality of any sermon. Music, after all, is also an event-in-time art form, with melody, harmony, and rhythm coming sequentially. No one builds a song; it is shaped and performed.
> —Eugene L. Lowry, *The Sermon: Dancing the Edge of Mystery*

Sermon form is a curious beast. In many ways, a sermon's form, or structure, is its least-noticed feature. Most hearers would be puzzled to be asked, "What was the form of the sermon you just heard?" Ask them about what the preacher said or about their own responses, and they can usually come up with an answer, but the form of a sermon slips by them as undetected as the meter of a hymn.

Despite the fact that it passes by relatively unnoticed, form is absolutely vital to the meaning and effect of a sermon. Like the silent shifting of gears in a car's automatic transmission, sermon form translates the potential energy of the sermon into productive movement, while remaining itself quietly out of view. "The power of a sermon," wrote Halford Luccock many years ago, "lies in its structure, not in its decoration."[1] Form is as important to the flow and direction of a sermon as are the banks of a river to the movement of its currents.

It is easy to get tripped up by our own language when we speak about this business of a sermon's form. We tend to talk about a sermon's content, on the one hand, and its form, on the other, as if form and content were two distinct realities. The picture we have in our heads is that of a preacher developing the content of a sermon and then hunting around for a suitable form, something like a shipping container, in which to box this content for delivery. In other words, content is the important stuff of the sermon; form is mere packaging, an afterthought.

Outside of the mail room, however, the notion of a form as a package does not work. In artistic creations (and sermons are artistic creations of a sort), form and content cannot be easily distinguished. Think of Michelangelo's *David*. What is "form" and what is "content" in that magnificent sculpture? Or recall the interplay of form and content in the shapes, patterns, and faces of Picasso's *Guernica*. Or again, see the blurring of form and content in the fluid grace of the youthful Michael Jordan as he sailed through the air toward the basket or in the almost magical movements of dancer Misty Copeland gliding across the stage in the ballet *Cinderella*. Both of these are aesthetic events as well as athletic achievements, and both blend form and content.

Instead of thinking of sermon form and content as separate realities, then, it is far better to speak of the *form of the content*. A sermon's form, although often largely unperceived by the hearers, provides shape and energy to the sermon and thus becomes itself a vital force in how a sermon makes meaning. Form is an essential part of a sermon's content and can itself support or undermine the communication of the gospel. If a sermon is structured in a manipulative, deceptive, or incoherent manner, then, regardless of what else is said in the sermon, manipulation, deception, or incoherence is spoken, too. On the other hand, if the form of the sermon is clear, lively, and inviting to the listeners, then clarity, life, and dignity become a part of the sermon's word to the hearers.

In the simplest of terms, a sermon form is an organizational plan for deciding what kinds of things will be said and done in a sermon and in what sequence. For example, if the preacher decides to open the sermon by posing a question or problem that is on the minds of the hearers and then to spend the rest of the sermon trying to answer that question with the help of the biblical text, this is essentially a decision about sermon form. In this case, the preacher has chosen what has often been called the Problem/Response form. If, on the other hand, the preacher decides to move back and forth between the text and the contemporary setting, first describing the historical situation out of which the biblical text arose, then showing how that situation is analogous to a contemporary situation, then going back to see what word was spoken by the text to its setting, then turning again to the contemporary circumstance to hear the text's word anew, this too is a choosing of sermon form. In this case the form will be a weaving of old and new, text and context, what-the-text-said-then/what-the-text says-now.

Since a sermon may assume many possible shapes and designs, many possible forms, the question for the preacher is how to create a form for a particular sermon that best embodies the aims of this particular sermon.

Outlines: The Traditional Approach

The traditional way to plan the form of any oral communication—a sermon or a speech or a lecture—is to create an orderly and logical outline, a schematic diagram of the parts and sequence of the message. Many homiletical textbooks of past generations enthusiastically endorsed the outlining process as the most efficient method for designing sermon structure. Developing an outline in advance, it is said, forces the preacher to make choices, not only about what will be said when but also about the logical connections among the various pieces of the sermon. Once a good outline has been produced, the preacher can simply fill out the parts to create the final sermon.

How is a good outline created? Let us examine a typical sermon outline and see how it was made. Imagine that the text for the sermon is Psalm 19.

Psalm 19

The heavens are telling the glory of God;
    and the firmament proclaims his handiwork.
Day to day pours forth speech,
    and night to night declares knowledge.
There is no speech, nor are there words;
    their voice is not heard;
yet their voice goes out through all the earth,
    and their words to the end of the world.
In the heavens he has set a tent for the sun,
which comes out like a bridegroom from his wedding canopy,
    and like a strong man runs its course with joy.

Its rising is from the end of the heavens,
    and its circuit to the end of them;
    and nothing is hid from its heat.
The law of the LORD is perfect, reviving the soul;
the decrees of the LORD are sure,
    making wise the simple;
the precepts of the LORD are right,
    rejoicing the heart;
the commandment of the LORD is clear,
    enlightening the eyes;
the fear of the LORD is pure,
    enduring forever;
the ordinances of the LORD are true
    and righteous altogether.
More to be desired are they than gold,
    even much fine gold;
sweeter also than honey,
    and drippings of the honeycomb.

Moreover by them is your servant warned;
    in keeping them there is great reward.
But who can detect their errors?
    Clear me from hidden faults.
Keep back your servant also from the insolent;
    do not let them have dominion over me.
Then I shall be blameless,
    and innocent of great transgression.

Let the words of my mouth and the meditation of my heart
    be acceptable to you,
    O LORD, my rock and my redeemer.

After exegeting this psalm, the preacher, to use the language of the previous chapter, fashions these focus and function statements:

Focus: God speaks to people in the wonders of nature, through Scripture and proclamation, and in everyday experience.

Function: To enable the hearers to discover and name the variety of ways in which God is speaking to them.

And then, on the basis of the focus and function statements, the preacher creates this outline:

Title: How Does God Speak to Us?[2]

I. God Speaks through Nature (*Psalm 19:1–6*)
   A. In the silent processes of life
   B. In the cosmic wonder of the universe

II. God Speaks through the Divine Word (*Psalm 19:7–10*)
   A. In the Bible
   B. In the preaching and teaching of God's people

III. God Speaks in our Life Experiences (*Psalm 19:11–14*)
   A. In our sense of failure and sin
   B. In our hunger to be faithful

Now, why did the preacher come up with this outline, this particular form, and not some other? In this case, it seems likely that the biblical text itself guided the preacher. In the exegesis, the preacher saw that the psalm seems to be composed of three parts, each part with its own main theme: verses 1–6 are about nature, verses 7–10 are about Scripture and proclamation, and verses 11–14 are about personal experience. So the preacher developed focus and function statements around that insight, and expanded the focus and function into the main points and subpoints of the outline; the result is a three-point sermon plan that matches the divisions the preacher saw in the text.

Even though this preacher would say that the outline is simply following the natural flow of the psalm text, it is important to observe that the outline was nevertheless created by the preacher and not by the text. The psalm, of course, did not designate the divisions, did not employ Roman numerals: I, II, III. The preacher brought those to the psalm. All sermon forms, even those that follow a biblical text verse by verse, are finally reshapings by the preacher, impositions of a new sermonic form on the text. Other forms could have been devised for this sermon and been just as legitimate. Psalm 19 can be analyzed from many angles, and nothing dictates that it must be divided in just this three-part way or according to these themes, or patterned after the sequence of the text at all. In this instance, the preacher was aided by the flow of the text, but finally this sermon structure came, as all sermon forms do, through a creative act of the preacher's imagination.

But is it a good outline? How can we know? The outline looks fine on paper, but do we know whether or not the sermon that will grow out of it will have a good form? Classical homileticians were quite concerned about this question, and over the years they developed a catalog of virtues for outlines, a series of tests to check the quality of the sermon outline. Here is a fairly typical checklist:[3]

Unity:	Each major point should support the main proposition.
Order:	The major divisions should be of equal importance.
Movement:	Each major division should carry the thought forward by saying something distinguishable from what has gone before.
Proportion:	The major divisions should be stated in parallel construction.
Climax:	The major divisions should be arranged in an ascending scale of impact.

If we apply these criteria to the Psalm 19 sermon outline above, does it hold up? Actually, the results are fairly encouraging. This outline certainly has *unity*, since all the divisions, all the points, relate to the same basic idea, namely, how God speaks to us. It also has *order*. Perhaps all divisions are not exactly equal, but the main points have roughly the same weight, and there are no trivial molehills mixed in with the mountains. *Movement* is perhaps a bit of a challenge, since each main division stands alone, and despite following the sequence in the psalm itself, the order of the divisions seems arbitrary. As presented in the outline, there doesn't seem to be any clear or logical reason why point II couldn't have come first, or last, rather than in the middle. But the preacher can handle this slight complication by being honest in the sermon and presenting the divisions as what they truly are: a list. The resulting movement from one to the next will be somewhat artificial but not impossible for the hearers to navigate. As for *proportion*, we can tell by the fact that each main section begins with the same phrase ("God speaks . . .") that these divisions show parallel construction. Now the matter of *climax* may be a question. Does this sermon outline really move in an ascending scale of impact. Maybe. Section III does bring the sermon home to the personal experience of the hearers, and that potentially carries a punch, but the preacher test-ing this outline would want to think a bit more about climax. All things considered, though, this outline appears, according to the traditional canons of homiletics, to promise a sturdy sermon form. So far, so good.

Questioning the Tradition

There are good reasons, though, to question whether or not outlining sermons is the best way to create a good sermon form. The problem is not really with the outlines themselves. They are, after all, just notes on paper, fairly innocent diagrams of sermon structure, and any sermon, even a very innovative and creative one, can be outlined. The problem, instead, is with the kind of thinking that is typically called for to create outlines.

To begin with, outlines often carry with them assumptions about the sort of logic that ought to hold sermons together. Whenever we see an outline, with its I, II, III or A,B,C, it is difficult to get away from the notion that these sections are major conceptual divisions of some overarching idea and that the other parts of the outline (1, 2, 3 . . . a, b, c . . .) are subdivisions and sub-subdivisions of various aspects of that overarching concept. In other words, like it or not, an outline pushes the preacher way over to the propositional side of preaching and away from the eventful side.

Some sermons, of course, are largely propositional. They do, in fact, aim to teach and to show how facets of some big idea are logically interconnected. But this is not true, and should not be true, of all ser-mons. If every sermon were presented this way—I, II, III—the mes-sage implied over time would be that the gospel is essentially a set of major ideas with rationally divisible parts. To be sure, every sermon should be logical, but there are many different kinds of logic—nar-rative, inductive, parabolic, conversational, and metaphorical, just to name a few. Outlines—at least in the way we have been trained to construct them—tend to reduce our options and to shuttle us down the chute of formal logic.

Homileticians have also charged that, despite all the brave talk about "movement," the process of outlining actually tends to produce sermons that don't actually move well but are rather static and turgid: next point, next point, next point, and another thing. We flagged that problem in our sample outline for the sermon on Psalm 19. We can imagine the preacher of this sermon forcing some movement by saying something like, "And the second way God speaks to us" or "God speaks to us not only in nature but also in God's word," but these weak transitional statements merely reveal that the movement between these sections must be artificially constructed. Section I does not really lead into section II and II into III. The preacher simply swings on the trapeze from one to the other, hoping that the hearers will be game to follow along. Fred Craddock is surely correct when he observes that any experienced preacher with nerve enough to reexamine critically one's old, outline-style sermons will almost surely discover that some sermons were three sermonettes barely glued together. There may have been movement within each point, and there may have been some general kinship among the points, but there was not one movement from beginning to end. The points were as three pegs in a board, equal in height and distance from each other.[4]

The most telling criticism of the outlining process, however, focuses not upon logic or movement but rather upon what an outline aims to organize in the first place. The outlining process tends to focus on organizing the content, but sermons need a form that provides a shape for the listening process. Ever since we were taught how to outline term papers in high school, most of us have been schooled to think of an outline as a means for arranging the material, the data we have gathered, for our paper, report, speech, or whatever. When we create a sermon form, though, we are not primarily arranging the material. We are, rather, asking, "How can people best *hear* the material in this sermon?" Sermon structure is an act of pastoral care. It is about shaping communication, not merely about organizing information. A sermon form is a plan for the experience of listening, not just an arrangement of data, and it is the listeners who are missing from the typical process of outlining.

The Search for an Ideal Form

Disenchanted with traditional outlining, many homileticians have begun searching for alternative means to create apt sermon forms. Quite a few works in the field of preaching over the last few decades have focused sharply upon the question of form,[5] and these books are set apart from their immediate homiletical predecessors by their claim that sermon form must be controlled not only by the data of the sermon but also around the dynamics of the human listening process.

Actually this development in homiletics is not entirely new, since throughout most of its history homiletics has borrowed many of its ideas about form from "secular" rhetoric, a discipline that has always given serious attention to the inner processes of human listening. What has renewed the question of sermon form among contemporary homileticians is actually the rediscovery, aided by studies in the psychology of human listening, of an old truth: sermon forms are not innocent or neutral. The shape of a sermon is not merely a convenient and logical way to arrange content; it is an invitation to—perhaps even a demand upon—the hearers to listen to the content according to a particular pattern. As such, form significantly influences what happens to the hearer in and through the sermon.

One of the charges against outlines, as we have seen, is that they tend to result in sermons shaped according to a single format, a I-II-III pattern of linear logic, thus reducing the formal options to one choice. Ironically, a few contemporary homileticians, in rejecting the outline scheme, have put in its place their own highly unified—one might even say rigid—view of sermon form. All of these homileticians are aware, of course, that sermons can and do assume many legitimate forms. But when these teachers of preaching thought deeply about how people actually listen to preaching, they came to the conclusion that the form of the sermon ought to be matched to the process by which the listeners actually hear the gospel and achieve creative and faithful insights (as opposed to the process of rational thinking presupposed in the outline process). Consequently, they sought out the one type of sermon form that could best engender this sense of discovery in listeners and pointed to it as a form to be prized above all others.

Craddock's Inductive Movement: Fred Craddock's landmark essay *As One without Authority*, referred to in the last chapter, has often been read this way, even though Craddock warned that he was simply proposing one option among many for sermons and that the "forms of preaching should be as varied as the forms of rhetoric in the New Testament."[6] Craddock argued so persuasively for what he termed the "inductive" form in preaching, however, that it was difficult for readers not to be convinced that this was the sermon form par excellence.

Put simply, Craddock proposed that sermons be shaped according to the same process of creative discovery employed by preachers in their exegetical work. When preachers study biblical texts, he said, they do not know in advance what those texts mean; they must search for meanings, putting clues together until meanings emerge at the end. Sermons, therefore, ought to re-create imaginatively this inductive quest so that the listeners can share the preacher's experience of illumination. The implication is that hearers best listen to and learn from sermons precisely the way preachers listen to and learn from biblical texts.

So instead of being told in the introduction what the sermon is about, listeners ought to move through the sermon as a process, putting together various bits and pieces of evidence, until they are able to discover the key claim of the sermon in the conclusion. Indeed, by the time the hearers arrive at the end of an inductive sermon, they ideally have become so engaged in this discovery process that they, and not the preacher, complete the sermon by naming its resolution in their own minds and lives. Just as preachers at their exegetical desks finally claim for themselves the meaning of the text, so hearers in the pews should be empowered to claim for themselves the meanings of those texts through the gradual step-by-step process of the sermons.

Now, what does this inductive sermon form look like in actual practice? Instead of being composed of points (I, II, III), a sermon would consist of a series of small segments, or movements, building cumulatively toward a climactic "Aha!" These smaller units are connected by transitional expressions that help the hearers put the pieces together, such as "It seems . . . , but still . . ."; "Of course . . . , and yet . . ."; or "Both this and this . . . , yet in a larger sense . . ."[7] Taken as a whole, then, the sermon form proposed by Craddock is an attempt to organize the flow of the sermon so that it "corresponds to the way people ordinarily experience reality and to the way life's problem-solving activity goes on naturally and casually."[8]

Craddock's own label for his proposed form, "problem-solving activity," is the real key to understanding this approach to sermon structure. In Craddock's view, the preacher should imagine that the hearers are going to solve a specific problem, and then design the sermon to give them all the necessary information, and in the proper order, to resolve that problem for themselves. It is crucial to remember that in Crad-dock's scheme the problem being solved in the sermon is always the question, What does this biblical text mean for us today? That question hangs in the air at the beginning, and the sermon rolls along the path-way of discovery, gathering clues, until it finally arrives at the place where the listeners are prepared to make a decision for themselves about the claim of the text upon their lives.

Lowry's 'Plotted' Sermon: Another powerful version of the problem-solving form has been suggested by Eugene Lowry in his influential book *The Homiletical Plot*. For Craddock, the one prob-lem to be solved was the problem of the text's contemporary meaning, but for Lowry, any "felt need" on the part of the hearers—whether originating in the biblical text, a theological doctrine, or a situation in life—can serve as the organizing task. Lowry believes that sermons should begin by describing this problem, dilemma, or bind so clearly that the hearers feel "ambiguity" and desire its resolution. He writes that "there is one essential in form which I believe indispensable to the sermon event, and that one essential is ambiguity."[9]

Now, sometimes, of course, the congregation is already aware of a problem and already feels its ambiguity. At a funeral, for instance, the circumstance of death poses its own deeply felt dilemma. The preacher does not need to raise the problem; it is already powerfully present. Most of the time, though, it is up to the preacher to generate this ambi-guity by kicking over the apple cart in the opening section of the sermon. A preacher who begins a sermon by saying, "Today I want to talk about love" is, in Lowry's view, "dull" because no suspense has been created at the sermon's beginning. Far better, he says, is this opening line: "Our problem is that so many times we extend our hand in love only to bring it back bruised and broken. To love is to risk rejection."[10] What makes that introduction better is that it creates imbalance; that is, it generates con-flict by raising to the level of awareness an experiential problem about love. The listeners, he maintains, will want so much to see that conflict resolved they will listen to the rest of the sermon to discover how it all comes out.

The job of the remainder of the sermon, claims Lowry, is "the resolu-tion of that particular central ambiguity,"[11] and he has a very specific notion of how the sermon should be shaped to get this task done. Ser-mons, he claims, should be designed around five basic movements, or "stages" (these five stages constitute, of course, a kind of "outline," but Lowry would be eager to claim that his outline is fueled by a different sort of logic than the traditional ones):

I.   *Upsetting the equilibrium (Conflict).* In this opening stage, which we have already described, the preacher poses the "problem" of the sermon in a way that can be felt by the hearers.

II. *Analyzing the discrepancy (Complication).* In this stage the preacher diagnoses the problem by exploring it in detail and articulating the reasons that it exists in human experience.

III. *Disclosing the clue to resolution (Sudden Shift).* Here is where the "Aha!" comes in Lowry's form. In this stage the preacher supplies the clue from the gospel that provides the resolution for the problem. Lowry is quick to point out, though, that since the resolution comes from the gospel and not from "worldly wisdom," this moment in the sermon has the air of surprise about it. There is a "reversal" of the hearers' expectations, and this clue comes "by means of sudden illumination."[12]

IV. *Experiencing the gospel.* In this stage, the clue disclosed in the previous stage is fleshed out in terms of its fuller meaning, a stage in which the good news grasps the minds and hearts of the hearers.

V.   *Anticipating the consequences (Unfolding).* In this final stage, the new discovery of the gospel is projected onto the future. "What—in the light of this intersection of human condition with the gospel—can be expected, should be done, or is now possible?"

In recent years, Lowry has changed his mind about this form slightly. Instead of the fivefold sequence, he now describes a fourfold sequence (Conflict-Complication-Sudden Shift–Unfolding) with the "experiencing the gospel" element (the good news) still present but potentially occurring at any one of a number of places in the sequence. In both the original and the revised versions, though, Lowry has provided, instead of a deductive structure fashioned with points growing out of a central idea, a fluid suspense-driven master form for sermons. He calls this form "narrative," since the four (or five) movements of the sermon work together like the episodes of a plot, but "narrative" is probably a misleading label. Lowry's fivefold form is shaped more according to the "creativity paradigm" familiar to researchers in the field of human problem-solving than it is styled after actual narrative plots, which are quite varied. Many creativity studies have found that people who discover innovative solutions to old problems do so according to a similar pattern. They customarily report that they wrestled long and hard analyzing the problem, only to have the solution come to them in a sudden and surprising moment of illumination. Once this solution has been received, however, it becomes part of the person's problem-solving repertoire and can be applied to future puzzles. It is not much of a stretch, of course, to see that Lowry's master-sermon form is simply a renaming of the steps in this typical pattern of human creativity.

Wilson's Four Pages: A third example of a master form, this one theologically driven, has been suggested by homiletician Paul Scott Wilson. Wilson builds his homiletics upon the classic theological distinction between law and gospel. The law is God's judgment upon human sin as well as the tragic quality of broken existence. The gospel is God's ultimate saving mercy and divine redemptive moments woven into everyday life. Wilson renames law and gospel in more accessible terms, "trouble" and "grace," and he claims that the move from trouble to grace reflects the basic structure (or, as he puts it, the "deep grammar") of the gospel.

So what does this mean in terms of sermon structure? Wilson calls for a sermon form which ensures that the sermon discloses trouble and grace both in the scriptural world and in the contemporary world, allowing for the energy that sparks between these two theological poles to animate the process of hearing the sermon. Having heard far too many sermons in which God plays little or no role, Wilson is keen to ensure that the action of God always appears. Homiletician Stephen Farris agrees: "The most important task of the interpreter is to ask, 'What is God doing in the text? The most difficult question for the interpreter to answer is, 'Is God doing anything similar in the world?'"[13]

After a number of years of experimenting with the clearest and best way to express his ideas about form, recently Wilson has settled on the clever and helpful image of "the four pages of the sermon."[14] The idea of the "four pages" is that sermons should be divided into four basic movements, and each of these movements should take up about one-fourth of the sermon time:

Page one—Trouble in the biblical text
Page two—Trouble in our world
Page three—Grace in the biblical text
Page four—Grace in our world

The sermon does not have to present these four pages in this order; the preacher is free to shuffle the pages around, thereby creating many possible sermon sequences. Normally, though, page four will come last in the sermon, because grace finally triumphs in the Christian gospel and, as Wilson puts it, the move *from* trouble *to* grace in a sermon helps ensure that grace is stronger and reinforces the overall movement of the faith."[15]

Homileticians like Craddock, Lowry, and Wilson have gone a long way toward restoring creativity and excitement in sermon form. Because they propose designing sermons around the process of the discovery and experience of the gospel, they overcome many of the problems of the static outline and provide the means for enabling hearers to be active and responsible participants in the preaching event.

There are also problems, however, in their suggestions about sermon form. To begin with, any scheme that purports to be able to lead a group of people to the place where they exclaim, "Aha! I have discovered a surprising new truth!" must reckon with the fact that human creativity is fragile and unpredictable. It may be the case that people who have exciting discoveries can look back on those experiences and recount the steps they took to get to the moment of insight. It is not at all clear, though, that marching someone else through those steps will generate the same "Eureka!" This is probably one of the reasons that Lowry revised his earlier fivefold scheme. Any form that expects or demands that a sudden reversal and surprising shaft of light break through on cue in stage three of the sermon is true neither to the full range of biblical texts nor the full range of the ways human beings listen, hear, and change.

A deeper issue for the problem-solving form comes, however, not from the fact that these forms do not always work as advertised to create fresh insight, but rather from the fact that, skillfully done, they usually do work to create listener interest. Sermons that begin with an intriguing problem (whether we call that problem "law," "conflict," or "trouble") and then move themselves gradually toward a resolution have high listener appeal, and the preacher will be tempted to form every sermon according to a pattern so well received.

However, a sermon's form, as we have argued, is a part of its meaning, and if a congregation is treated week after week only to the problem-solving design, it is inevitably being subtly taught that the purpose of the gospel is to resolve problems or that the best experience of hearing the gospel is a deeply felt "Aha!" Sometimes the gospel does not resolve ambiguity; it creates it. Sometimes the gospel does not come to us as an Aha!—an unexpected word surprising us or turning our world upside down—but instead as a familiar and trusted word of confirmation, as the "old, old story." The Bible itself, taken as a larger narrative, does not in fact move from problem to resolution, or from "trouble" to "grace," but begins with creation, with what God says is "very good." Trouble happens later. Wilson has objected that his critics who say that his ideas about sermon structure constitute a problem-resolution model have missed the point that "the gospel is relationship."[16] But, as a matter of fact, sermons that are routinely built according to the pattern of *"from* trouble *to* grace" are finally theologically nuanced versions of the problem-resolution form.

There are also other reasons that Wilson's theologically rich "trouble" and "grace" scheme is not as encompassing and unifying as it may seem at first. It is most helpful, of course, to keep the categories "trouble" and "grace" before us as a reminder that even the structure of a sermon is theologically freighted and that, to be fully Christian, a sermon must include some aspect of the human condition and some announcement of the action of God. Wilson also underscores the important truth that any proclamation of grace oblivious to human brokenness is cheap grace and any hammering away at human trouble and sin that does not also speak a word of grace is mere moralizing.

Finally, though, the categories "law" and "gospel" (or "trouble" and "grace") alone are not comprehensive enough to serve as the master organizers of sermon structure. To begin with, in the Bible, the terms "law" and "gospel" are not always polar opposites. The law both judges human sin and reveals the gracious will of God for human life. The Ten Commandments not only enumerate our transgressions; they are a manifesto of freedom ("I am the Lord your God, who brought you out of the land of Egypt, out of the house of slavery. You are free from the slavery of other gods. As those freed from bondage and brought into the land, you have all things and do not need to covet, murder, steal, or bear false witness"). In other words, from one angle of vision, the law of God exposes our broken condition, but from another angle the law opens up a vision of a just and hopeful world, and this is the gospel of God. To put this in Wilson's terms, in the Bible trouble can also be grace and grace can also be trouble. Job's woes—were they all trouble or was there a measure of grace? The prophets point out trouble, but their words and deeds also often cause trouble, and this "troubling of Israel" is full of grace. When Jesus eats and drinks with sinners, the result is a bushel of trouble and a bounty of grace. The cross of Jesus is trouble and grace all mingled together.

Second, "trouble" and "grace" are powerful and expansive biblical constructs, but unless they are stretched out of recognizable proportion, they are specific theological categories that do not cover the full range of Christian witness. "Trouble" and "grace," as Wilson ably describes them, are primarily categories of the larger doctrine of redemption or salvation. The doctrine of redemption is crucial, of course, but not every aspect of the Christian faith falls under the doctrine of redemption. Creation and providence, the eternity and beauty of God—these are Christian themes that are connected to but are not equivalent to redemption.

In short, the gospel is too rich, complex, and varied to be proclaimed through a single sermon form. Craddock himself, no doubt aware that some of his earlier readers had become practitioners of the inductive problem-solving form to the exclusion of others, firmly argued, in a later book, that the repetition of any one sermon form tends to constrict the fullness of proclamation:

> Form shapes the listener's faith. It is likely that few preachers are aware how influential sermon form is on the quality of the parishioners' faith. Ministers who, week after week, frame their sermons as arguments, syllogisms armed for debate, tend to give that form to the faith perspective of regular listeners. Being a Christian is proving you are right. Those who consistently use the "before/after" pattern impress upon hearers that conversion is the normative model for becoming a believer. Sermons which invariably place before the congregation the

"either/or" format as the way to see the issues before them contribute to oversimplification, inflexibility, and the notion that faith is always an urgent decision. In contrast, "both/ and" sermons tend to broaden horizons and sympathies but never confront the listener with a crisp decision. Form is so extremely important. Regardless of the subjects being treated, a preacher can thereby nourish rigidity or openness, legalism or graciousness, inclusiveness or exclusiveness, adversarial or conciliating mentality, willingness to discuss or demand immediate answers.[17]

Motion Pictures

The contemporary homiletician who has perhaps given the most sustained attention to the relationship between sermon form and the listening process is David Buttrick. Actually "the listening process" is too tame a phrase to describe Buttrick's main concern, which is the deeper issue of how sermons work to form faith in the consciousness of the hearers. "Sermon structures," he writes, "ought to travel through congregational consciousness as a series of immediate thoughts, sequentially designed and imaged with technical skill so as to assemble in forming faith."[18]

That rather complicated sentence receives a lengthy and elaborate exegesis in Buttrick's massive textbook *Homiletic*, much of which is devoted to the question of sermon form. Buttrick's ideas about good sermon form are based on a simple analogy: The human mind works something like an auto-focus camera. Everything out there in the world is streaming through the lens of human consciousness, but, as every photographer knows, not everything can be captured on film. The photographer must pick something to photograph and must allow the camera to focus on some object, thereby creating both foreground and background. Just so, the mind selects some field on which to focus, either using a wide-angle lens, thus taking in a broad range of meaning, or narrowing its view to a single small area. It can employ "filters" to highlight certain structures of meaning and can even determine "composition" and choose "angles of vision."[19] When all is set, the shutter opens, the image is captured in memory, the shutter closes, and the film is advanced to the next frame.

This is all an analogy, of course, but Buttrick finds in it much guidance for the preacher. Preachers are something like photographers' assistants, setting up a series of interesting scenes and then urging the hearers to take pictures of them. When preachers interpret the Scripture, they discover there *"fields of understanding* produced by symbols of revelation," and the task of preaching is to present those in such a way that the hearers can capture them on the mind's film. "Preaching," claims Buttrick, "mediates some structured understanding in consciousness to a congregation."[20]

What does this have to do with sermon form? Sermons involve a sequence of ideas. First the preacher speaks of this idea, then another idea, then the next idea, and so on. As the preacher presents one idea after another, the hearers are busily snapping away with their mental cameras. "Here is the first idea," the preacher says. *Click.* "Here is the second idea," and, again, *click.* Now, when the sermon is finished, what do the hearers have? If the sermon is poorly constructed, all they have is a cluttered box of random snapshots. If the sermon is well formed, though, they will have something like a filmstrip, a series of pictures that possess a lively sense of movement from one to the next and that work together to produce coherent understanding.

Sermons, then, are "a movement of language from one idea to another," and because of this Buttrick likes to call the individual ideas, or units, of the sermon "moves." Because of his understanding of how human consciousness works, Buttrick insists that these moves must be built according to a single blueprint. Every move is required to possess three indispensable parts:[21]

1. *Opening statement.* The preacher must state, in one clear sentence, the main idea of this move, what this move is about (e.g., "We are all sinners"). This invites the hearers to "take a picture of this." In addition, the opening must show how this move is connected to the one before, indicate the point of view of the move, and establish the move's emotional mood.
2. *Development.* In the middle section of the move, the main idea is elaborated, sometimes through clarification or illustration and sometimes through the raising of objections.
3. *Closure.* In a terse final sentence, the main idea of the move is restated, thereby signaling to the hearer that this move is

complete. Thus, the shutter on the hearer's camera closes, and the film advances in readiness for the next move.

Buttrick is persuaded that, given the diminishing attention spans of contemporary people, about four minutes is the most people will devote to a single idea, so each move must complete its work within that limit. A well-designed twenty-minute sermon, then, consists of an ordered sequence of no more than five or six of these three-part, precision-designed moves.

So far, we have only viewed the rudiments of Buttrick's theory of sermon form (the whole scheme, presented at length in *Homiletic*, is quite complex), but we have seen enough both to admire Buttrick's scheme and to raise some critical questions about it.

On the positive side, Buttrick compels us to think long and hard about what is happening inside the heads of listeners as we preach. He has a high view of the power of language and form to make things happen, and he is convinced, correctly, that a sermon shaped one way forms faith quite differently from a sermon shaped another way. This makes sermon form a theological and ethical issue, and not merely a rhetorical one.

Moreover, Buttrick, like Craddock, Lowry, and Wilson, has shed additional light on the crucial matter of movement in sermon form. Buttrick's approach does not really provide a single form but instead gives us a comprehensive way to think about sermon forms as processes of thought, which can yield many different structures. It is impossible to encounter Buttrick's method and not be attuned to the power of sermons to help, or to hurt, people as they move through the gradual and ordered process of coming to understand the gospel.

However, Buttrick's approach raises at least two troubling questions. First, do ideas really get formed in human consciousness in the way Buttrick claims they do? They *can*, I suppose, but surely not in every case. Buttrick wants every move to state the idea, to develop the idea, and then to restate the idea. Some of the best ideas I have, though (like the idea that God is gracious or the idea that my family loves me), simply did not "happen" in my consciousness that way. What Buttrick has done is to produce an abstract schematic description of one way of thinking and to declare that process as normative for each section of a sermon. Less direct, more poetic ways of coming to understanding get washed away.

The second concern about Buttrick's understanding of form is whether it is adequate to conceive of a sermon as "a movement of language from one idea to another." Is a sermon only a string of ideas? Some moments in good sermons are like the congregational singing of "A Mighty Fortress" at a funeral. There are ideas involved, to be sure, many of them, but these ideas are so woven into the fabric of memory and experience, grief and hope, that they cannot be sorted out and should not be reduced to a single concept. It would seriously miss the mark to ask, "What is the main idea in singing this hymn?" If a sermon contained no ideas, or a bewildering jumble of disconnected ideas, it would mean nothing at all. But surely sermons are more than a series of idea-laden boxcars moving down the track.

A Variety of Faithful Forms

As the debate among homileticians about sermon form continues, it has become increasingly clear that a sermon's form should be fashioned out of the interplay of two factors: the claim of the biblical text and the needs of the listeners—that is, the gospel as it comes to us from the biblical text and the listening capacities and patterns of those who will hear the sermon. The dynamics of human listening, while certainly an important and often neglected ingredient in the creation of sermon form, must not serve as the only basis, and not even as the starting point, in considerations of sermon design.

If we begin to create forms for sermons by trying to discern how people listen in general to oral communication, we will inevitably produce abstract anthropological descriptions of the patterns of human listening into which preaching must then be fit. We are constantly tempted to say that people *always* listen (or at least most *deeply* listen) narratively, inductively, in order to resolve conflict and ambiguity, or something of the sort. The inescapable conclusion, then, is that sermons must be poured into narrative or inductive or problem-solving or move-system molds because that, after all, is how human listening is shaped. Homiletician Richard Lischer, objecting to this move from anthropology to homiletics, writes:

The implicit hope is that if only we could find the perfect glass slipper of form, not only would the sermon be transformed into a beautiful princess, but we ourselves would also be transformed. Some would understand rhetoric as a natural ally of homiletics. But when rhetoric is accompanied by an implicit anthropology, as it always is, it poses a danger to homiletics. Homiletics then finds itself in crisis to the extent that it takes its cues from principles not its own.[22]

Lischer's warning flag is a necessary one to wave. Form, as we have seen, is not neutral, and if we look to the culture to tell us what form our sermons must assume, then, like it or not, we will end up preaching the culture instead of the gospel. On the other hand, if we decide to avoid the culture altogether and search for a purified sermon form in heaven or in the Bible, we will look in vain. There is no such thing.

Indeed, the Bible itself demonstrates how quite diverse literary forms are borrowed from the culture to serve as vehicles for proclamation. One way to view the New Testament is as the record of the earliest attempts to express the gospel in comprehensible form, and when we examine its range of texts, we quickly discover that the gospel has found expression in a variety of forms. In this passage, a logical argument is being developed; in that text, a straightforward narrative is being told; over here, an enigmatic parable is being unfolded; and over there, a hymn is being sung. All these forms—story and syllogism, poem and pronouncement, epistle and apocalypse—are found in the culture, but in every case the borrowed form is employed to serve the proclamation of the gospel. No one form is adequate to display the fullness of the gospel. Many forms are used, each selected in turn to express some aspect of the gospel on a particular occasion.

The same dynamic has been present throughout the history of Christian preaching. "In the history of its preaching," writes Lischer, "the church has moved from form to form. . . . No form of sermon design has proven normative—only the rhetorical situation remains."[23] Whenever the gospel has been faithfully proclaimed, the intersection between the claims of the faith and the specific circumstances of the hearers has evoked suitable but ever-varying forms.

A good sermon form, then, grows out of the particularities of preaching this truthful word on this day to these people. Think of those occasions when a person must speak an important truth to another. Perhaps it is a joyful but risky truth, like "I love you." Or perhaps it is a hard truth, like "Your work is not satisfactory and must improve if you are to stay here." The one who speaks words like these must decide how to speak them. In some ways the nature of the message itself demands its own form. "I love you" must be said personally, directly, straightforwardly. In other ways, the form must be fitting for the one to whom the word is spoken. We say "I love you" differently to a person who already knows of our love and will hear this as confirmation than we do to a person who has reason to think that we do not care for them and who will receive this word as a shock. How we speak a word of truth is the result of an interplay between the word spoken and the ones to whom it is said. The preacher is attempting to bear witness to the truth claims of the gospel that have been heard through a specific biblical text. The crucial question for form is, How can the preacher bear witness to these claims in such a way that these people can hear them? The preacher, therefore, must be concerned about the truth being preached, but always in light of how this congregation will be able to hear it. Likewise, the preacher must be concerned about how this congregation will listen, but always in relation to the hearing of this truth. Many strategies and oral genres will be employed—story, logical presentation, historical account, rhetorical questioning, poetry, and so on—but always because they are adequate to accomplish the task of bearing witness to the gospel for these people in this setting. Every sermon form, then, must be custom-tailored to match the particular preaching occasion.

Finding a Satisfactory Sermon Form

The preacher is a witness who brokers, as we have said, between the biblical text and the listeners, between the testimony the Scripture wishes to make and the people who will receive and hear this testimony. Each side of this transaction has a stake in sermon form. The nature of the testimony itself calls forth certain ways of speaking, and the capacities and needs of the hearers require other ways of speaking. A good sermon form results at the intersection of these two forces. How does the preacher find, or create, a good form for a given sermon? Sometimes just the right sermon form jumps out at the preacher, practically as if it were shouting, "This is the way to shape this sermon; no other form will do as well!" On other occasions the preacher simply begins to create the sermon, not knowing exactly how the sermon will arrive at its destination, letting the structure emerge as both preacher and sermon feel their way along toward the end. Most of the time, however, good sermon form results from careful thinking and planning in advance. Good sermon form is an artistic achievement, and no universally accepted and always reliable process exists for creating a satisfactory sermon form.

Here are three suggested steps designed to raise the central questions that form must address. In some ways, this suggested process might seem like just a fancy way to do outlining, since it does aim at thinking in advance about the pieces of a sermon and how they can best be arranged. But it is also an attempt to allow the listening process to play a major role in the decisions about sermon form. The result, if all goes well, is a form that is able to hold the sermon content but that also puts that content into action in such a way that it strikes the ear with power.

1. Start with the focus and function.

The place to begin in creating a sermon form is with the focus and the function statements —what the sermon aims to *say* and what the sermon aims to *do*. If we keep our eye firmly on the focus and the function, the sermon form that develops will have movement, unity, and suspense.

It will have *movement* because the focus and the function statements actually name the sermon destination. Where is the sermon going? It is going toward the place where the focus has been said and the function has been accomplished. The sermon is not finished until it has arrived at this destination, and the sermon form is a map tracing the pathway the hearers will travel, moving from where they are when they start the sermon journey to where they will hopefully be at the end of the sermon.

It will have *unity* since everything in the sermon will be shaped toward getting the focus said and the function done. There should be no "side trips" in the sermon. A good form will include only those steps needed to get to the focus and function destination. Everything else should be weeded out.

It will have *suspense* because there is the sense of incompletion until the focus has been said and the function accomplished. Both emotionally and intellectually, the sermon achieves "the sense of an ending" when it arrives at its destination. Until then, the hearers are hopefully intrigued and pressed forward by an intuiton of unfinished business.

Let's see how this works. Returning to an example from chapter 4, recall the focus and function statements for a sermon on Romans 8:28–39:

> *Focus:*   Because we have seen in Jesus Christ that God is for us, we can be confident that God loves and cares for us even when our experience seems to deny it.
>
> *Function:* To reassure and give hope to troubled hearers in the midst of their distress.

These focus and function statements grew, of course, out of the exegesis and, specifically, out of what the preacher saw as the claim of the Romans text. But now we view them as the *destination* of this sermon. If all goes well, when the sermon is completed the focus will have been said and the function will have been done. The preacher will have enabled the hearers to move from wherever they are at the start of the sermon to a new place, a place where (as the function states) they have reassurance and hope in the midst of their distress, because they have heard (as the focus states): "God is for us; we can be confident that God loves and cares for us even when our experience seems to deny it."

To enable the hearers to travel from here to there, the sermon form is going to guide them in a sequence of steps. We are going to call these steps "Moves," borrowing a term (but not the full definition) from Buttrick, because each one of these steps advances the flow of the sermon, that is, *moves* the sermon along toward the destination. So now the preacher asks, What are these "moves" and in what sequence should they be placed? What is the best form for saying and doing these things?

2. Divide the overall tasks of the sermon, as specified in the focus and function, into smaller "Moves."

Focus and function statements express the overall tasks of the sermon, and these tasks cannot be accomplished all at once. They will be done in smaller Moves, bit by bit, over the whole span of the sermon. Thus, the preacher should try to break the focus and function down into a set of smaller undertakings.

Our example focus statement is "Because we have seen in Jesus Christ that God is for us, we can be confident that God loves and cares for us even when our experience seems to deny it." This is what the sermon as a whole will say, but we cannot say it in one gulp. Instead, we can break this focus statement down into several smaller tasks, or Moves, that will have to be accomplished in the whole sermon. If the preacher is going to get this focus across, then somewhere in the sermon the preacher will have to perform the following Moves:

Move A: *Using Romans 8 as a lens, say where and how we have seen in Jesus Christ that God is for us.* The sermon will need to spend some time exploring the theological claim of the biblical text and making the case that what we have seen in Jesus indeed points toward the truth that God is with us and for us.

Move B: *Name and describe experiences that seem to deny God's love and care.* It won't do in this sermon merely to say that our experiences sometimes raise questions about the love and care of God. The preacher needs to describe some of those experiences and to show how such experiences raise these questions.

Move C: *Describe clearly how what we have seen in Jesus Christ is able to create present confidence in God's love and care.* This will be a difficult task. The preacher needs to make the contemporary connection and needs to do more than just argue that the hearers ought to be confident in God's love and care. The preacher needs to show how this confidence is actually generated today.

Now let us turn to our example function statement: "to reassure and give hope to troubled hearers in the midst of their distress." If the sermon as a whole is to get this function across, then along the way the sermon must complete the following:

Move D: Provide reassurance, based upon God's continuing love and care, to troubled hearers.

Move E: Evoke a sense of hope for people who struggle with tough circumstances.

Note that these last two Moves, both related to the function, are emotionally charged. The preacher cannot get away with saying, "So, we can clearly see from this passage from the apostle Paul that we can be reassured of God's love and care and have hope." Reassurance and hope are not matters of logic; they are matters of experience and feeling, and the preacher who wants to accomplish the function of this sermon will need to speak at the affective level, not just the cognitive one.

Depending on the circumstances of the hearers, the preacher may have to take up one more task related to the function:

Move F: Call into question all shallow reassurances that do not deal honestly with suffering.

If these hearers have been victimized by superficial theologies of "sunshine and sweetness," then these views will be out there in the congregation creating active resistance to the sermon. Sermons that do not address strong resistance rarely get heard, so the preacher will need somewhere in the sermon to try to turn the volume down on the static and clear out the clutter.

3. Decide the sequence in which these Moves should be arranged.

Now we must decide the best sequence in which to place the Moves we have just named. If we are building a house, decisions about sequence are usually fairly obvious and a matter of necessity. We must draw the plans before we order the materials, pour the foundation before placing floor joists, and erect the wall frames before constructing the roof.

In sermons, though, the choices are not nearly so clear. Sermons are oral events that take place in the imaginations and hearts of the hearers, and in building sermons we are not locked into the same necessities as a house builder. We can even construct the roof first, if we want to, and ask the hearers to suspend it in midair in their imaginations while we build the sermonic house beneath it. Decisions about sermon sequence are made almost exclusively on the basis of the needs and capacities of the listeners, and the preacher goes through a process of thinking through how the listeners would hear this or that possible sequence. "Should I begin by describing the biblical text," the preacher may ask, "and then show how that text speaks to our experience? Or will they hear the text better if I begin with a portrayal of human need and then show how the text speaks to that? But, then again, if I begin with human need, will they only hear the text as a quick fix for their problems rather than a new way of seeing life altogether?" Arriving at a good sermon sequence is finally a judgment call about how people can best listen to and respond to the focus and function of the sermon.

For our sample sermon on Romans 8, we have named five, maybe six, Moves (A, B, C, D, E, and perhaps F) that must be done if the focus and function are to be accomplished. What is the best order for them to be addressed in the sermon? The preacher has to decide the best strategy, and here is how one preacher might decide to arrange this sermon:

Possible Sermon Sequence 1

Move B: *The Problem.* In this design, the preacher has decided to start with the "tough stuff," the difficult experiences of the hearers that seem to deny God's love.

Move F: *False Responses to the Problem.* Having named the problem, the preacher names the typical shallow religious responses to this problem and then describes how these are insufficient.

Move A: *The Deeper Response of the Gospel.* Now the preacher turns to the text from Romans 8, describing how Paul gives a deeper response to suffering.

Move C: *The Gospel for Us.* The preacher describes how the promise of Romans 8 is also spoken to us today.

Move D: *Provide Reassurance.* As we noted, this involves moving the sermon to an emotional level. The preacher will, through story or confident and consoling words, provide reassurance based upon God's continuing love and care, to troubled hearers.

Move E: *A Sense of Hope.* Continuing on the emotive level, the preacher will build upon reassurance in the present toward a sense of hope for people who struggle with tough circumstances.

What this preacher has done is to take the six necessary tasks, the six Moves, and organize them into a sequence that will allow each one, at least in this preacher's view, to be done at just the right moment in the sermon. Notice that this preacher has clearly decided that the place to begin is with the felt need of human crisis, and that the remainder of the sermon should be a careful working through of the gospel response to that crisis. Basically, then, this preacher has crafted a problem-response sermon form to be accomplished in six Moves.

But this is not the only way to order these tasks. Here is another preacher's attempt to create a design. Same biblical text, same focus and function, but a different form:

Possible Sermon Sequence 2

Move F: *Name Inadequate Responses to Suffering.* In this sermon design, the preacher has decided on a different starting point. The preacher will talk about the "Hallmark Sympathy Cards" and all ways that our culture tries to gloss over suffering.

Move B: *Raise Objections Based on Real Experiences of Suffering.* Now the preacher will challenge whether the sentimentalities named in Move F really address the depth of suffering in human experience.

Move A: *Explore Paul's Witness in Romans 8.* Here the preacher turns to the biblical text and explores its word about suffering.

Move C: *Connect the Witness of the Text to Contemporary Experience.* Here the preacher connects the word of Romans 8 to the hearers' present experience.

Moves D and E Combined: *Move the Promise of the Gospel to the Emotive Level.* As a last Move, the preacher turns the claims made so far into the emotional realities of reassurance and hope.

Both of these sermon forms employ the same set of Moves, but each displays a different order. The first preacher decided to use a fairly straightforward "problem-response" form. The problem is named, false responses are cleared out, and then it is on to the Romans text for a deeper response. The second preacher, however, decided to take a somewhat different approach and, therefore, to craft a different form. This preacher chose to start not with the problem itself but with some of the false comforters in the culture that offer sentimental greeting-card responses to human suffering. Next, experiences of real human suffering are brought forward to show how superficial these sentiments are, and then the preacher turns to the text for a deeper answer. So if the first preacher crafted a "problem/response" form, this second preacher created a "here-is-the-prevailing-cultural-view/here-is-the-word-of-the-gospel" form. In the first sermon, the gospel responds to an aching question that the listeners have; in the second sermon, the gospel argues against a popular cultural attitude.

Both forms are good; both grow out of the sermon's focus and function. They differ because each preacher discerned that a certain sequence would work best to help the congregation move toward the sermon destination. Deciding which form to employ is a matter of discernment on the part of the preacher. If the sermon is to be an act of Christian proclamation, the hearers must not be passive. They should participate with the preacher in the creation of the event of proclamation, and the preacher should choose the sermon form that best allows the hearers to exercise their ministry of active and creative listening. If the hearers cannot follow the structural movements of the sermon, they will experience it as toil. Recently, when a group of researchers interviewed hearers about what they hear in sermons, many of the hearers complained about sermons that are unfollowable, that do not unfold in some orderly way. One layperson reported the following experience:

> There was a time, and it wasn't very long ago, when we had a guest preacher, and it was absolutely horrible. I'm used to orderly, structured listening, and going somewhere. This person rambled and was everywhere, and I was so exhausted. I was so tired trying to hear, "What are you trying to say?" So that just made me very tired and I thought, "Please don't bring that person back here anymore."[24]

Good Sermon Form: Two Examples

Another example of good sermon form can be seen in Edmund Steimle's superb Christmas Eve sermon on Luke 2:1–20, "The Eye of the Storm."[25] The full text of this sermon can be found in Appendix A.

The focus of this sermon is that the beautiful story of Jesus' birth in a manger, its "all is calm, all is bright" character, should not lull us into a romantic view of the Christ child disconnected from the conflict, pain, suffering, and violence of Jesus' life—or ours. The function of the sermon is to replace the sentimental and nostalgic "I'm dreaming of a white Christmas" understanding of Jesus' birth with the deeper truth of the nativity as God's response to a world of conflict and confusion.

Steimle had, then, a difficult task. He was to face a sanctuary full of people on Christmas Eve, including many families with children, and challenge, on the basis of the biblical text, a warm, homey, and cherished view of Christmas. He decided to form his sermon as follows:

Move A: *Present a Governing Image: Hurricane Hazel and the eye of the storm.*
   In this Move, Steimle described his experience of Hurricane Hazel in the 1950s. The storm hit with fearsome force. There were drenching rains, screaming winds, uprooted trees, and broken power lines crackling on the pavement. Then, suddenly, there was breathless calm—the eye of the storm—followed by the renewed fury of the storm.

Move B: *Apply the image to the biblical story.*
   In this Move, Steimle compared the story of Jesus' birth in Luke to his experience of the hurricane, a moment of calm in the midst of raging winds before (the anger of God at Israel, the biblical flood, the exile, the Roman occupation) and violent storms to follow (the massacre of the innocents, the rejection of Jesus by his own people, the crucifixion).

Move C: *Show how the Christmas story was the "eye of the storm" for the early church.*
   In this Move, Steimle explained that the stories of Jesus' birth were never intended to be gentle departures from the world of pain and conflict but rather were told and cherished precisely by early Christians well acquainted with conflict.

Move D: *Show how the Christmas story is the "eye of the storm" for the church today.*
   In this Move Steimle named some of the contemporary storms swirling around the hearers—poverty, violence in

the Middle East, families breaking up—and claimed that if the Christmas story is merely a nostalgic means for forgetting these storms, then it is not worth the effort of listening. But the Christmas story, he went on to say, is not a sentimental peace but like a peace in the eye of a storm, a peace that passes all understanding.

We can see that Steimle carefully constructed the form of this sermon. He was concerned not simply with saying something, but with saying it in such a way that his hearers could visualize it, be compelled by it, and perhaps let go of an inadequate view of Christmas and grasp the text's view of Jesus' birth as their own.

Another fine and more complex example of sermon form is displayed in Barbara Brown Taylor's compelling sermon "The Lost and Found Department,"[26] a sermon based on the three parables of Jesus in Luke 15: the Lost Sheep, the Lost Coin, and the Lost (Prodigal) Son. The full text of this sermon can be found in Appendix B.

In her exegesis, Taylor became convinced that the usual interpretation of this text—namely, that it is basically about repentance—is not quite on target. The main thrust of these parables, she discerned, is not about repentance but rejoicing: heaven's rejoicing and our rejoicing over the lost who are found and restored. This interpretation of the text raised a preaching problem for her. She knew that her congregation, having already heard many sermons about these parables, would have the traditional interpretation planted firmly in their minds. They would tend to think of themselves as "little lost lambs" or "prodigal sons and daughters," and would assume that the intent of these parables is to urge them to repent and to throw themselves on the mercy of God. But Taylor heard the text moving in a different direction. So how did Taylor craft a sermon that can change people's minds about a familiar biblical text?

To answer that question, let us look first at her focus and function for this sermon:

Focus: Contrary to our assumptions, Jesus' parables in Luke 15 do not call us to mend our evil ways and repent but to search for the lost and to rejoice when they are found.

Function: To change the hearers' previous conceptions of the parables in Luke 15, and to encourage them to assume the joyful role of seeking and finding the lost.

Here is the form she chose to use to get the focus and function accomplished:

Move A: *The Traditional Interpretation of Luke 15*
Calling Luke 15 "the gospel within the gospel," Taylor points out, "We love these stories because we imagine ourselves on the receiving end."[27] We think of ourselves as the lost lamb, lost coin, or lost son, always ready to repent and fall on the grace of a loving God. "They are stories about me," she says, "and I treasure them."[28]

Move B: *Challenging the Traditional Interpretation*
But then, Taylor challenges the traditional interpretation in two ways. First, she points out that the original hearers of these parables, the religious leaders, were not nearly as charmed by these stories as we seem to be. They were deeply offended by Jesus' ministry to sinners, not nostalgic types like "a hooker with a heart of gold," but real sinners like street prostitutes and drug dealers. The religious leaders were not unconcerned about the plight of sinners, but they thought they ought to set a good public example, and Jesus violated this standard. Second, Taylor points out that it is not at all clear that repentance is at the center of these stories. She says that "the lost sheep does not repent as far as I can tell and the lost coin certainly doesn't. They are both simply found. . . ."[29]

Move C: *Responding to the Challenge: Three Possibilities*
Taylor makes a creative move at this point in the sermon. Having described problems with the traditional interpretation of the text, she names three possibilities for responding to these problems:

1. Jesus was improvising these stories, so we shouldn't get too concerned when the details don't quite fit. In short, let the original interpretation stand.

2. Jesus meant these stories to be open-ended, and later editors reshaped them to make sure that repentance was emphasized. That's why the repentance theme doesn't quite line up with the details of the stories.
3. We have been missing the point all along. These "are not parables about lost sheep and lost coins at all, but parables about good shepherds and diligent sweepers."[30]

Move D: *Going with the Third Possibility*
In this Move, after pointing out that Jesus, when he says to his hearers, "Which one of you, having a hundred sheep . . . ," is inviting them to think of themselves as shepherds and not as lost sheep, Taylor invites her hearers to do the same. In essence, she asks her congregation to go with the third possibility suggested in Move C. "If you are willing to go with the third possibility—if you are willing to be a shepherd—then the story begins to sound different."[31]

Move E: *Experiencing the Joy of Finding*
Now Taylor faces a hard task. She wants to make the point that, when we do take that third possibility, when we see ourselves as shepherds, then finding the "lost sheep" produces great joy in and of itself, regardless of whether the sheep is repentant or not. This means she wants to create joy as well as understanding, and she must address the hearers on the emotional level as well as the cognitive level.

She decides to do this by telling a long story about going on a ten-day wilderness hike with a group of strangers. One woman in the group was an extremely needy and irritating person, and Taylor details the bothersome demands she constantly made. Then, around the fifth day out, the group got lost in the wilderness, and, after ten hours of wandering, finally made camp in the darkness and the rain. But when a count was made, the problem woman was not present. She was missing, and the leader of the group had the job of going out into the gloom with a flashlight to find her. After several anxious hours, the leader finally returned carrying the "lost lamb," and the entire camp erupted into rejoicing. No one cared or asked if the woman had repented and had promised to be a more cooperative person. There was joy purely over the fact that she had been found.

By telling this story, Taylor aims to seal the focus and function of the sermon. She hopes the story will not only reinforce the new perspective on the text but will also have an emotional wallop, evoking the experience of joyful finding.

Move F: *Conclusion: Tying the Threads Together*

Normally, at this point the preacher would wrap things up quickly, simply naming the insights and emotions of the story in Move F. Taylor, however, chooses to take a communicational risk, and she concludes the sermon this way:

> [W]hen I am working so hard to . . . stay found, it is difficult not to judge those who seem to capitalize on staying lost. I want to believe that they are not merely lost people, but that they are bad people, because then I could write them off and save myself some grief. I want to concentrate on the good people, the ones who want to be found. . . . I think about heaven ignoring those good folks in favor of one sinner . . . and I want to sue God for mercy.
>
> Then I hear someone behind me who calls me by my name, and big brown hands grab me by the scruff of the neck, hauling me through the air and laying me across a pair of shoulders that smell of sweet grass and sunshine and home, and I am so surprised, and so relieved to be *found* that my heart feels like it is being broken into, broken open, while way off somewhere I hear the riotous sound of the angels rejoicing.[32]

This is a beautiful but risky way to conclude the sermon. What Taylor wants to do is to show that our previous attitudes toward these stories—namely, that they are gentle stories about good people like us who either repent or don't need to, people like us who look down on real, unrepentant sinners—actually reveal that we are not the repentant sinners we fancy ourselves to be, but unrepentant and lost. When we are found by the shepherd, even though we are unrepentant, all heaven rejoices. The risk comes because this is a tricky and difficult move, and it also involves closing the sermon with an image of us as the lambs who are found, an idea that got rejected earlier in the sermon. Taylor is trusting the power of these images to pull the reader through the labyrinth to the desired goal.

Energizing the Form

The process of creating sermon form described in this chapter helps us to make some initial decisions about basic sermon structure. But all we have at this point are the bare bones of the sermon. We know the sermon destination (the focus and the function); we know the smaller tasks that must be accomplished along the way if the focus and function are to be achieved; and we have sketched a map of how to get there, that is, we thought through the best sequence, the necessary Moves that the sermon will follow to get to its destination. A full sermon form, however, is more than a destination and a sketch of how to get there. Now we need to put some flesh on these bones and some energy and life into the form by thinking through how these tasks are dynamically linked together and what it will actually take to get these tasks done. These are our concerns in chapter 6.

6

Refining the Form

Poets and preachers are moved whenever they remember that forms of words are expressions of the ceaseless creative activity of God without whom no words can be made and used in meaningful conjunction.

—Robert E. C. Browne, *The Ministry of the Word*

In the last chapter we discussed the creation of basic sermon form. We saw that a form is essentially a map for the journey of the sermon, a plan showing the sequence of Moves to be taken along the way toward the destination. As the sermon moves through each of the Moves, a cluster of communicational tasks is performed, and when all of the Moves are complete, hopefully the focus of the sermon has been said and the function of the sermon has been accomplished.

Some preachers need no more than the basic form to round out the sermon. They can get down to the business of creating the full sermon, using only the basic form to chart their way on the journey. Just as some people can add fractions in their heads, some preachers can intuitively put flesh on the bare bones of sermon form.

But turning a map into a real journey, turning a sermon form into a real sermon, is not always clear and easy. There are unexpected turns, unscheduled stops, and sometimes even detours that don't always show up on a map, and these have to be taken into account. So, we need to explore how the preacher takes the series of Moves named in the basic form and actually translates them into a full and rich sermon.

By way of analogy, imagine that the human resources director of a company plans to inform an employee that the company would like

171

to promote her to a new position but that this promotion will mean relocation to another city. Additionally, the human resources director wants the employee to know that she is free to accept or reject this promotion without penalty, but that realistically another opportunity like this may not develop for a long time.

The director's task of communicating the new job possibility is like one Move in a sermon form. Now, the director knows what he is supposed to do, but that is a far cry from knowing what to say and how to say it. Only the clumsiest director, given this task, would push open the woman's office door and blurt out, "We'd like to promote you to regional sales manager and move you to Detroit. You don't have to take it, of course, but this may be your last chance for a long time. What d'ya say?" That would technically fulfill the assignment, but it would not accomplish the director's mission. The employee would no doubt be overwhelmed, hit by a bombshell rather than graced with a promising option. A more skillful and sensitive director would think through how to break the news in a way that both the company's hopes and the woman's true choices would be understood and thoughtfully considered.

It is precisely this thinking through of communication that a faithful preacher, a reliable witness, needs to do as well. Bearing witness to the claim of the gospel upon the lives of the congregation requires discernment about the way that claim will be heard and received. Refining the form of a sermon is the process of thinking through in very nuanced ways how to present that claim in such a way that people can truly hear it and respond to it. This is a question of clarity, of course, but it is also a question of freedom. A sermon should present the gospel so that people can understand it, and it should also present the gospel so that people are liberated to respond to it. Sermon forms can be, if we choose, strategies for manipulation, deception, and coercion. But when they are shaped in obedience to the gospel, they become arenas for free and human decision making. Fleshing out a basic sermon form is, in many ways, an act of pastoral care.

Measuring the Distance

The process of refining and expanding the basic sermon form begins by examining each Move of the proposed form and sizing up just how big this Move will be for the hearers to take. Look, for example, at the first Move that one of our hypothetical preachers in the last chapter designed for the sermon on Romans 8:

Move 1:   The Problem. Start with the "tough stuff," the difficult experiences of the hearers that seem to deny God's love and care.

What this preacher hopes to accomplish in the opening Move of the sermon is clear. This preacher has decided that the good news in Romans 8 can best be heard in response to the cry "Where is God in our suffering?" So, the initial Move of this sermon is designed to disclose places where the hearers, at least implicitly, are already uttering this cry in their own experience.

This is a well-planned first Move for this sermon, a necessary one to take in the overall journey of the sermon, especially when we remember the destination, the sermon's focus and function:

Focus: Because we have seen in Jesus Christ that God is for us, we can be confident that God loves and cares for us even when our experience seems to deny it.
Function: To reassure and give hope to troubled hearers in the midst of their distress.

But devising a sermon Move in the lab is quite different from carrying it out in a live sermon. What will describing the "tough stuff" of life actually mean for the real congregation who will hear this sermon? Another way to put this is, "What sort of change is the sermon asking for here, and what will it mean for the hearers to make this change?" Every sermon Move implies some sort of change on the part of the hearers. Perhaps they will learn something new, deepen their understanding of something familiar, see something in a fresh way, feel something, or be motivated to do something. The preacher needs to assess where the hearers are in relation to this Move and should measure the distance the hearers will be invited to travel in this section of the sermon.

So what change does our sample sermon demand? It invites the hearers to recall certain experiences from their own lives and to understand and feel these experiences as moments of doubt about the providence of God. Now, if the listeners already have a keen and urgent awareness of "experiences that seem to deny God's love and care" and have come to church with these experiences keenly on their minds, then obviously no change is called for. The hearers have already traveled this leg of the journey, and this Move is unnecessary. But chances are good that the hearers are not in fact there yet, that the congregation is not screaming at the preacher, "We want to know the meaning of our negative experiences," and this Move is needed.

But where are the hearers in relation to this Move? The preacher considers several possibilities:

- Perhaps the hearers have had charmed lives and are simply not aware that many people have "experiences that seem to deny God's love and care." In other words, they don't know about such experiences and need to be informed about them. The preacher thinks about this possibility, but then rejects it. Most people, by the time they reach adulthood anyway, have had an ample measure of loss, pain, inexplicable suffering, and other doubt-provoking experiences; it hardly seems likely that they would be ignorant of this.

- Perhaps the hearers have had many doubt-provoking experiences, but they are probably not actively thinking about them as they come to worship. The preacher considers this a much stronger likelihood, and, if this is true, then this Move in the sermon becomes a means for naming and bringing to the surface the hearers' memories of these experiences.

- But then the preacher presses the question a bit deeper. Yes, the hearers have had doubt-provoking experiences, but it is probable that they have quite different attitudes toward these experiences. Some of the hearers will be more than ready to claim their experiences of suffering and loss as God-denying moments. A child died, a marriage dissolved, a business collapsed, a sense of personal worth was crushed, an accident left paralysis and pain in its wake. These experiences are raw and open wounds in these hearers' faith, and they want them named and addressed.

Other hearers, though, may be reluctant, even fearful, to let these open wounds touch their understanding of God. They sense the potential destruction that unresolved suffering can do to the structures of faith, so they keep their creed and their doubts at arm's length. They cannot, must not, admit to doubt, not because they are stubborn but because they are afraid that doubt, once loose, would consume them. If the preacher charges through this section of the sermon, heedlessly naming painful experiences as times of doubting God's care and love, these listeners will respond with fear, anger, or, more probably, by closing their ears.

Still others have also had experiences of suffering in their lives but have worked through them to some sort of resolution. Perhaps it is a healthy resolution, perhaps not, but some of the hearers will have discovered ways to remain faithful in the teeth of suffering. The preacher, then, cannot presume that for these listeners suffering automatically provokes an unanswered theological question.

The more deeply we know the hearers, the sharper our thinking will be. As we have said before, the one who bears witness to the gospel in preaching comes from the community of faith and is a part of that believing community. The more intimately one is involved in the struggles of a particular community of people to be faithful to the mission of Christ, the more fully one can know how to shape sermons so that the gospel can be heard by these people. We are not really adding at this point a new ingredient, the hearer, to the process of sermon development. As we maintained earlier, the hearers are already present in the interpretation of Scripture. The preacher is sent by them to the text on their behalf, and their needs, fears, questions, commitments, theological views, relationships, struggles—all that makes up their lives—actively shape the preacher's interrogation of the text. The preacher has already heard the claim of the text specifically in relation to those who will hear the sermon. So we are not bringing the hearers in only now as an afterthought. Instead, we are bringing what we know intuitively to the surface and trying to discover how the sermon, as it flows, Move by Move, from beginning to end, may faithfully express the interaction between text and hearer already present in the exegesis.

So, just exploring the first Move in the sermon form, the preacher realizes that the hearers will begin this sermon journey at several different points of departure. Some will welcome the change demanded in this first Move, others will resist it, and still others will see themselves as already having moved past it. Is there a way to develop this Move so that all the hearers can make this part of the journey?

Sometimes the answer, frankly, is no. Not every sermon, or every sermon Move, can or should attempt to speak with equal power and pertinence to every hearer. Most of us, as hearers, have had the experience of being deeply addressed by one sermon, or part of a sermon, and not so directly spoken to by the next one, knowing that others in the congregation were having the opposite experience. Part of the ethic of Christian worship is giving up the idea that every sermon, every prayer, every hymn must be focused upon me and my needs. Sometimes hearing the gospel actually means "overhearing" the gospel being spoken directly to others whose circumstances are unlike our own. From the vantage point of the preacher, the encounter with the biblical text often yields a word that speaks more immediately to some in the congregation than to others, and trying to speak to everyone all the time can drive us into bland generalities. If, on the other hand, the preacher always addresses the same group—the strong or the adults or the families or the men or the women or the resourceful or the lonely or those who do not believe—then the fullness of the gospel is not being proclaimed.

In our example, the preacher may well decide to try to bring all of the hearers along on this first Move of the journey, even though they start in different places. If so, the preacher will search for language that acknowledges the differences in the hearers. The preacher may make a first draft of the sermon beginning something like this:

> It is sometimes said that if you live long enough, life will take you through some rough places and fearful valleys, and it is true. Everyone here this morning who has any measure of life experience has had some seasons of pain, trouble, loss, and doubt. It goes with the territory of being human.
>
> For some of us, these experiences are like exposed nerves. Touch them, and we still cry out in pain. When we are honest, we raise our fist at heaven and wonder why a loving God would let us and others suffer this way. For others of us, we have made our peace with bad memories and painful experiences, but we still carry them with us. Heavy baggage indeed. Still others of us would rather turn our heads from the shadows and focus on

the light. What good, we wonder, can come from dwelling on the negative?

But regardless of how we feel about these experiences, the fact is, we have all had them. We all walk with a limp.

Naming the Resources

So, the preacher has thought through where the hearers are in relation to the first Move of the sermon, and has even produced a first draft, but the preacher senses that more needs to be done. The draft is good, but it doesn't get down deep enough. The preacher now asks, "What else do I need to add to this part of the sermon that will help the listeners hear?" The preacher is now asking about resources to flesh out this Move. When the preacher thinks more deeply about this Move, it sinks in that what is missing is something that will do more than just name the fact that they have had doubt-provoking experience but, rather, will actually evoke for the hearers their experiences of loss, suffering, and separation, experiences that cause crises in their faith. What sort of material can do that? What kind of communication evokes memories?

Again the preacher considers several possibilities. The preacher thinks first of all of narrative resources. A story can release the spring of memory, and the preacher takes stock of the stories that may be appropriate here. Perhaps a well-known example from history would be useful, something like the story of poet John Milton becoming blind at age forty-three, including the well-known plea from his poem about this experience, "Doth God exact day-labour, light denied?" Here is a person's experience in which the theological question of providence was explicitly raised, and the recounting of it could well spur the hearers to recall similar events in their own lives. Upon reflection, however, our preacher decides that this is not the best resource to use. Historical examples such as the one from the life of Milton raise the crucial issue, all right, but they seem too remote for this sermon and this congregation. They may come across more as examples from cultural and literary history than as pieces of real life.

So the preacher decides something closer to home is needed, and one such experience, the preacher knows, involves the recent and tragic death by breast cancer of a young woman who was a strong and devoted leader in the congregation. This event will surely be on the minds of many during this sermon. On second thought, though, the preacher realizes that it would be unwise to mention it directly. Not only would it be unfair to the woman's family, who are still present in the congregation, the story of this woman's death is, in a way, too close to home because unfinished grief would make it impossible for the sermon to be anything but a response to this one incident.

Finally the preacher decides that the best way to draw in the wide variety of hearers is not by a single narrative at all but through a series of vignettes, each one briefly picturing the sort of human circumstance that could prompt a crisis of faith. These vignettes, drawn from the lives of everyday people, would be punctuated by pauses in the sermon, inviting the hearers to fill in the silences with their own experiences. So the preacher revises the draft of the sermon opening, adding some of these vignettes:

> It is sometimes said that if you live long enough, life will take you through some rough places and fearful valleys, and it is true. Everyone here this morning who has any measure of life experience has had some seasons of pain, trouble, loss, and doubt. It goes with the territory of being human.
>
> - A marriage that began with dreams and romance ended with anger and alienation. "What God hath joined together" came apart at the seams, and we wonder where God was in the coming apart.
> - A cruel disease is at work in our bodies, stealing strength and hope, and we wonder in the pain about the loving care of God.
> - There is an empty place at the table where once one we loved shared bread and life, and we wonder about a God whose world holds such loss.
> - There are deep wounds inflicted by parents who cared too little or who gave violence instead of love, and we wonder if God is also this kind of parent.
>
> For some of us, these experiences are like exposed nerves. Touch them, and we still cry out in pain. When we are honest, we raise our fist at heaven and wonder why a loving God would

let us and others suffer this way. For others of us, we have made our peace with bad memories and painful experiences, but we still carry them with us. Heavy baggage indeed. Still others of us would rather turn our heads from the shadows and focus on the light. What good, we wonder, can come from dwelling on the negative?

But regardless of how we feel about these experiences, the fact is, we have all had them. We all walk with a limp.

Now, obviously, different preachers in different settings would make different decisions about all of this. In some close congregational settings, the telling of the story of the woman in the congregation who died of breast cancer would not be a violation of confidentiality and would in fact be the most faithful way to raise the issue. In other congregations, biblical examples of doubt would carry great authority and power. What is important to see here is the process by which a preacher thinks through each Move of the sermon, each portion of the basic form. Each Move of the form names a task, and the preacher asks what it will mean for the sermon to perform this task with *these* people. In the light of this, the preacher makes decisions about what kinds of materials are needed: stories, descriptions, definitions, teaching sections, hymns, prose quotations, dialogue, images, practical examples, rhetorical questions, personal confession, persuasive argument, poems, verses of Scripture, exegetical information, or whatever.

What is happening here is that we are beginning to understand a sermon as a "system of communication" and the form of a sermon as a description of that system. "System of communication" is an ugly phrase, to be sure, but it is a helpful one nonetheless, since it makes clear that every portion of a sermon works in concert with all of the others toward a unified effect. Each Move of the sermon picks up one piece of the total sermonic task, and we must decide what resources are necessary in order for each piece of the larger job to get done. This steers us away from general and misguided advice about sermon form (found in some homiletical manuals) based upon arbitrary and mechanical concerns (for example, "every sermon 'point' should have an illustration") or pseudo-psychological considerations (for example, "the congregation always needs a 'break' between points").[1] Abstract rules like these miss the mark. All choices about form are ad hoc decisions, since each Move of a sermon calls for the preacher and the hearers to perform a labor specific to this sermon and this sermon only.

More Examples

Here are some examples, based on actual sermons, demonstrating how several preachers went about the process of refining and elaborating basic sermon form.

1. William Willimon, in a sermon on the story where Jesus tells the rich man, "You lack one thing; go, sell what you own, and give the money to the poor" (Mark 10:17–22), wanted to include a Move in the sermon form in which the hearers could become critical of all attempts—their own and others'—to tone down this word into something more comfortable, less demanding. The problem was, if Willimon had directly attacked this tendency to reduce the demand of Jesus, some of the hearers may well have considered Willimon, as preacher, to be an uninvited, unwelcomed adversary and retreated to safer ground. So Willimon decided that what was needed was not direction but indirection. Rather than criticizing the hearers, he instead gave voice to his own resistance to the word of Jesus, letting the congregation "overhear" his ironic and amusing attempt to wiggle free of the text's demand. Here is that portion of his sermon:

> "Jesus loved him and said, 'Go, sell all you have and give it to the poor!" He lacked "one thing needful," something beyond the bounds of conventional morality and realistic, practical ethics.
>
> Of course, if I had been Jesus that day, that's not what I would have said. I might have asked the well-heeled young man for an endowed fund for student scholarships, a bigger pledge for the church budget, not everything. This I call pastoral care, compassion. Unlike Jesus, if I had looked upon the young man, I would have been sensitive to his personal limitations, his need for some earthly security, his desire for something practical, workable. I've had courses in pastoral counseling. I know that even though the man is well off financially, he is still a poor, struggling beggar—spiritually speaking, psychologically speaking. He, like all the rest of us, is doing the best he can.

And that's good enough for me. So my flock, when it comes to me for counseling or guidance, doesn't expect to be told something "irrational" like, "Go, sell all you have and give it to the poor." It expects to be assured that they are doing the best they can, that whatever they have already decided in their hearts is right, is fine with me.

. . . "What must I do to inherit eternal life?"

"Well," Jesus should have said (if Jesus had the benefit of a seminary education), "What do you think is practical—considering your socioeconomic circumstances? What feels right to you?" . . . And yet Mark says that Jesus spoke an unpleasant word to the Rich Young Man because he loved him. I fear that I (and most of my church), in the name of "love," have decided to make people's lives a little less miserable rather than a lot more redeemed.[2]

2. Henry Mitchell once developed a sermon on Philippians 4:8 KJV ("Whatsoever things are true, whatsoever things are honest, whatsoever things are just . . . think on these things"). In one of the sections, or Moves, of the sermon, he wanted to enable the hearers to understand what he viewed to be the central concept of the text: namely, that Christians, when they follow Paul's counsel and think about true, honest, just, and pure things, are using their faithful memories to participate in the creation of the world in which they live. The task of this Move, then, was to teach this concept clearly, and Mitchell decided that what he needed were some teaching examples that would render plain this Pauline idea. He chose two: an analogy from the world of television and an example from the history of Mitchell's own slave ancestors. The result in the sermon was as follows:

To put it another way, Paul's word is advising us to make wise choice of our re-runs. Whatever previously aired programs you may see this summer, you may be sure they are the best and not the worst of any series. It occurs to me that my ancestors had just such a selective process at work. They were instinctively seeking things to praise God for, largely as a result of their African religious roots. That made them live it over and over again. One small blessing lived through a hundred times could make a huge difference in the quality of their lives, if not the variety. The joy of a visit from a relative on another plantation, or the health of an infant once hardly expected to live were very big on their always-summer schedule. Without being aware of why it was so, they were driven to build secret "praise houses," and to praise and shout. . . . They survived because of it. It's still good for survival: Think on these things.[3]

3. Barbara K. Lundblad, when she interpreted the story of young Samuel and old Eli in the temple (1 Sam. 3:1–18), saw in this text an expression of the interplay between old and young in the faith, especially in terms of the blessing of wisdom that those who are old can give to those who are young. In order to express this claim, she needed to include in the sermon form two sections: (1) a Move in which the hearers were enabled to see Eli not as a "cardboard" biblical figure but as a real man, encountering the struggles of aging, and (2) a Move in which the hearers saw Eli use his maturity to bless the much younger Samuel. She decided that what was needed in these two Moves was a weaving together of the biblical information about Eli with very contemporary descriptions of aging so that the hearers would simultaneously participate in the biblical narrative and experience its present relevance. Here are those two Moves in her sermon:

> Then, there is Eli. An old man whose eyesight was so dim he could no longer see. His old age was not filled with the joy of family, for his own sons had done evil in the sight of the Lord, evil which he was either unwilling or unable to stop. Time itself is measured out for him . . . no longer are there plans, plans for career, or college, or raising children. But even more painful, as [Joseph] Sittler says, "the interpersonal filaments snap loose one by one." The people who have been friends, colleagues, partners over a lifetime are gone. One by one the filaments snap. No one remains alive who knew me when I was a child . . . no one who was a classmate in college or a colleague in the earliest days of my work. An older woman told me not long ago of the agony she felt over tossing out bundles of old letters. She simply had to get rid of the boxes in her apartment . . . there was no room. "But," she added, "sometimes I think to

myself, if I don't have something in writing, I won't be sure I was really around thirty years ago. Who is left who remembers I was there?"

The filaments had snapped in Eli's life. His ministry, his life work, his faithfulness—all were in question. He had passed on nothing good to his sons. (The congregation he had served for thirty years was now down to a handful of members . . . the books he had written were now sold on the bargain table for $2.98 or given away to the Salvation Army.) There was only past tense, and it was not worth remembering.

But there was one nagging phrase which begs Eli to stay a while longer. It is not even about Eli, but about the young boy Samuel . . . the boy who came to Eli in the night at the sound of a voice in the darkness. "Now Samuel did not know the Lord, and the word of the Lord had not yet been revealed to him." How could the boy ever imagine that it was God's voice calling to him in his sleep?

It was the aged man of dim eyesight who alone was there to speak the word of the Lord . . . to tell young Samuel that there was such a thing as the "Word of the Lord." It was Eli, the melancholy priest whose life seemed over, who alone was the link between the ancient stories and the squint-eyed, sleepy boy standing beside his bed.

. . . And so it was that Eli spoke from a place deeper than his own broken spirit, deeper than the despair over children gone bad, deeper than his own doubts . . . from that very deep place of the spirit which perhaps only the very old really know. For they have seen life in its fulness and its emptiness; they know life's possibilities but also life's limitations. Such things the sleepy boy could not yet know. "It is the Lord," said Eli, "go, lie down."[4]

4. As he developed a sermon on Revelation 3:14–22, Edmund Steimle decided that a teaching Move was needed in the sermon. A key line in this text reads, "Behold, I stand at the door and knock; if any one hears my voice and opens the door, I will come in to him and eat with him, and he with me" (RSV). Steimle knew from his exegesis of the passage

that this image presents to the church an urgent and demanding call to repentance. Steimle also knew that the popular understanding of this verse is as a more cuddly picture of a gentle and inviting Christ. The task of this teaching Move in Steimle's sermon, then, was to replace this popular misunderstanding with the text's own intention. How does one enable people to give up a familiar understanding of a Bible verse in favor of a harsher, more challenging word? Steimle decided that he first needed materials that would bring the popular view to mind but that he also needed some solid evidence from the text itself to counter that view. Here is the Move as he ultimately composed it:

> For generations of Christians the image of Christ standing at the door and knocking has been influenced by Holman Hunt's painting of a gentle-faced Christ, lantern in his hand, knocking quietly on the door of an old house; and also by William W. How's familiar hymn:
>
>> O Jesus, Thou art standing Outside the fast closed door,
>> In lowly patience waiting
>> To pass the threshold o'er . . . O Jesus, Thou art pleading
>> In accents meek and low.
>
> Now, whatever comfort that hymn and that painting may have brought to generations of Christians and no matter what lofty sentiments may have been stirred up in us, they both distort almost beyond recognition the actual situation in which that familiar line occurs, "Behold, I stand at the door and knock."
>
> To begin with, the face is not gentle. Here is how John of Patmos pictures the face of the Lord Christ as he speaks to the churches in the opening chapters of the Book of Revelation: "Then I turned to see the voice that was speaking to me, and on turning I saw seven golden lampstands, and in the midst of the lampstands one like a son of man, clothed with a long robe and with a golden girdle round his breast; his head and his hair were white as white wool, white as snow; his eyes were like a flame of fire, his feet were like burnished bronze, refined as in a furnace, and his voice was like the sound of many waters . . .

from his mouth issued a sharp two-edged sword, and his face was like the sun shining in full strength."

And the voice, like the sound of many waters is speaking hardly in "accents meek and low." It is an impatient voice, an angry voice, addressing the Church at Laodicea: "I know your works: you are neither cold nor hot. Would that you were cold or hot! So, because you are lukewarm, and neither cold nor hot, I will spew you out of my mouth. For you say, I am rich, I have prospered, and I need nothing; not knowing that you are wretched, pitiable, poor, blind and naked. . . . Those whom I love, I reprove and chasten, so be zealous and repent." Then—precisely then—comes the familiar line, "Behold I stand at the door and knock." It is an urgent last call to a self-satisfied and lukewarm church rather than a privatized picture of a gentle Christ, "in lowly patience waiting to pass the threshold o'er" of our hearts.[5]

5. In a sermon preached on the National Day of Mourning after the 1995 bombing of the federal building in Oklahoma City, Annette Sowell wanted to make the theological point that God was present in the midst of this tragedy. Instead of simply making this as a broad theological claim, she decided that what was needed were very concrete images of how and where God was present. Here is that portion of her sermon:

> And so Jesus sends doctors and nurses into neonatal ICU units and rescue workers into bombed-out buildings and policemen into the debris of a daycare center, so they can hand out to firefighters sent by God the little ones who have suffered and already been taken to heaven.
>
> Jesus sends an amateur photographer to snap a picture that the world might be forever reminded that there are more good people in this world than bad people.
>
> Jesus sends dedicated teachers and administrators into classrooms to teach children that knives and guns and drugs are not the way to live and breathe the spirit of God.
>
> Jesus sends the Red Cross and the Feed the Children Foundation to feed and care for the children and their families.

Oh yes, through it all, there is God. God with skin on . . .

And, make no mistake about it . . . through it all, there is God, sitting in a jail cell on a military base in Oklahoma, with a man who will be punished by the laws of this land. Our God weeps for us all.[6]

6. One of the more difficult tasks of sermons is translating a theological claim into everyday experience. It is one thing to say that the gospel calls us to love, forgive, trust, believe, or whatever; it is quite another thing to help people see what this could look like in their lives. In a sermon on the unusual story of Jesus' cursing of the fig tree (Mark 11:11–25), I was attempting to communicate the claim that I had heard in that text: living in the kingdom's power means praying for, working for, and expecting fruitfulness in places where the world sees only barrenness and expects nothing. As I developed the basic form of this sermon, I knew that one of the necessary Moves would be to enable the hearers to see and to experience what this claim looks like when it is lived out in everyday circumstances. I decided that a story in which a person actually did what the text described was the best resource for this task (for a more complete discussion of the use of stories and experiences in sermons, see chapter 8). Here is that portion of the sermon:

Sometime ago I found myself in a conversation with a man seated next to me on an airplane, a conversation that took a rather serious turn. He told me that he and his wife were the parents of a son, now in his thirties, who was confined to a nursing-care condition for a number of years because of an injury to his brain. "We had stopped loving him," said my companion. "It's a hard thing to admit, but we had stopped loving him. It's hard to love someone who never responds. We visited him often, but our feeling for him as a son had begun to die. Until one day we happened to visit our son and discovered a visitor, a stranger, in his room. He turned out to be the pastor of a nearby church whose custom it was to visit all the patients in the nursing home. When we arrived we found him talking to our son—as *if* our son could understand. Then he read Scripture to our son—as *if* our son could hear it. Finally he had prayer with our son—as *if* our son could know that he was praying. My first impulse was to say, 'You fool, don't you know about our son?' But then it dawned on me that, of course, he did know. He knew all along. He cared for our son as if our son were whole, because he saw him through the eyes of faith, and he saw him already healed. That pastor renewed in us the capacity to love our son.

Rejoice! Rejoice that in the power of the kingdom come in Jesus even those broken in disease are never out of season in God's love.[7]

7. Sometimes a sermon Move seeks to enable the hearers to feel something as well as to understand something. Evoking feelings usually requires special language: stories, images, songs, poems, or perhaps the language of silence gradually filling with meaning. In a sermon about the meeting of the risen Christ with the two followers on the Emmaus road (Luke 24:13–35), John Vannorsdall described how the followers, unaware that they were speaking to the risen Christ, told the stranger on the road of their dashed hopes. "We had hoped," they said, "that he was the one to redeem Israel." Vannorsdall saw himself and his hearers in the role of the followers, and he wanted the hearers not only to understand the disappointed hopes of the disciples on the Emmaus road but also to feel their own broken visions and crushed hopes. He knew that to do this he would need language that would touch the hearers' imaginations. This is what he composed:

> There was a time when we thought that the world could be a better place. We were capable of visions, you see. We could imagine a world of green lawns rather than a street full of junk, a world where neighbors greeted one another rather than pass silent with hidden faces, a world in which the aged were wise and cherished, where bullies were defeated, where games were for fun rather than profit, and dancing was the purest pleasure. We had a vision of a world of clean, white snow, smelling of Spring, carpeted with Autumn's color. There was a time when we thought the world could be a better place.

There was a time when we thought that we could be better persons. We could imagine our families proud of us rather than ashamed. Imagine a crucial time when we would dare to tell the truth and everyone would be amazed and say, "Thank God the truth's been told at last." We could imagine a time when we would be the champion for some kid beaten on the street, or be the lawyer fighting for the innocent and oppressed. We would be the scientist discovering a way to feed the hungry, an engineer making heavy work light. There was a time when we thought we could be better persons.

There was a time when we believed that God had a plan for his people. His plan was to bless marriage with joy and children, to free us of our sins and guilt, fill our lives with peace, to remake the world without war, a world in which the woods were cool on a summer's day and the animals played with one another. There was a time when we believed that God had a plan for his people.

"We had hoped," said the two on the road to Emmaus, "that he was the one to redeem Israel."[8]

Out of the Stockroom

In the previous chapter, and in all of this one to this point, we have presented the question of sermon form as a creative activity, a thinking through the interaction between the claim of a specific sermon and the listening process of particular hearers. Every sermon event possesses its own set of variables and peculiar circumstances, and therefore we have insisted that every sermon form must be freshly minted and custom made.

Surely, though, there must be some outer edge to the possibilities for sermon forms. The idea of running a never-before-seen, never-before-tried form out onto the test track every Sunday strains our creative energies and boggles the mind. Is there not a limited set of tried-and-true sermon that can prove serviceable for most occasions? There may have been severe problems with the notion that all sermons should have three points, each with an illustration mounted on it like a bulb inserted into a chandelier, but at least that form worked as a sturdy, time-honored template.

Indeed, many older homiletical manuals provided handy lists of sermon-form "types.'" These lists characteristically included a half dozen or so frequently used patterns of sermon form. The problem with them was that they were presented apart from any discussion of how an apt sermon form emerges through the interplay between the claim of the biblical text and the receptivity of the hearers. In other words, there was no theory, no theological or communicational grounding, for how sermons should be formed; there was only a list of "stockroom" forms. The implication was that preachers were to rummage through the stockroom until they found an attractively shaped form and then fit the sermon into it.

This is not to say that these lists were not of value. In fact, such lists continue to be very worthwhile when we get away from the notion that they are boxes in the stockroom and view them instead as answers to the kind of dynamic questions about sermon form we have been asking. In other words, when we think through, for each and every sermon, all the issues about sermon form, the end result of our thinking will often be not some utterly new and wildly innovative form but, rather, a form that has been employed by many preachers many times before, and quite effectively.

Here, then, are some of these frequently appearing sermon forms, along with some commentary about the kind of sermon each is likely to "fit."

1. If this . . . then this . . . and thus this.

In this form, each Move of the sermon builds logically on the previous Move. The full claim of the sermon comes at the end, as the final link in a chain of smaller claims. This is a fairly heady form, best suited to sermons in which the function is a teaching one.

2. This is true . . . in this way . . . and also in this way . . . and in this other way too.

Luccock called this form the "jewel sermon," and Sangster called it the "facet sermon" because the preacher presents the central claim of the sermon and then turns it in the light so that its various facets can be seen. This form is particularly apt for those sermons with claims of some internal complexity or for sermons in which the central claim affects various hearers in different ways.

3. This is the problem . . . this is the response of the gospel . . . these are the implications.

Sometimes called a "law-gospel" or "problem-solution" form, this form begins by exploring the human dilemma and announces the claim of the sermon in response to that. It is most effective when the hearers have some shared sense of need or crisis.

4. This is the promise of the gospel . . . here is how we may live out that promise.

Rather than beginning with a particular human dilemma, this form starts by announcing the claim of the text and then explores the convictional and ethical demands of that claim. Some call this the "indicative-imperative" form, and it is most appropriate when the function of the sermon contains ethical implications.

5. This is the historical situation in the text . . . these are the meanings for us now.

In this form, the circumstances of the text are given (e.g., Amos's word to the socioeconomic situation of Israel in the eighth century BCE), followed by the word of the text for today (e.g., Amos's word to our socioeconomic situation). This may be done in two large Moves (then/today) or as a series of interweavings (then/today, then/today, then/today). Another variation is to employ a "flashback" (today/then/back to today). This form is best suited to those texts in which the preacher has identified what James Sanders has called a "dynamic analogy"[9] between the text and the contemporary situation. No historical situation is repeated exactly, but a dynamic analogy results when we identify in some ways with characters or circumstances in the text and thus participate in the tensions and resolutions of the text.

6. Not this . . . or this . . . or this . . . or this . . . but this.

This sermon form usually begins with some kind of question or quest, such as, "What could Jesus possibly have meant when he said, 'Blessed are you when people hate you'?" The sermon then proceeds by suggesting possible erroneous or incomplete answers, gradually eliminating them until the full claim of the text can be heard. This form is most effective when the original question is an enigmatic one or when the function of the sermon is to provide new insight on a familiar issue. Variations on this form are *This . . . and this too* and *Either this . . . or this.*

7. Here is a prevailing view . . . but here is the claim of the gospel.

This is sometimes called the "rebuttal" form, but that name unfortunately carries a debating connotation. At its best, this form describes, as fully and as sympathetically as possible, a prevalent cultural attitude toward something and then allows the claim of the gospel to enrich, correct, challenge, replace, or renew that view. It is an apt form when the function of the sermon calls upon the hearers to see something in a new way.

8. This . . . but what about this? . . . well, then this. . . . Yes, but what about this? . . . and so on.

This form represents a dialogue in a monological format. Each Move of the sermon is followed by a questioning or probing of that Move, modeled on the style of inquiring conversation. The form is most effective when the claim of the sermon is complex, nuanced, or controversial.

9. Here is a story.

The story form of preaching actually represents a cluster of related forms:

> *A single story.* Although it is rare, sometimes the entire sermon is simply the telling of a story, either a retelling of a biblical story or the recounting of a contemporary story. The story itself carries its own insight.
>
> *Story/reflection.* In this form, a story is told and then reflected upon for insight and guidance.
>
> *Part of a story/reflection/rest of the story.* Sometimes a preacher will recount the first part of a story and then stop before the story is finished. The tension of the unresolved story is then explored in some manner before the story is finished. A variation on this is to break the story into several narrative/reflection episodes.
>
> *Issue/story.* This is a version of the "problem-response" form listed above. In this case, a story serves as the response to some issue or question presented in the opening Move of the sermon.

10. Here is a letter.

In this form, the sermon is composed as a letter, addressed either to the congregation or to someone else. The sermon follows normal epistolary form. This form is especially effective in evoking the sense of personal address and in disclosing the affective dimensions of the gospel.

11. This? . . . or that? . . . both this and that.

This form presents a sermon claim that is either paradoxical or two-sided, such as "Jesus was a servant; Jesus is Lord; Jesus is Servant-Lord," or "Disciples are wise as serpents; disciples are innocent as doves; disciples are both wise as serpents and innocent as doves."

This list could be extended, of course, but there is no need to do so. Already variations, combinations, and other possibilities are probably coming to mind. The important thing to remember is that we do not begin with one of these abstract forms and then try to force the sermon to fit it. We begin with the focus and function of the sermon and try to create the right form. These standard patterns are for the preacher like chord patterns for a musician. We study them, and they are there in our repertoire, but the sermonic song itself seeks its own best form.

The Importance of Variety

The diversity of rhetorical forms among biblical texts, combined with the flexibility of the process we have described for creating sermons, will inevitably produce a wide variety of sermon forms. As a matter of practical experience, preachers must guard against gravitating toward a narrow range of sermon patterns. As preachers, we tend to create sermon forms that match our own ways of listening and learning, and therefore we must self-consciously move beyond our own preferred patterns.

Although the reasons for this are not entirely clear, it is widely known that hearers possess many different styles of listening. A sermon that includes many personal references and pastoral experiences will be for one listener a powerful and touching word, while another hearer will find it intellectually thin. A free-flowing, artistic, image-rich sermon will stimulate some hearers to see the faith in new ways, while others will find the same sermon opaque and confusing. A carefully ordered, tightly argued sermon will be received by some as a model of clarity and the occasion for deep insight, while others will find such a form dull and confining.

I once spoke with a minister who was puzzled because some members of his congregation had complained that he was "not preaching the Bible" in his sermons, despite the fact that he spent hours each week on exegesis and richly supplied his sermons with the results of his labor. The problem, as it turned out, was not that his sermons lacked a biblical dimension but that the form of his sermons did not match the listening styles of many of those in his congregation. They were listening for "biblical principles"; he was supplying them with biblical images. They were listening for information from the passage; he was attempting to re-create the experience found in the passage. They were listening for direction; he was supplying indirection. The biblical text was governing his sermons, but not in ways that many of his hearers could listen for it or recognize it.

Preaching was once thought of as an activity much like putting eggs into baskets. The "eggs" were the key ideas, or points, of the sermon; the "baskets" were the minds of the hearers. Preachers did the placing; hearers did the receiving. Thus, preachers were active; hearers were passive. If the preacher worked skillfully and carefully, a fairly substantial number of eggs could be placed, without breakage, into everybody's basket during the course of a sermon. If a preacher wanted an indication of how effective a given sermon was, the hearers could be asked, after the sermon, how many of the main points they remembered. In other words, "How many eggs do you have?"

Studies in human communication have confirmed, however, what insightful preachers knew all along: the hearer is not at all passive in the listening process. The space between pulpit and pew bristles with energy and activity. As the preacher speaks, the hearer races ahead in anticipation of what might be said next, ranges back over what has already been said, debates with the preacher, rearranges the material, adds to the message, wanders away and returns (sometimes!). In short, the hearer is a co-creator of the sermon. Preachers may be passing out eggs, but hearers are making omelets, and a sermon preached to seventy-five people is actually transformed by them into seventy-five more or less related sermons.

Now, the wonderful and frustrating truth about the cooperative artistry that goes on between preacher and hearer is that it demands both dissonance and consonance. If there is not at least some measure of dissonance between preacher and hearer, some degree of surprise and even conflict in their interaction, there will not be enough energy to maintain lively communication. Too much consonance produces dull predictability. On the other hand, there must be enough common ground for the task to be mutual, for too wide a variance between preaching and listening styles results in a breakdown in communication. This is what happened to the minister just mentioned whose congregation could not hear the biblical influence in his preaching. Dissonance overwhelmed consonance.

What impact does all this have on the task of forming sermons? In light of the fact that any given group of hearers, no matter how compatible and homogeneous they may seem, can be expected to contain a complex and diverse set of listening styles, we are tempted to factor out the whole issue as hopelessly confusing, design our sermons the best we know how, and let the hearers fend for themselves. If they cannot hear our style, let them go down the street to another church and find a match.

The realities of the situation, however, do not warrant such an overreaction. Listeners do have diverse listening styles, and these are complex and not-fully-understood processes, but these styles are to be seen more as band spreads than as single frequencies. In other words, while it is true that certain hearers may prefer to listen to sermons that are shaped in a particular way, may say they get more out of a certain style of preaching, and may in fact find such sermons clearer and more compelling precisely because they are designed in a way that more or less matches their listening style, it does not follow that this is the only style of sermon they can "hear." If they are exposed to a sermon in an alien form, they may resist it somewhat, not like it as much, or even reformulate it so that it fits more comfortably into their listening equation, but the fact of the matter is that they can hear it if it is not completely outside their range. Not only that, but the chances are good that they will begin to develop a deeper capacity for listening to sermons shaped that way. The preacher who speaks week-in, week-out to a congregation is learning how to preach effectively to them, but they are learning also, discovering how to listen to this preacher. Over time, and under the surface, preacher and listeners are gradually adjusting to achieve the best communication fit.

Even so, differences will remain. There will always be in any given congregation those who prefer straightforward, one-two-three sermons and those who do not. There will be those who need the sermon to remain open-ended and those who need full closure. When we recognize these differences among people, we begin to see that forming sermons is an act of pastoral care. It is important for those preachers who tend to design the sermon journey in a free-flowing, loosely connected way, with many side trips and scenic excursions into symbolic imagery, to depart from that form on occasion and to create a more tightly structured form for the sake of those in the congregation who travel better that way. Likewise, the preacher who tends toward the firmly guided sermon journey, with conceptual mileposts clearly marked, needs on occasion to supplement that sort of form with other, more fluid designs.

The gospel comes to us in a wide variety of forms, and the preacher who faithfully bears witness to the gospel will allow the fullness of the gospel to summon forth a rich diversity of sermon forms as well.

7

Beginnings, Connections, and Endings

> Sometimes when I was starting a new story and I could not get it going, I would sit in front of the fire and squeeze the peel of the little oranges into the edge of the flame and watch the sputter of blue that they made. I would stand and look out over the roofs of Paris and think, "Do not worry. You have always written before and you will write now. All you have to do is write one true sentence. Write the truest sentence that you know." So finally I would write one true sentence, and then go from there.
> —Ernest Hemingway, *A Moveable Feast*

A great deal of ink has been spilled in the pages of homiletical literature over the matter of how to begin a sermon. This degree of attention paid to sermon beginnings, or "introductions," as they are traditionally called, is somewhat curious, since much of what needs to be said about them applies equally to every other part of a sermon. A sermon introduction has a job to do, but so does every other part. An introduction requires certain kinds of materials to get its job accomplished, but, then again, the same is true of every other sermon Move. From one perspective, a sermon introduction is not at all a special case. A sermon's journey involves several Moves, and the introduction simply happens to be the first one.

The Sermon Introduction

From another perspective, however, sermon introductions merit special attention; homileticians are of the general opinion that the opening move in a sermon's development is an extremely important one. Every Move of the sermon embodies a task, true, but the task of the introduction is unique and crucial to the outcome of the sermon. A sermon must begin well, it is said, and the introduction must get its special job done in good order, or the whole sermon will be impoverished.

The problem is that the very same homileticians who argue the urgency of the introduction have never been able to agree about what precisely is the distinctive task of an introduction. Almost everybody seems to be convinced that sermon introductions do something extraordinarily important, but what exactly do they do? When we read about sermon beginnings in the homiletical manuals, two "commonsense" notions about the task of introductions surface repeatedly, and since they are so frequently cited they deserve critical examination.

1. Often the notion is advanced that sermon introductions ought to be attention getting. Introductions, in other words, have the task of pricking the ears of the hearers. They serve the same purpose as a drumroll or a trumpet fanfare; they provoke curious interest in what may come next. "We are simply trying," Gerald Kennedy says of the introduction, "to get our people to want to hear what we have to say."[1] George Sweazey is even more direct and graphic as he draws imagery from the old-time radio days:

> The congregation may be settling down after the sermon hymn, staring around the room. If a Scripture reading just before the sermon was not interesting, minds may have wandered. People may expect to enjoy the sound of the minister's voice as mood music for daydreaming. The audience is hanging in the balance, poised to be lost. The minister's opening words have to mean, "Wait a minute! Don't touch that dial; this is something you want to hear!"[2]

This notion that a sermon introduction is to arouse the listener's interest seems so obvious that we almost overlook the fact that it is based upon the rather pessimistic assumption that hearers, at the outset of a sermon, are uninterested or distracted and need to be whistled to attention. The truth, though, is that most hearers, unless they have been knocked into semiconsciousness by an unbearably tedious liturgy, come to the moment of the sermon with an air of expectancy and a genuine readiness to listen. One of the graces of preaching is that hearers, though they have perhaps often been disappointed by the sermons they have heard, still approach each new sermon prepared to believe that this day they will hear an urgent and important word. Randall Nichols is surely correct when he observes:

> Time after time, we have all heard that the purpose of an intro-duction is to "get people's attention." Now really, when was the last time anyone saw a preacher step into the pulpit at sermon time and not have everyone's attention? The rather more pain-ful fact is that we already have their attention and their willing-ness as a free gift—for a while. What we have is *their offer* to participate in the preaching that is about to happen. . . . There will hardly ever be a time when the preacher does not start with the people's attention; there may be many times indeed when it is completely gone five minutes later.[3]

It is deceptive, then, to think that the purpose of a sermon introduc-tion is to snap the listeners to attention. The listeners, for the most part, freely choose to give their attention, and this gift, eagerly granted, must not be squandered by the preacher. Sermon introductions do not grab the hearers' attention; we already have that. It would be more accurate to say that sermon introductions must not lose the listeners' attention, but that wisdom applies to every other part of the sermon as well.

2. Others have claimed that the task of the sermon introduction is to do what its name implies: to *introduce* the whole sermon, to be a pre-view of coming attractions. This means both providing a taste of what the whole sermon will say and disclosing something of the plan the sermon will follow in saying it. Ilion T. Jones described it as follows:

> The introduction to a sermon may be compared to the chart which the ranger draws on the blackboard before he takes a group of tourists over a trail through a national park. This chart is not merely to help them decide whether or not they wish to take the trip, but to give a prospectus of what is ahead.[4]

Thinking about this from the vantage point of the hearer, the intro-duction becomes an announcement of the agenda that the sermon will follow and that the listener can expect. Since the hearers are told what the whole sermon will be about and how, in broad terms, the sermon will develop, they can anticipate what will be required of them as listeners and set the dials on their receptivity accordingly.

In this light, Randall Nichols has proposed replacing the customary term "introduction" with a concept borrowed from the world of therapy, "contract":

> An introduction's purpose is to establish between preacher and hearers a "contract for communication," a shared agreement that in the message to follow we will be talking about certain things in certain ways, trying to get to certain points of understanding or action and each contributing this or that to the unfolding process. The idea of a "contract" is familiar enough in pastoral care and counseling, where it refers to the agreement to work toward certain goals and in certain ways between care giver and care receiver. It operates the same way in preaching; both are incidents of the same communication phenomenon.[5]

In this view the preacher leans across the pulpit during the introduction and says, in effect, "Today I plan to talk about thus and so in such and such a way. Would you like to listen?" This appears to be a clear advance over the idea that introductions are supposed to grab people's attention because it presents a more positive image of the listeners. Instead of picturing them as distracted and lethargic, we now see them as people who are attentive, prudent, perhaps cautious, and who deserve to be told ahead of time what is in store for them. They can then choose either to listen actively and intelligently or to let their minds roam to other thoughts.

But do hearers really need—or want—to be told in advance what is to follow in a sermon? Or, to put it another way, does a sermon get heard better when the listeners know ahead of time what to expect? David Buttrick does not think so, and he is sharply critical of the "tell them what you're going to do" approach to sermon introductions on the grounds that such an approach destroys the spirit of discovery and the suspense so vital to rich human communication:

> Introductions should not give away the structure of a sermon ahead of time in a pedantic fashion. If playbills in the theater were to print a synopsis of plot which we could read before

the curtain rises, suspense would be destroyed; we would know what is going to happen ahead of time. Human thought is intriguing precisely because human beings think and speak differently, so that we are continually surprised by turns of mind or sudden shifts in imagination. Destruction of suspense (the possibility of the unexpected) is positively unkind.[6]

Proponents of the preview concept of sermon introductions would no doubt freely admit that such a strategy is destructive to suspense but would claim this as a virtue rather than a failing. Suspense may be crucial to Broadway plays and detective novels, they would say, but sermons, after all, aim at clarity and forthrightness, not intrigue and suspense.

As a matter of fact, though, good sermons, as we have noted in our discussion of form, vary widely right on this point. Some good sermons pull back the veil on their claims early and then spend the remainder of their time elaborating upon those claims, while other, equally effective sermons develop slowly and gradually toward the moment when their claims can be disclosed as the result of a process of discovery. No Christian sermon should be coy, artificially building suspense by withholding required information or playing with the hearers by keeping them guessing unnecessarily. Every sermon, though, requires decisions about timing: when should certain things be said so that they can best be heard?

The problem, then, with the preview notion of sermon introductions is that it imposes on all sermons a decision about timing that is suitable for some sermons but not for others. Suppose I want to tell you about an argument I had with a colleague, a dispute that was angry and bitter but that led finally to reconciliation and a deepened friendship. How do I tell you about it? I can imagine some circumstances in which I might begin this way: "I want to tell you about a disagreement that developed between me and Matthew. It was tough for a while, but now that it's over I count Matthew as one of my closest friends. What happened was. . . ." I can also imagine, in other circumstances, simply beginning, "Three months ago I got a telephone call from Matthew, and he seemed upset. Then. . . ." In the first instance, I am giving you a thumbnail sketch of the whole incident and then filling in the details. You know in advance how the incident will turn out; you listen to the rest of the story not in order to discover *what* happened but how it happened. In the second instance, you know neither what happened nor even what my story is about. You listen, though, confident—for the moment, anyway—that this tale is about *something* and that whatever it is will emerge in due course.

In the first instance I have deliberately chosen not to be suspenseful, to lay my cards on the table at the beginning. I have decided to do this because I have some goal in mind in telling you this incident that does not need, or would be harmed by, suspense. Perhaps you too are involved in a dispute, and I wish to give you an encouraging example of a similar tangle that developed for the best. So I inform you right at the outset, "This one turned out all right." In the second instance, however, I have another kind of aim in mind. Perhaps I want your empathy and desire that you feel the pain of Matthew's anger as I did. I want the dispute to surprise and disturb you in the same way that it surprised and disturbed me. So I let it unfold, preserving the shock and drama of the narrative. I do this not to be deceptive or coy but rather because suspense is essential to the emotional effect of the incident.

The point here is that I have described two quite different ways to introduce the same narrative, and your experience of hearing my story will vary accordingly, but both beginnings are effective in their own ways. Choosing which of the two is the "better" way to get my story going involves assessments about the circumstances of our conversation and the use I hope to make of the incident. The same is true of sermon introductions. Sometimes it is better to tip the sermon's hand at the beginning; sometimes it is better to wait and let the shape of the sermon's claim emerge as the sermon unfolds. It will not do, then, to think of the purpose of a sermon introduction as always previewing the form and content of the sermon to follow. So sermon introductions do not have the responsibility of arousing the hearers' interest, and they are not necessarily charged with the task of disclosing in advance the agenda of the sermon.

What, then, are the special responsibilities of the introduction? We can identify four.[7]

1. A sermon introduction should make, implicitly or explicitly, a promise to the hearers.   When people listen to another person speaking, they are taking in what is being said, but they are also running

ahead of the speaker, anticipating where the speaker's words are leading. The phone rings, and we answer it. "This is Amanda Smith calling," says the voice on the line, and already our minds are racing off on
a search process, guessing who Amanda Smith is and what she may say
next. "I'm with the Civic Improvement Council, and we are conduct-
ing our annual spring fundraising campaign," she continues, and we
are way ahead of her. In her next sentence—we just know it—she will
ask us for a contribution.

We listen faster than people speak, and our minds are constantly
scampering ahead of the speaker, positioning ourselves in that spot
where we have reason to believe the conversation is going. Indeed,
when impatient listeners get paired up with sluggish speakers, the listeners, continually guessing where the speakers' words are heading
and often growing weary of waiting on them, may even be tempted to
finish the speakers' sentences for them.

When we begin a sermon, the listeners are also running ahead,
anticipating where this sermon may lead. Whether we know it or not—
and even whether we like it or not—the listeners are using the opening
statements of the sermon to form a guess about what the rest of the
sermon holds in store. The hearers, then, are not only listening *to* the
sermon; they are also listening *for* the sermon they have been led to
expect. So, our first rule for sermon introductions is more a description
of what actually happens than it is a law to be obeyed. Whether they
want to do so or not, preachers are giving hints and are therefore making promises to their congregations in the opening sentences of their
sermons about where the remainder of the sermon will be heading.
The fact that this happens in the expectations of hearers regardless of
our intent does not mean, however, that the preacher has no control
over what promises are made and what expectations get formed.

As we discussed, some homileticians are persuaded that preachers
best exercise their responsibility here by eliminating any mystery surrounding this moment and setting forth a synopsis of the rest of the
sermon. As I have argued, though, that overstates the case. Full disclosure is not essential, nor is it always desirable. What listeners need
at the beginning of a sermon is not necessarily a thumbnail prospec-
tus of the whole sermon but rather an orientation, a reliable direction
for listening. In some sermons, this orientation may be quite full and
complete; in other sermons, it may be only a hint of what is to come.

Listeners need to know only that they are traveling on the right path, not necessarily the contours of the path itself. That is why I have chosen the word "promise" as a descriptive term for the introduction. To make a promise is to point toward a certain kind of future without necessarily specifying precisely how that promise will be fulfilled.

So, in simple terms, a preacher should begin a sermon in such a way that the hearers can accurately anticipate something of what the whole sermon will be about. Depending on the particular sermon and its circumstances, this promising can range from a subtle but reliable hint to a rather full disclosure of the sermon plan.

How does the preacher decide what promise to make in the introduction? Actually, that decision has already been made when the preacher formulates what we have called the focus and function statements. These statements articulate what the whole sermon will say and do, and the task of the introduction is to point toward those aims.

In order to see, in practical terms, how introductions make promises, let us examine a few sample sermon beginnings. We can start with an example in which the promise made by the preacher is quite obvious. This introduction comes from a sermon based on selected verses from Galatians 5 and 6:

> When I was invited to preach in this series on the overall theme of "Freedom, as expounded in Paul's letter to the Galatians," it was suggested that I emphasize the theme of freedom and political responsibility. While I am very much aware that freedom for the Christian has to do with such things as freedom of the individual conscience, freedom from internal fears, freedom from guilt, and other personal matters, these are not the subject matter this morning. All freedoms, as Christians conceive of them, are interrelated, but from time to time we hold certain kinds of freedom up for more detailed scrutiny, and that is what we are doing this morning with freedom and political responsibility.
>
> Question: Can one draw insights about political freedom out of Paul's letter to the Galatians—without cheating? Answer: It's not easy. I wasn't sure at first that it could be done. Politics is not the stoutest arrow in Paul's quiver, and he says things elsewhere, notably in Romans 13, that are often cited by

Christians as reasons to side with the *status quo*. But as I have worked with this letter, it has seemed clearer and clearer to me that, while Paul is obviously not writing with our own political situation in mind, he says some things that are applicable to it.[8]

This is a fairly full and straightforward introduction. What does this preacher promise? Anyone hearing this beginning can reasonably expect the rest of the sermon to explore the implications of the theological concept of freedom in Galatians, not in the usual sense of individual concerns but in relation to political circumstances. Indeed, the preacher makes this promise quite explicitly, and if the rest of the sermon did not do this (it does, as a matter of fact), the hearers will have been misled.

Now let us turn to an introduction in which the promise is less explicit. This introduction comes from a sermon based on the story of the healing of the blind man named Bartimaeus (Mark 10:46–52):

Please ask no up-to-date questions of the great account of the deliverance of Bartimaeus from his blindness, which is not an up-to-date account. Do not say, "Was it a disease of the eye? Did Jesus do the first corneal transplant? Was Bartimaeus psychosomatically blind, perchance, his physical blindness caused by emotional illness?" These are smart questions, all right, but the wrong questions, and questions the Mark account provides no answers for. Instead, try to stand down nineteen centuries to another world view held by another people in another land. Listen to the story the way the story was told.[9]

In this case, the preacher does not tell us how the sermon will unfold. Indeed, we are not yet even sure about the theme of the sermon. We are told more about what the sermon will not do (answer our modern questions about Bartimaeus's blindness) than we are about what it will do.

Nonetheless, this preacher has made an implicit promise: In this sermon, inappropriate modern questions will be ignored, and the Bartimaeus story will be explored for insight on its own cultural and historical ground. The listeners do not have an inkling about what these insights may be, but they have every reason to believe they will hear something new and unexpected from the story in the remainder of the sermon. They will have their previous understandings of this story challenged by this new angle of vision.

Here is yet another example of an introduction, this time from a sermon on prayer:

> Why do we pray? Why is it we say into this vast space or cry out into the darkness that which is deepest upon our hearts? Why did David fast and weep as his son lay dying? Why did Jesus go to Gethsemane? Why do any of us bow our heads or raise our hands or fall to our knees and call upon such silence as surrounds us in hopes of hearing a word for us? The reasons are both too many to fit into the space of a Sunday morning sermon and at the same time too inaudible to find their way into words. Why do we pray?[10]

What is the promise contained in this introduction? The preacher is making a qualified promise to answer the question "Why do we pray?" I say "qualified" because the rhetorical question that closes the introduction ("Why do we pray?") is prefaced by the disclaimers that the reasons are both "too many" for a single sermon and "too inaudible" to be expressed in words. The hearers, then, have every reason to expect the question to be addressed, but they are not promised more than the sermon can deliver since they are notified that the answers will be partial and open-ended.

This understanding of the promise-making dimension of sermon beginnings exposes one of the typical flaws of many introductions. Often preachers, usually in well-intentioned attempts to begin sermons in an exciting fashion, generate sparkling, ear-catching, arresting, even glitzy introductions. Such introductions undoubtedly intrigue the hearers, but they also make promises to the hearers that go unfulfilled, and, as John Killinger maintains, they are "like the story of the boy who cried 'Wolf! Wolf!' when there was no wolf. The preacher says, 'Listen! Listen! You are going to hear a great sermon.' But after a few deceptive beginnings, when there was nothing of substance to follow, the crowd learns not to pay any attention."[11]

2. A sermon introduction should make a promise that the hearers are likely to want kept.   Since sermon introductions are heard by listeners as promises about what is to come in the sermon, it is important for the promise to be one that the hearers find valuable. We do not need to arouse the hearers' interest at the beginning of a sermon, but we do need to maintain it by promising a sermon that bears meaning for their lives. Consider the following introduction for a sermon on John 20:11–18, the story of the encounter between Mary Magdalene and the risen Christ on Easter morning:

> The story of the meeting between Mary Magdalene and the risen Christ on that first Easter is a very strange one indeed. Mary is weeping, not only because her Lord is dead, but also because she has found his tomb to be empty. Turning toward one whom she assumed was the gardener, she said through her tears, "Sir, if you have carried him away, tell me where you have laid him, and I will take him away."
>
> His reply was but a single word: "Mary." In the hearing of her name, she moved from sadness to amazement, from the assumption that she was speaking to a caretaker to the awareness that she was in the presence of her living Lord. But then, just as her tears were giving way to an embrace, Jesus said a disturbing and curious word. As Mary reached out to Jesus, crying, "Teacher!" Jesus drew back from her. "Do not hold me," he said, "for I have not yet ascended to the Father. . . ."
>
> "Do not hold me." What an odd statement from the risen Christ. What could he possibly have meant? Throughout the centuries students of the scripture have been puzzled by these words and have offered many suggestions about their meaning. Are any of these suggestions correct? What *did* Jesus mean?

This preacher, through the introduction, is promising a sermon that will explore the history of interpretation of John 20 in quest of an accurate rendering of Jesus' statement, "Do not hold me." Is this a promise that the hearers are likely to want to see kept? That depends, of course, on who happens to be listening to this particular sermon. Some congregations, no doubt, would be eager to sift through Johannine exegesis in search of the best interpretation of Jesus' words, but most hearers probably would not find this prospect very appealing. They may feel they ought to be intrigued by this quest. After all, these are Jesus' words, and we should want to know what they meant. What nags at them, though, and what is unheeded in this introduction, is the question "Suppose we do find out exactly what Jesus meant? So what?"

Presumably this preacher believes that determining what Jesus meant potentially makes some kind of difference to people today. If so, at least some hint about this should be a part of the promise of the introduction. Here is another preacher's introduction to a sermon on the same biblical text:

> As I was mulling over this sermon on the meeting between Mary Magdalene and the risen Lord outside the empty tomb, I happened to be flying from Chicago to New York on a fantastically brilliant, clear night. Even at 33,000 feet, the thousands of sparkling lights on the ground below seemed so close you could almost sense the people living in and around them: people watching TV in the early evening, friends visiting, children doing homework, people at their basement workshops, cars darting here and there. And I thought suddenly, how utterly absurd to imagine that any of them could care one bit about the scene outside an empty tomb, or about what Mary said to Jesus, or what Jesus said in reply, as compared with their interest in their favorite television program, the rising cost of food in the supermarket, the latest bit of town gossip, or the fortunes of the local high school basketball team.
>
> And yet virtually all of them would be concerned about the tension between the old and the new, the good old days and the perplexing present, the tension between old life-styles and new ones, between old moral standards and new ones, between a fairly stable and simple past and an almost terrifying present with its rapidly changing customs, morals, standards.
>
> And most of them would want to cling to the old and resist the everchanging new. When radical change comes along and hits us almost every day, it's understandable that we seek reassurance and stability by clinging to the past. And that does bring us directly to the story of Mary Magdalene and Jesus outside a tomb on Easter morning.[12]

The sermon that follows this beginning also explores the meaning of Jesus' enigmatic statement "Do not hold me," but notice that the introduction promises something other than an abstract examination of interpretive options for the meaning of that phrase. This introduction promises that the sermon will wrestle with the biblical text in order to throw some light on an issue of direct importance to the hearers: namely, the tension we all experience between the old and the new. This is a promise that most hearers will desire to see kept.

Now, there is an obvious objection to this idea that sermon introductions ought to make promises that hearers want to see kept. Does this not lead to a comfortable, demand-free, tell-them-only-what-they-want-to-hear approach to the gospel? What about those occasions when the sermon, if it is faithful to the biblical text, must bring a hard word, a painful word, a demanding word? What about those aspects of the gospel people *need* to hear but do not necessarily *want* to hear?

We can explore this problem by thinking about ourselves and our own listening tendencies. It is surely true that all of us prefer to hear things that bring us pleasure over things that cause us discomfort. We prefer praise to criticism, encouragement over demand, endorsement rather than judgment. If this is all that we truly want, the advice to make promises in sermon introductions that people want to see kept is bad advice, because it simply panders to the self-serving preferences in human listening.

As a matter of fact, though, our wanting is more complex than this. A part of ourselves wants to hear only comfort, but another part of us wants to hear the truth whatever the cost. The first part struggles against the second, sometimes winning the battle but never entirely eradicating the hunger for the truth. If someone comes to us and says, "I have some concerns about you that I would like to discuss," we wince, anticipating a critical word. At one level we do not want to hear what is coming next, but at another level we do want to hear. If we do not trust this other person, or if we believe this word will damage us beyond repair, we close our ears. But if we do trust the other, and if we have reason to believe that this critical word, though painful, will finally prove to be beneficial, we brace ourselves and listen.

When we place this reality about human listening into the context of the Christian community, it becomes deeper and richer. The story of the church is one of closed ears and resistance, to be sure, but it is also a story of hearing and repentance. It is unrealistic to suppose that congregations (or preachers) are always ready to hear the demanding side of the gospel, but it is cynical to assume that in sermons people want to hear only those things that reinforce their ease and buttress the status quo. Congregations do not hear sermons in the abstract, but rather in the midst of the larger experience of their faith. We confess our faith in terms of a story that values God's judgment as a part of God's love; without being naive about the obstacles involved, we can nonetheless affirm that congregations want to hear sermons that promise challenge and demand.

So when we say that sermon introductions should make promises that the hearers want to see kept, we are not making a distinction between "pleasant" sermons and demanding ones but rather a distinction between relevant sermons and irrelevant ones. Some sermon introductions promise only that the rest of the sermon will move chess pieces around on the board of some self-enclosed religious language game. Something deep inside the hearers cries out, "So what?" and the listening process halts. Other introductions, however, say, implicitly or explicitly, that if we listen to this sermon, it will intersect some crucial issue in our life together. It may bring joy or it may bring judgment; it may call us to express our love or to confess our sin; it may reinforce our beliefs or undermine our illusions; but it will make a difference in our real lives. There is also another lesson to be learned here. Given the choice, people are simply unwilling—perhaps even unable—to hear a thoroughly destructive message. The demands of the gospel are not given to destroy but to give life. The preacher who opens a sermon by swinging a scythe of punishment will only find that the hearers learn quickly how to step out of the way. A church member reported that her preacher began a sermon by saying, "I'm going to have to step on some toes this morning." Note the arrogance of that beginning: Not the gospel, not the claim of the biblical text, but "I am going to step on some toes." The response of this church member was, "He says something like that in almost every sermon, and what he doesn't know is that our toes are hardened by now." The point is that hearers pick up immediately whether the preacher, and the sermon, intend to do good or ill. Again, the distinction we are making about sermon introductions is not between a beginning that promises an "easy" word versus a "hard" one, but between the promise of a destructive word versus the promise of a redemptive one.

3. A sermon introduction should make a promise at the same communicational level as the rest of the sermon.   The promises we make in sermon introductions carry with them certain tonal qualities. If the sermon begins by raising some issue in thoughtful and precise language, the hearers have every reason to expect that the rest of the sermon will also be thoughtful and precise. If the introduction arouses an emotional response, the rest of the sermon must not suddenly switch to a highly cognitive treatment of the issue.

Consider the following introduction for a sermon on Mark 5:21–43:

> In the middle of today's Gospel there is an uncommonly moving scene (Mark 5:25–34). A woman whose life has been bleeding away for twelve years pushes through a tremendous crowd, comes up behind Jesus, touches his garment. Instantly the bleeding ceases; she feels in her body that she has been healed. Jesus is aware that power has gone forth from him; he quickly asks: "Who touched my garments?" The disciples are amazed, almost amused: "You see the crowd pressing around you, and yet you say, 'Who touched me?'" But he keeps looking around, keeps looking until the woman comes in fear and trembling and tells him the whole truth. And Jesus explains to her what has happened: "Daughter, your faith has made you well; go in peace. . . ."
>
> "Who touched me?" Three years ago, for the first time, that question laid hold of me, made me shiver. I cannot get it out of my mind. Increasingly it has told me something: something about Jesus, something about myself, something about Christian living. A word about each.[13]

What is the promise in this introduction? From one perspective we can see that this preacher has promised to open up Jesus' question "Who touched me?" in three ways: what it says about Jesus, what it says about a person, and what it says about Christian living. When we consider the tone of this introduction, however, it becomes clear that there is more to the promise than this. Note the emotion-laden language: "uncommonly moving," "bleeding away," "feels in her body," "fear and trembling," "laid hold of me," "made me shiver," and so on. Language like this signals to the hearers that this introduction is proceeding at the affective level as well as the cognitive level, and the implied promise is that the sermon will do the same. In short, some sermons promise an intellectual and analytical thinking through of some issue, but not this one. This sermon aims to let Jesus' question "Who touched me?" "lay hold" of the hearers too, perhaps even make the hearers "shiver."

The introduction to the sermon, then, should match the communicational level of the rest of the sermon. As David Buttrick claims, "Introductions . . . orient a congregation's hermeneutical understanding. After an introduction, people should be ready to hear a sermon, and to hear in a certain way."[14]

4. A sermon introduction should anticipate the whole sermon, but it should also connect directly to the next Move of the sermon. "A good introduction," claims John Killinger, "is conductive. It leads people into the sermon."[15] In the larger sense, this statement means that introductions lead people into the *whole* sermon. A sermon beginning, as we have seen, makes a promise, and the task of the rest of the sermon is to fulfill that promise. In addition to leading the hearers into the whole sermon, though, there is a smaller sense in which the introduction simply leads people into the next part of the sermon. When the introduction is done, the hearers should have an idea about where the total sermon is going, and they should also be ready to take the next Move.

David Buttrick imagines a sermon on 1 Corinthians 11:17–32, a text that discusses the meaning of the Lord's Supper in the context of a bitter dispute among the Corinthian Christians. The whole sermon is aimed at dealing with the issue of peace and conflict in the church, so the introduction should anticipate that. In the second part of this sermon, though, the part directly after the introduction, the preacher intends to discuss the Lord's Supper in particular. The introduction should also anticipate that. Buttrick composed three possible introductions:[16]

Introduction 1:

The little church in Corinth was such a problem. As with
many churches today, it was sadly divided. Factions! There
were rich and poor, slave and free, bluenose and libertine—
all bunched together in a bundle of conflict. Corinth was the
kind of church ministers avoid, unless they've taken courses
in "conflict management." For every faction got together,
chose leaders, and snarled at every other faction. Corinth was
a church divided.

This introduction gets rather nicely at the general issue of the
whole sermon: conflict in the church. It does not, however, prepare
the hearer for the next Move: a discussion of the Lord's Supper. "As
the introduction stands," Buttrick observes, "a sudden . . . shift to the
Lord's Supper will seem an abrupt non sequitur." So Buttrick tries
another beginning:

Introduction 2:

The Lord's Supper is a sacred moment for most congregations.
We gather at the Lord's table with solemnity. "This is my body,"
the minister announces, and we break bread together. For centuries, the table has been set as Christians gather to share one
cup and receive the bread of life. So, the Lord's Supper is special, a special sacred moment in the life of the congregation.

The problem with this introduction is the opposite of the problem
with the first try. It anticipates the next Move of the sermon just fine,
but there is no hint here of the concern of the whole sermon. This
introduction promises only a discussion of the Lord's Supper. "As a
result," claims Buttrick, "when the sermon does turn toward a discussion of conflict and unity, the introduction will seem trivial or even
misleading." Buttrick then formulates a third introduction:

Introduction 3:

Some years ago, there was a movie about a family reunion.
The family was a contentious bunch. They scrapped and split

and never got along. Yet, every year, they scheduled a party, a family reunion. At a long table, they'd all sit down together. But, you couldn't help noticing the sidelong glances, the cold shoulders, the obvious slurs. Perhaps that's the way it was in Corinth. Though they gathered at one table and shared one cup together, they were at odds. Corinth was a divided church.

This introduction manages both to anticipate the theme of the rest of the sermon, conflict in the church, and to lead the hearers fluidly into the next Move of the sermon, a discussion of the Lord's Supper. It is, therefore, a better sermon beginning than the first two examples because it introduces both the sermon as a whole and the very next segment of the sermon.

Making Connections

Many names are used to describe the component parts of a sermon: Moves (the term used in this book), points, steps, episodes, units, panels, pages, and so on. Regardless of the label applied to these parts, the underlying idea is that a sermon consists of a series of segments arranged in a logical sequence. We might even picture a sermon as a long corridor with a set of doors leading to separate rooms, much like a school hallway. The "rooms" are the points, Moves, chunks, or whatever we choose to call them, and the "corridor" is the logical thread that holds them together and provides movement from one to the next. We start down the hallway and enter the first room, where perhaps a story is told, a history lesson is given, an image is developed, or a concept is explained. Then we reenter the corridor to move to the next room, where something else is said, seen, learned, and experienced.

We need now to think through what happens "out in the hallway," to consider the material that appears between the major segments of the sermon. To use another image, we can think of television sports announcers doing a football game. There are usually at least two, a play-by-play announcer and a color commentator. The job of the play-by-play announcer is to describe the main action of the game, and the job of the color commentator is to talk between the plays, adding details that help the viewers appreciate and understand the main action. Preachers fill both roles. They preach the main material of their sermon—the play-by-play—but they also offer comments between the plays about how to understand, receive, and appreciate the main material.

Traditionally these small in-between pieces of the sermon have been called "transitions," since they mark the points of transfer from one section to the next. Many preachers mistakenly do not consider them to be very important, and it is common for transitions to be dull and mechanical insertions into the sermon flow ("in the second place," "the next thing I want to say," "in conclusion"). When we view this transitional material from a communicational point of view, however, it becomes clear that these connectors (as we will call them) between the segments of the sermon are absolutely vital to the sermon's clarity, vitality, and movement.[17] Although they are usually brief, connectors accomplish four crucial communication tasks.

1. **Connectors provide closure for the preceding segment of the sermon, thus reassuring the hearers that they are on the right track.**   Each Move of the sermon contributes something to the sermon's overall development, and if a hearer is to navigate the route successfully to the end of the sermon, the listening task of each Move must be accomplished effectively. A connector, first of all, concludes a sermon Move, often by naming whatever it is that is most important about that Move. Here, for example, is a typical connector:

> So, we see that the early church lived its life on tiptoe, expecting that the kingdom would come any minute, ringing down the curtain on history and sweeping all of creation up into the victorious hand of God. No wonder Paul could say, "Rejoice . . . the Lord is at hand!" But for us today the time has grown long, really long. We may sing "O Come, O Come Emmanuel" in Advent, and we may even get interested in one of those "Left Behind" novels, but truthfully we have become weary scanning the horizon, searching for the coming triumph of God. We pray in the Lord's Prayer, "Thy kingdom come . . . ," but we aren't holding our breath.

This connector obviously follows a portion of the sermon in which the expectations of the early church regarding the imminent end of time were explored. The first thing this connector does, then, is to repeat the essence of that section: "So, we see that the early church lived its life on tiptoe, expecting that the kingdom would come any minute."

What does this do for the hearers? For those who have been following this section of the sermon well, it provides reassurance that they have, indeed, gotten the message. It is like the experience of following a set of handwritten directions to a friend's party. "Go six miles down Bogan Road," they say, "and take the third left after the bridge. When you make this turn, you will see a blue house on the hill." So we travel six miles down Bogan Road, we count the streets past the bridge, and we make the left turn at the third one. We think we are going correctly, but when we see the blue house, we *know* that we are on the right road. Just so, when we hear, in a sermon connector, a reinforcement of what we think we have just heard, we *know* we have listened well. For those hearers who have become confused, however, or whose minds have wandered, the connector provides an opportunity for them to reenter the sermon flow, to get back on track.

2. Connectors indicate how the upcoming section of the sermon is logically related to the previous section. Look again at our example connector, especially at the phrase "But for us today." That little word "but" signals to the hearers that the next section of the sermon will be a logical contrast to the section before. The hearers thus anticipate a tension being established between these two sections of the sermon.

Many types of logical connections may exist between sermon segments. Some of the more common ones are as follows:

> *The "and" connection.*   This type of connector joins sections that build cumulatively. It says, in effect, "This is true, and this is also true." Such terms as "in addition," "moreover," "again," "not only . . . but also," "besides," and "another" are characteristic of this kind of connector.

> *The "but/yet" connection.*   This type of connector creates logical contrast and typically employs such terms as "but," "yet," "however," "upon second thought," "despite this," "still," or "on the other hand."

> *The "if . . . then "connection.*   This type of connector indicates that the validity of the next section of the sermon depends in

some way on the previous segment. Characteristic terms include "so," "because," "since," "thus," "therefore," and "if . . . then."

The "reconsider" connection.   This type of connector signals that a segment of the sermon will go back over the same ground as the previous section, but this time with another point of view. Typical are such terms as "look again," "in a deeper sense," and "perhaps," and rhetorical questions such as "Why is this so?"

The "new departure" connection.   This relatively rare type of connector actually breaks the logical chain of the sermon by announcing a discontinuity between sections. Typical expressions include "leaving this behind," "the real question, though, is," and "what if?"

3. Connectors anticipate the content of the next section of the sermon.   A good connector not only names the essence of the previous section; it also hints, at what is to follow. This enables the hearers both to listen *to* the next segment and to listen *for* its message. Note again our example connector. The clause "But for us today the time has grown long" gives the hearers advance notice that the next section of the sermon will discuss the difficulty of maintaining, in our own time, the early church's sense of kingdom expectancy.

4. Connectors add a bit of "color," guiding the listeners in how to understand and what attitude to take in regard to the sermon.   The sermon has just been describing the early church's lively expectation of the arrival of God's reign and is anticipating a section of how we now lack that expectation. But how does the preacher think the listeners ought to feel about this shift in the sermon? Should they be ashamed that they can no longer maintain the early church's eschatology? Should they pooh-pooh the naivete of first-century Christians and be glad that they are living in a scientific age? When the preacher says,

We may sing "O Come, O Come Emmanuel" in Advent, and we may even get interested in one of those "Left Behind" novels, but truthfully we have become weary scanning the horizon, searching for the coming triumph of God. We pray in the Lord's Prayer, "Thy kingdom come . . . ," but we aren't holding our breath . . .

the preacher is providing some color commentary and suggesting that the listeners might want to think of themselves as standing right on the dividing line between the New Testament and the contemporary world, between those who hope for God's reign and those who have given up hope.

So connectors provide closure for a sermon segment, indicate the kind of logical "glue" that bonds that section to the next one, aim the listeners in their expectations about what is coming next, and provide a little guidance in what posture to take toward the sermon. Our example connector accomplished these tasks in complete fashion. The first two sentences provided the closure, the word "but" named the logical bond, the final few phrases anticipated the content of the next section of the sermon, and the lines about "Left Behind" novels and "don't hold our breath" put the hearers in the position of those caught between the claims of Scripture and the realities of life many centuries later. All four tasks belonging to connectors were accomplished overtly.

If all of the connectors in a sermon were as fully expressed as our example, though, it would mean communicational overkill. Sometimes a single word ("but," "nevertheless," "hogwash!"), a simple gesture (a raised eyebrow, a shrug of the shoulders, a shake of the head), or just plain silence will be all that is necessary. What we are trying to accomplish in the connective moments of a sermon is to provide enough guidance to the hearers to ensure that they are following the movement of the sermon. If we provide no help or insufficient help, the listeners are likely to hear the sermon as a series of confusing and disconnected episodes. We know why one thing follows another, but they do not, and we must allow the logical movement of the sermon to become plain.

On the other hand, if we provide too much help, the hearers can become bored or feel that we are being too simple or condescending.

Deciding how complete to make the sermon connections is a matter of judgment. If, for example, we are considering the sort of connector needed after a sermon section in which the material is completely clear and the message is transparent, we are probably better off to omit any closure statement. The listeners already have the point and do not need any restatement. If, however, the material is complex or ambiguous, a solid closure statement is important. On the whole, erring on the side of fullness and clarity in connectors is to be preferred to less complete sermon connections that leave the movement of the sermon in doubt.

The Final Word

There are two urgent questions about sermon endings: when to conclude and how to conclude.[18] Regarding the first, Luther is reported to have advised, "When you see your hearers most attentive, then conclude." That is hyperbole, of course, but there is wisdom in his exaggeration nonetheless. The fact is that hearers intuitively know when a sermon is finished. In the same way that people know when a story is done, a joke is complete, or a conversation is over, they also have the "sense of an ending" about sermons. When a listener says something like "There were two or three places in that sermon where the preacher could have stopped but didn't," this is not necessarily a complaint about dullness or length. Hearers have an intuitive grasp of a message's symmetry and wholeness, and when the listeners' need for completion has been resolved, they unconsciously close the book on their hearing. If the sermon continues after that point, if the preacher runs clearly marked stop signs, it will surprise and often irritate the hearers. Sermon conclusions that come after the hearers have finished listening can only serve as pallbearers.

Highly skilled preachers can adjust their sermons on their feet. They can almost palpably discern the hearers' sense of closure and round out the sermon with dispatch if need be. Most of us, however, do not possess this skill. Once we have begun the sermon, we are like tightrope walkers whose only choice is to continue all the way to the other side, even if the crowds have departed and the safety net has been taken down.

For most of us, then, the decision about timing the sermon's conclusion must be made during preparation and not in the pulpit. Our best friend in this regard is a crisp, clear, coherent, and economical sermon form. A sermon with a sharp focus and function will aim to say one thing well and to do one thing well, and the form should be the vehicle for efficiently accomplishing those aims. If we look critically at the form of our sermons and discover that we are actually trying to say more than one thing or do more than one thing, we probably have two or more sermons competing for the same space. One of them will inevitably win the hearers' attention, leaving the others to tug desperately at the listeners' ears crying, like Esau, "Have you but one blessing? Bless me, even me, too." Someone in the congregation will surely say, "There were two or three places in that sermon where the preacher could have stopped, but didn't."

In regard to how to conclude sermons, the key factor is what the sermon aims to do, what we have been calling the function statement. Sermons obviously, and joyfully, always do more than preachers intend for them, as the hearers make their own uses of what is proclaimed, but this is not the same thing as saying that sermons should have no aims, or only vague goals. As preachers we do intend for each sermon to accomplish something, and that intention is gathered up in the function statement.

Generally speaking, sermons aim to teach, to evoke a feeling, to call for action, or some combination of the three. These are obviously intertwined objectives. To teach a new idea, for example, also evokes feelings and motivates action, so we should not think of these as discrete categories but as places of emphasis. Let us examine four actual sermon conclusions to see how each ending matches the basic function of the larger sermon.

1. This conclusion appears in a Palm Sunday sermon in which the preacher began the sermon by asking whether Palm Sunday was a happy and optimistic parade, an occasion of despair, or a tragedy. The preacher spent time in the sermon giving rich interpretations of those three terms—optimism, despair, and tragedy—because he wanted the hearers to know what is at stake in these terms and to realize that Palm Sunday could only be understood theologically if it was viewed as a tragedy. The sermon, while not lacking in feeling and ethical implication, was primarily a *teaching* sermon in the best sense. Here is the conclusion:

> Optimism is all right, I suppose. We should walk on the sunny
> side of the street, away from the dark side of life. And despair
> is understandable, and all of us despair sometimes, but it's an

easy way out. Neither optimism nor despair are large enough, profound enough, to trace the outline of what any of us would recognize as an image of what our lives can be.

Tragedy, on the other hand, is clean. It tells the truth. It clears our heads. Tragedy strengthens our backs. Palm Sunday is a tragedy. It's the day that Jesus the Christ, knowing the facts of life, does what he is called to do, and does it without rancor; does it simply; without apology. A tragedy. Strong and clean. Worth celebrating. "Blessed is he who comes in the name of the Lord."[19]

In this conclusion no new information is given. Every statement in the conclusion is a reiteration of something already said in the sermon. The conclusion is, in essence, a summary of what has been taught in the sermon. It gathers together in two concise paragraphs all that has been learned, and it serves well the teaching function of the whole sermon.

2. The following conclusion is a part of a sermon on Ezekiel's vision in the Valley of Dry Bones (Ezek. 37:1–14). In this sermon, the preacher did some teaching about the biblical text, relating it to the blowing of the Spirit at Pentecost and also to current political and ethical realities. She cited the racial crisis in South Africa, recounting in particular the experience of blacks in the small town of Mogopa, who were ordered by the government to leave their town to be resettled in a "homeland." The government sent bulldozers and destroyed Mogopa, turning it into a modern Valley of Dry Bones.

This preacher wanted the hearers not only to understand the text and to perceive the "dry bones" places in the contemporary world, but she also, and primarily, wanted the hearers to feel the presence of God's Spirit blowing now through all hopeless and hungering places, bringing new life. Here is the conclusion:

God breathes into the clay and into the dry bones and into the people of Mogopa and into the disciples . . . and into your life, too, where you are sitting today. For it is the same breath, the same spirit. A protesting and a comforting presence. This breath of God connects us with the people of Mogopa, with the disciples in Jerusalem. This breath means that faith is

more than memory or wishful thinking. This breath is tied
to the stories passed down—yet it is the Spirit alone which
breathes into the bones of history to call the stories to life.

Send your breath, O God, to our sisters and brothers driven
from Mogopa. Send your breath that they may live. Blow
within them a protesting and comforting presence. Send your
will, O God, to shake our churches that they may be more than
buildings, more than bones of history. Blow within us so that
we will dare to speak the truth against the lies. Send your spirit,
O God, into the parched, hopeless valleys of our own lives—
the same spirit promised by Jesus. Blow within us so that we
mean what we pray: "Thy Kingdom come, thy will be done on
earth as it is in heaven." Amen.[20]

Note that this conclusion is a dramatic and passionate one. The
preacher uses rousing language, powerful language, prayer language.
This is not a strategy, not a device, but a cry. The preacher has heard
this text speaking to the deepest places in human life. The sermon
speaks to those places, and the conclusion is an appeal both to and
from the heart.

3. Here is another conclusion for a sermon that speaks at the affective level. The biblical text is Isaiah 40:31 KJV ("But they that wait
upon the Lord shall renew their strength; they shall mount up with
wings as eagles; they shall run, and not be weary; and they shall walk,
and not faint"). In the sermon the preacher interpreted the phrase
"wait upon the Lord" to mean trusting God to do what we, in our own
strength, cannot do. This preacher, however, wanted to do more than
explain the meaning of the text; he wanted to encourage the hearers
to feel and to experience this trust of God. So he closed the sermon by
telling a story about his own struggle with heart disease. His physician
prescribed swimming exercises, and as he engaged in this activity he
learned a lesson about trust. "The most important thing I learned," he
said, "was the fact that all the while I was swimming . . . I was assuming
that the water would hold me up. . . . Forty years ago, as a teenager, I
wasn't able to swim a mile nearly so easily as now, having learned this
lesson. Likewise the deadly tension and tightness of subtly striving and
worrying without waiting has gone." He carried this image of the trusting swimmer into the conclusion:

> They that lie back on the water of life and wait on the Lord between strokes shall renew their strength. They that lie trustingly in the bosom of providence, knowing that God will care for them while they recuperate—these are they that shall renew their strength in every way, physically, mentally, and spiritually. They shall even mount up with wings as eagles and soar through life in joy and victory. They shall both run and swim marathon distances, and not get weary. They shall walk and walk and walk and not faint.[21]

In this conclusion we do not so much learn something as we feel something. The language is poetic, biblical, and image-rich, matching the affective aim of the sermon as a whole.

4. This conclusion is a part of an Advent sermon that has as its aim behavioral change. Wishing to call the congregation to Christian service and action, the preacher ends the sermon this way:

> A new birth is required if we are to see the signs of his presence. We need new eyes that perceive what is hidden, new hearts of courage to risk all in order to gain what the world deems lost. This new birth is the good work that Paul says God has begun within us. What does it mean for everyday life? The list of specifics is long and filled with risk. It means caring about human problems that most people would rather ignore. It means speaking up for the poor who are not present to speak for themselves. It means calling for forgiveness when others call for blood. It means insisting upon justice when others are prepared to settle for order. It means giving money and time without asking, "What's in it for me?" It means turning our backs upon the idols of pleasure, convenience, and class. It means being satisfied with nothing less than the coming of the kingdom of God.
>
> Keep the Advent faith, and you will sometimes feel terribly alone. But you are not alone, for we read, "God is leading Israel in joy by the light of his glory, with his mercy and justice for company" (Bar. 5:9 NAB). Jesus is the light of his glory. Jesus is the sign and seal of his mercy and justice. He has been here before. In stark and bitter loneliness, he cried the victim's cry,

"My God, my God, why have you forsaken me?" In the triumph of Easter, God raised him from the dead and made him the new man for all men. He is God's pledge that your work is not in vain. He is God's pledge that you need not fear the future, that you can welcome change, for it is by change that the kingdom comes. Prepare the way, then—not for an unknown power, not for a stranger, but for the Lord who has been, and will be, your companion on the way.[22]

There are clearly affective and cognitive aspects to this conclusion, but the main feature is a listing of specific actions that the hearers may take: caring about human problems, speaking up for the poor, calling for forgiveness, insisting upon justice, unselfishly giving money and time, and so on. An alternative way to have concluded this sermon would have been for the preacher, instead of providing a list of possible actions, to have told a story about one person putting the claim of the sermon into practice.

Good sermons do not really end, of course, with the preacher's concluding words. They continue to work in the minds of the hearers (and the preacher, too) and in the life of the community of faith. "I count a sermon a success," said one member of a congregation, "if I think about it again during the week." That is a modest standard, perhaps, but not a bad one. Sermons that are too neatly finished, that have a "well, that's that" feel about them, that have no loose ends for the hearers to struggle over, communicate a tidiness that the gospel itself does not possess. "If I could understand religion," commented Baron von Hugel, "as I understand that two and two makes four, it would not be worth understanding."[23]

Two excellent sermons can be found in the appendices: Cleophus LaRue's "Why Bother?" (Appendix C) and Ginger Gaines-Cirelli's "Special Effects" (Appendix D). Each of these sermons is analyzed in regard to form, beginnings, endings, and connectors.

8

Images and Experiences in Sermons

The Christian faith always has to do with flesh and blood, time and space, more specifically with your flesh and blood and mine, with the time and space that day by day we are all of us involved with, stub our toes on, flounder around in trying to look as if we have good sense.

—Frederick Buechner, *Whistling in the Dark*

The sermon is no place for a virtuoso performance; it is a place for believers to explore together their common experience before God. The stories I tell from the pulpit are not just "my" stories but "our" stories, which are God's stories, too. The stool of my sermon rests evenly on those three legs. If any one of them is missing (or too long or too short), the whole thing will wobble and fall.

—Barbara Brown Taylor, *The Preaching Life*

The reign of God, Jesus said, may be compared to a farmer who sowed good seed in a field or to a ruler who wished to settle accounts with his servants. Jesus also said that the kingdom of God is like leaven which a woman took . . . a grain of mustard seed . . . treasure hidden in a field. . . a merchant in search of fine pearls . . . a net thrown into the sea . . . a woman searching for a lost coin . . . a man going on a journey who called his servants and entrusted his property to them. Jesus came preaching in stories and parables, and when he spoke of the reign of God he often did so in familiar images drawn from ordinary experience. Christian preachers ever since have followed Jesus' example and have continued to communicate the gospel through narratives, images, metaphors, and similes drawn from everyday life.

224

There is nothing surprising about this, of course. The gospel makes claims upon life as people actually live it, and Christian witness naturally gathers in experiences and examples from the common round of human existence. Indeed, any sermon that remained entirely in the realm of abstract thought, never touching the real world of fields and crops, offices and commutes, parents and children, employers and workers, feasts and banquets, toil and play, illness and death would hardly qualify as Christian preaching at all. But what sort of experiences and images should we bring into sermons? How should we incorporate them? What are the effects we hope to achieve? Beneath the seemingly simple and spontaneous use of ordinary experience in preaching lie rhetorical and theological issues of great complexity. Stories, images, analogies, and experiences are not mere decorations in sermons; they are active ingredients of communication. They cause certain things to happen in the minds of the hearers and are thus powerful, but also potentially disruptive, poetic elements. An image can clarify, and it can also mislead. An example can ground the truth of the gospel in actual experience, but it can also make the gospel seem merely mundane. A story can be richly evocative or insipid, sentimental, and cloying. A well-chosen experience can enable people to envision new possibilities for discipleship, but a contrived one can manipulate them and be a form of verbal entrapment.

Moreover, whenever we include a slice of life in a sermon, we are making implicit theological claims whether we know it or not. By the kinds of experiences and images we choose to employ in sermons, we are forming, implicitly or explicitly, specific connections between the nature of contemporary life and the character of the gospel. A sentimental sermon story, for example, implies that the gospel itself is sentimental. A sermon full of experiences involving only clergy telegraphs the message that real faith is reserved for the "professional" Christians. Or suppose that a preacher decides to relate in a sermon several stories of people who learned to trust God in the midst of difficult and painful circumstances. If this preacher is honest about these experiences, the accounts will include some of the ambiguity and unresolved questions surely present whenever people struggle from suffering toward faith. A truthful relating of the experiences, in other words, carries with it the theological claim that the yes of the gospel does not instantly make the no of human doubt and struggle disappear. If, on the other hand, the preacher files the rough edges off these experiences and transforms them into stories with simple, happy, and purely victorious endings, an unrealistic triumphant picture of the gospel is conveyed, with little room for unfinished suffering and continuing struggle.

So if we are to be wise in using stories, examples, experiences, and images in preaching, we must take many factors into account. What we need is an understanding of how these elements function in sermons, the range of effects they potentially evoke in hearers, and what implicit messages about the character of the gospel they may communicate. We need to ask, in other words, What are these elements supposed to do in sermons?

The answer we give to that question depends, of course, on our prior understanding of the overall purpose of preaching. Early homileticians, schooled in classical rhetoric, generally assumed that the ultimate purpose of preaching was persuasion. Since preachers were supposed to be persuasive, these homileticians thought of stories and examples mainly as rhetorical devices employed to make the sermon more convincing.[1] They borrowed, from the ancient rhetoricians, technical names (e.g., example, parable, sign) for the various types of stories, metaphors, legends, figures, and analogies that a preacher might employ, and they provided elaborate descriptions of the uses, functions, and probable effects of each. Preachers were viewed as carpenters, working with words instead of wood, whose job was to build solidly convincing sermons. Stories, examples, analogies, and so on were seen as very specialized tools to accomplish that task of persuasion.

Breaking the Windows

A quite different understanding of the role of images, examples, and stories in preaching emerged, however, in the homiletical textbooks of the nineteenth and early twentieth centuries. The assortment of technical names and categories was largely abandoned in favor of the single encompassing term "illustration." Every imaginable sort of contemporary element in a sermon was called a "sermon illustration"—stories, historical anecdotes, examples, word pictures, analogies from nature, and even persons presented as role models. The ancient homileticians at least gave their carpenter-preachers tool chests filled with many specifically named and specially designed rhetorical tools. Now, however, the hammers, saws, and awls were replaced with a single all-purpose device: the illustration. This remains true today in the popular vocabulary of preaching. Published anthologies of sermon stories and examples are called collections of illustrations, and preachers typically speak of every means of bringing everyday life into their preaching as illustrating their sermons.

The rise to prominence of the word "illustration" was neither neutral nor innocent. Beneath this change in terminology lay a deeper shift in the overall understanding of the purpose of preaching. To illustrate means "to bring light," and homiletics, as it moved from the Enlightenment toward the twentieth century, was gradually displacing the earlier concept of preaching as persuasive rhetoric with an understanding of preaching as the clear, logical, and rational presentation of ideas derived from the gospel. The "persuader" was, little by little, being pushed out of the pulpit in favor of the "explainer." If the main job of the preacher was to make the truth of the gospel lucid and understandable, then a good, light-bearing illustration was an obvious aid for this task.

Ironically, even those homileticians who would have been horrified theologically by the idea that preaching the gospel was simply the logical presentation of a systematic set of concepts tended, nevertheless, to reinforce that very view in the practical sections of their textbooks.[2] Every sermon was supposed to develop a "thesis," and illustrations were seen as devices designed to illumine and clarify that thesis. Intriguingly, the older language of persuasion did not disappear all at once; it was simply relegated to a far less important role. Nineteenth- and early twentieth-century homiletical manuals typically provided lists of the purposes of illustrations, and such phrases as "they help to persuade people,"[3] they "can break down resistance,"[4] and "illustrations are used to make the truth persuasive"[5] still occurred. These persuasive purposes, however, were now placed far down on the lists,[6] and top priority was given to the matter of creating understanding. The number-one purpose of illustrations, these textbooks maintained, was to "make the truth concrete,"[7] to "make the message clear,"[8] and to "help the congregation understand"[9] the main ideas of the sermon.

Now and then, when homileticians of this period were searching for a way to explain this clarifying function of illustrations, they employed a revealing image (sort of an illustration about illustrations).

Illustrations, they said, are "windows on the word." The sermon, they argued, is a house built with timbers of reason and logic, and illustrations are the windows bringing in the clear sunshine of comprehension. The nineteenth-century preacher and homiletician Charles Haddon Spurgeon employed this image when he advised his preaching students, "The chief reason for the construction of windows in a house is . . . to let in light. Parables, similes and metaphors have that effect; and hence we use them to illustrate our subject."[10] The idea here is fairly obvious: A sermon moves along, logically developing this or that concept, but at some point along the way the concept becomes too obscure or conceptually difficult for the hearers to handle it without assistance. So the preacher opens a window by supplying an illustration, thereby throwing some light on an otherwise shadowy topic.

It is fairly easy to see now that this whole business of calling all experiential elements in sermons "illustrations" and thinking of them as "windows on the word" rested upon a didactic, rationalistic, and conceptually oriented understanding of preaching. As a matter of fact, though, preaching as an event in the Christian community is not, and never has been, exclusively such an activity. Even on those occasions when preachers tried their best to construct and preach rationalistic sermons, the church happily managed to hear in those sermons, over time, something more and something other than didactic messages. One evidence of this is that the rationalistic theory of illustrations, which made such logical sense in the homiletical textbooks, never would quite work between pulpit and pew. There were telltale cracks in these windows on the word.

Preachers who preached sermons week after week intuitively knew all along there was something misguided about the theory. This view of illustrations looked good on the drawing board, but there were problems in actual practice. When preachers tried to use stories, examples, and images as clarifying devices, opening illustrative windows here and there in the logical progression of the sermon (some homiletical manuals methodically prescribed "one illustration for each point"), they quickly encountered a troubling side effect: the illustrations often overpowered the rest of the sermon. Hearers were frequently more engaged by the illustrative material than they were by the main thread of the sermon. In other words, people cherished and remembered the windows and promptly forgot whatever it was that the windows were supposed to be illuminating.

At first, homileticians suspected that the trouble was not with their theory but with the preachers and their practice. Preachers, they said, were using too many illustrations and the wrong kind of illustrations. They were filling sermons with strings of cute, ornamental stories that distracted from the central business at hand. Sermons were becoming "glass houses" with too many windows, attractive from the outside but structurally unsound. Dire warnings were issued about the "overuse" of illustrations, and preachers were constantly advised to avoid padding their sermons with trivial "sermon anecdotes" and even to use solid illustrative material "sparingly," "judiciously," and with "caution," lest the illustrations thrust "themselves into the light instead of casting light."[11] Frankly, some preachers *were* using indulgent, disconnected, and merely decorative anecdotes in sermons (and some preachers still do), but the main reason congregations were more engaged by the illustrative material than by the conceptual parts of sermons is that stories, images, and examples contain more communicative power and energy than the terms "illustration" or "windows on the word" would allow.[12] Hearers are engaged by illustrations because illustrative material, when it is well chosen, communicates the faith in subtle and complex ways. Illustrations can be windows on the word, to be sure, but they can also be arenas for encountering, discerning, discovering, and experiencing the word as well. As the notable teacher of preaching Fred Craddock maintained, "[i]n good preaching what is referred to as illustrations are, in fact, stories or anecdotes which do not illustrate the point; rather they are the point. In other words, a story may carry in its bosom the whole message rather than the illumination of a message which had already been related in another but less clear way."[13]

Craddock's statement represents a strong trend in recent homiletics to rethink the entire matter of the role of illustrative material in sermons. We may, as a matter of convenience, want to keep the word "illustration," but we can no longer think of it as a single, unified category. There are many types of illustrative material, each of which has a specific and different potential function in a sermon. Some illustrations clarify concepts, but not all of them do. Some assist persuasion, but others produce quite different effects. Preachers must know how each type of illustration functions in order to be able to select the best material for a given sermon.

Homileticians have always recognized that well-crafted sermons possess unity, each element of the sermon working in concert to create the whole, but contemporary homileticians have sought to refine this insight by understanding precisely how each part of a sermon, including the various types of illustrative material, works together with all the other elements to achieve an integrated act of communication. When a slice of contemporary experience, a story, a metaphor, or an image is brought into a sermon, it is in order to accomplish some particular task that contributes to the larger sermon objective. The major flaw in the windows-on-the-word view of sermon illustrations was that it harnessed all illustrative material to one and only one communicational task: the clarification of concepts. Illustrative material possesses a much larger communication repertoire than that. What we are searching for, then, is an understanding of illustrations large enough to help us perceive their true communicational range.

Restocking the Tool Chest

In chapter 6 we saw that creating a sermon involves dividing the overall objectives of the sermon (the focus and the function) into a series of smaller tasks and then deciding what kinds of materials are needed to accomplish each one. For some tasks, what is needed are quotations from Scripture, sections describing theological concepts, analyses of issues, or the like. For other tasks, however, illustrative material of some sort is required. In order to see when this is so and what kinds of illustrative material may be called for, we need to explore the potential functions of the several types of illustrations. We need, in other words, to take out of the preacher's tool chest that one, clumsy, multipurpose tool called "illustration" and replace it with the very specialized illustrative tools available to us.

Essentially, an illustration operates in a sermon as a figure of speech works in a sentence. More specifically, most sermon illustrations function as one of three different kinds of speech figures: simile, synecdoche, or metaphor. These three figures of speech correspond to three basic kinds of illustrations: the analogy (simile), the example type (synecdoche), and the metaphor.

The Analogy

An analogy-style illustration works in a sermon like a simile works in a sentence: some issue, theme, idea, or action in the sermon is compared to something else. Here is a simile: "Don't ask George to do anything in a hurry. George is like molasses." Now "George" and "molasses" are obviously two quite different realities, and normally we would not think to mention both of them in the same breath, but a simile brings them unexpectedly together for the sake of comparison and understanding. Even though they are very different, there is this one area of similarity: their common lack of speed. When you tip a molasses jar and watch it creep sluggishly over the lip, you get a sense of George in action. A simile, then, specifies a particular area of overlap, and it uses the words "like" or "as" to make this connection. "George" and "molasses" are like each other in one, and presumably only one, way: they are both agonizingly slow.

A simile is a very disciplined figure of speech. It has surgical precision. If we try to press a simile beyond the bounds of its intended comparison, things go quickly awry. Suppose someone says, "When she finally comes to a decision, she is like a bulldog." Now how is she like a bulldog? The obvious and intended point of comparison is that she is like a bulldog in that she is tenacious and doggedly determined when she makes up her mind. But if a listener somehow got the idea that she is like a bulldog in other ways as well—prone to bury bones in the backyard, say, or to chase cars in the street, the image has clearly gone astray. In other words, similes are helpful only when they stay sharply focused like a laser on the one intended point of comparison between the two terms.

This points us toward the basic purpose of an analogy-style illustration: to create clear and emphatic understanding by zeroing in on how some aspect of life that we know about is like some aspect of the gospel we need to know about. Here, for instance, is an analogy-style illustration:

> I was raised in a small midwestern town near the Canadian border. Our winters were famously long and harsh, sometimes even cruel. On the main square of our little town was a bank with one of those rotating signs reading the time on one side

and the temperature on the other. In the depths of winter, the temperature side often had a minus sign in front of the number.

Early every spring there would always come a day when the sun would shine long enough on the square that, just for an hour or so, the temperature on the sign would rise just above freezing. But then the afternoon shadows would fall, the temperature would drop, and we knew that we had many more weeks ahead of frigid weather. But that day was nevertheless a day of note, even of joy, in our community. People all around town would talk about how the bank's temperature sign had shown, for the first time in months, a temperature above freezing. We had seen that day the first signs of the breaking of the power of winter.

Just so, on Easter we saw in the risen Christ the first signs of the breaking of the power of sin and death . . .

Notice that the story this preacher told was not about theology. It was about *meteorology*. But it was *like* theology, and because it was like theology it helps the hearers understand something about the nature of the resurrection.

Here is a another simile-style analogy illustration:

> As a boy, I loved to go puddle gazing, wandering from one puddle to the next, wondering how so much of the sky could be reflected in such small bodies of water. Today I often marvel at how so much of the story of heaven and earth is captured in small biblical tales such as the story of Jesus and the paralytic.[14]

Now, the experience of seeing the vastness of the sky in a tiny puddle and the wonder of seeing the story of heaven and earth in a small biblical passage are not the same thing. The preacher suggests that they are *like* each other. They operate on parallel tracks and are analogically related to each other because, in both of them, the vision of something large is captured in a small space. That is, for the moment at least, the one and only connection we are supposed to make between this feature of the Bible and the preacher's childhood puddle gazing.

The effect of this type of illustration is to provide vivid understanding. Its chief function is to give clarity, but it does so with a bit of a wallop. The analogy-style illustration, with its graphic clarifying function, is the sort of illustration the homiletical manuals of several generations ago had most in mind when they emphasized the word "illustration" and claimed that its primary purpose is to make a concept plain.

Here is another analogy, this one from a sermon by the famed Scottish preacher James S. Stewart. At the point in the sermon where the illustration appears, Stewart has introduced the idea that an active memory of God's loving presence in the past can sustain a person in those times when God seems to be absent.

> I remember once near Interlaken waiting for days to see the Jungfrau which was hidden in mists. People told me it was there, and I should have been a fool to doubt their word, for those who told me lived there and they knew. Then one day the mists were gone, and the whole mountain stood revealed. Next day the mists were back, but now I had seen, and knew myself that it was true. . . . [L]et us trust our own moments of vision: what matter if there are days when the mists come down and the face of God is hidden? We have seen, and we know for ever that this is real, so real that by it we can live and die.[15]

Although this experience is vivid and the language Stewart uses has obvious emotional power, the primary purpose of the illustration is to create understanding. Stewart strikes an analogy between the theological idea of faith in the unseen and the experience of seeing the mountain.

Analogy-style illustrations are perhaps the most common type of illustrative material in sermons. Sometimes they are complete stories; more often they are simply vignettes of experience or single images ("Like a rural tent-revival preacher, John the Baptist thundered from his desert pulpit" or "Jesus was at a fancy dinner party in the home of Simon the Pharisee, a party much like those covered on the 'Fashion' page of the *Tribune*"). Here is an analogy-style illustration from a sermon on Zechariah 8:1–8, in which the preacher takes one contemporary image (the kingdom of God is like a public park) and develops it at length:

What is the Kingdom of God, according to the prophet Zechariah? It is a public park! It is a park where old people are
no longer cold and lonely and ill and senile, but participants
in a community. It is a public park where the elderly can sit
together and bask in the sun, and talk and laugh over the good
old days in full vigor and clear mind and satisfaction of life.

The Kingdom of God is a public park where little children can
run and play in its squares, in safety and fun and delight. . . . It is
a place where no child is abused or unwanted or malnourished,
and where there is not even a bully among the group, shoving
and taunting the littler ones until they break into tears. The
Kingdom of God, says Zechariah, is a public park where the
streets are safe for children.[16]

In every analogy-style illustration—regardless of whether it is a
complete narrative, a fragment of experience, or simply an image—
something familiar is held alongside something less familiar, and a
comparison is made: *This* is like *that*.

The danger in using an analogy, as we have seen, is that it will spill
over the boundaries of its single point of comparison and thus overflow
its narrow educational purpose. For example, countless preachers, trying to communicate the character of faith, have told stories about their
children trustingly leaping off tables and refrigerator tops into their
open arms. What they intended to say, of course, was that this sort of
unwavering trust in a parent is something *like* faith in God, but the
illustration tends to slosh over the walls of the intended analogy and
to communicate that leaping heedlessly into danger is faith or that the
relationship between a parent and a child is in every way the same
reality as the relationship between God and people. Again, the often-
employed comparison of the resurrection to the emergence of a but-
terfly from a cocoon tends to perform all sorts of unintended mischief,
including trivializing the resurrection and implying that it was merely
the outcome of a natural process.

If we decide that we need an analogy-style illustration in a sermon,
how do we ensure that we select one that is suitable, that accomplishes
its intended purpose? Homiletician David Buttrick has suggested that
such illustrations ought to be able to pass three simple tests:

1. The analogy between an idea in sermon content and some aspect of the illustration must be clear. [I would add to this the caution that what is clear to the preacher may not always be as clear to the hearers, so preachers should ensure that, in the telling of analogy-style illustrations, the point of comparison is not left in doubt.]
2. There ought to be a parallel between the structure of the content and the shape of an illustration.
3. The illustration should be "appropriate" to the content [meaning that serious and important concepts should not be paired with small, trivial, or mawkish illustrations].[17]

Buttrick applies his three tests to the following stock illustration, intended to clarify the idea that God-in-Christ chose to come to us as one who was poor and lowly rather than in power and with status:

> In an art gallery, side by side, are two paintings. One is by the famous artist Rembrandt; it is the portrait of a great man, an important world leader. But the other painting, by an unknown artist, is of a peasant kitchen—a rough board table, and a bunch of asparagus waiting to be cooked. Which painting do people stand and stare at? Not the portrait of the great man; no, they stand transfixed before the picture of the peasant kitchen and the picked asparagus. So God might have come to us in power, in the flesh of a famous man, but instead God came as. . . .[18]

On the basis of his three tests, Buttrick judges this to be a failed illustration. Why? There is a clear analogy between the illustration and the theological concept—a peasant kitchen is lined up with Jesus' birth—so the first test is passed. The second test is also successful because the illustration and the concept share a similar two-part structure; the contrast between high and low, between nobility and peasantry, operates in both. In Buttrick's view, it is the third test that causes the analogy to stumble. The illustration is not appropriately matched to the theological idea it is supposed to illustrate, claims Buttrick, because, "unfortunately, without realizing it, the preacher has turned Jesus into a bunch of asparagus!"[19]

That assessment may be slightly overdrawn, but Buttrick's basic point is well-taken, and his three tests are on target. An analogy-style illustration seeks to teach an idea with vividness, to provoke deeper understanding of a concept. Buttrick rightly wants to caution preachers about the potential for confusion created when an illustration leaks stray messages through its seams.

The Example

An analogy-style illustration, as we have seen, compares something we don't understand ("A") with something we do understand ("B") to help us figure out A. A and B are different things, related by analogy. An example-style illustration is different. It doesn't give us a slice of life that is like what we are talking about. Rather it gives us a slice of life that *is* what we are talking about. The preacher does not compare A and B but instead gives us a little taste of A itself. If the preacher is talking about following Jesus, the preacher does not say it's *like* something else. Instead the preacher tells us the experience of a person who actually follows Jesus.

Example-style illustrations work in sermons like the figure-of-speech synecdoche works in a sentence. In synecdoche a part of something is used to represent the whole. When we say, "My ship set out across the waves," we really mean that our ship set out across the ocean. We name one part of the sea—the waves—to poetically evoke the whole. Notice one of the important differences between synecdoche and simile. Similes make comparisons; synecdoche does not. The sea is not *like* the waves; the waves are a part of the sea itself. Synecdoche says, in effect, "This is the heart of the thing itself."

Example-style illustrations, then, do not say, "This is what something is *like*," but instead, "This is what it is, this is the heart of the thing itself in human life." No experience, no story, no example ever embodies, of course, all there is to know and experience about a concept like grace or hope or sin or love or repentance or forgiveness or faith. But we can point to places in human life where grace or hope or sin or love has been experienced and allow those experiences to stand as signs of the larger truth toward which they point.

Example-style illustrations are crucial in preaching because they put flesh on theological concepts. Like analogies, they make concepts clearer, but that is not their main purpose. They give the hearers a taste, a vicarious experience, of the reality being presented. It is one thing to explain a doctrinal idea—say, sanctification—but it is quite another thing to be able to say, "Here is sanctification as it is experienced in human life."

A good way for a preacher to discover the potential of examples is to take the manuscript of a sermon and mark all those places where theological concepts, challenges, and claims appear. The preacher should ask, "If the hearers took these statements seriously, what would the results be in their real lives?" If we cannot say what a sermon idea would look like in human life, the chances are good that we are pushing a mere abstraction in our listeners' direction. If we call upon them to take a theological idea seriously, to believe it and to live it, then we have the responsibility to help them envision specifically what that would mean for them.

Here are some theological statements that could typically be found in sermons, and some questions the preacher could ask:

Statement: "God has given us the opportunity to be responsible and loving partners in the redemption of creation."

Question: Suppose the Jones family, sitting in the middle of the congregation, decided to join with God in the redemption of creation. What exactly would they do?

Statement: "All around us we see signs of God's care."

Question: Where? Can you name some of these signs of God's care?

Statement: "Still today Jesus says to each of us, 'Blessed are the peacemakers.'"

Question: Specifically, how does this call of Jesus come to the people out there in the congregation? To the single parent? To the schoolteacher? To the soldier? To the legislator? To the woman who has cancer? To the elderly man whose eyesight is dimming and whose memory is failing? To the child beginning school this year? To others? What might it mean for these people if they decided, in some new way, to be peacemakers?

Statement: "In our time, too, it is sad to say, people are prone to worship idols, false gods who are nothing more than projections of their own selfish desires."

Question: Which idols? How do we know they are "gods"? What evidence do we have that they are being "worshiped"? What are the telltale rituals, ceremonies, and solemn vows? What allows us to say that they are "nothing more than projections of their own selfish desires"?

Statement: "As disciples of the crucified Christ, we are called to stand with all who suffer because of hatred, with all who are victims of the world's cruelty."

Question: Are there some ways in which these hearers are already doing this? If so, how? Beyond the powerful examples of people whose lives deeply embody this claim—the Mother Teresas and the Martin Luther Kings—are there less dramatic but nonetheless significant ways in which Christian people can "stand with those who suffer"?

These questions are, of course, difficult ones. That is why many sermons contain far more analogy-style illustrations than examples. Analogies are easier to find. It is much harder to find examples that actually embody theological claims and concepts in human experience. This difficulty, however, does not release us from the responsibility to articulate the theology of our sermons in the terms of specific contemporary experience. The task of preachers, Robert E. C. Browne once observed, is to know and to proclaim the gospel in such a way that the hearers can be empowered to know life in terms of doctrine and doctrine in terms of life. "It is not," he claimed, "that doctrine is supremely important and that life proves its importance; it is that life is supremely important and doctrine illuminates it."[20]

Suppose we are developing a sermon around the theological theme of Jesus' call to bear a cross. In the sermon we say that "bearing a cross" does not mean heroically enduring some misfortune that unexpectedly comes our way but rather *choosing* to take suffering upon ourselves in the service of others. There is the concept, but what does it look like in real human life? An illustration is needed, perhaps one like this:

In the newspaper last week there was a story about the process families go through in adopting children. The account related the usual details: the huge number of couples wanting to adopt, the much smaller number of "desirable" children, the extremely long waiting lists, the high legal fees, the red tape, the resulting increase of interest in "surrogate parents," and so on.

The story also told of the experience of the Williams family. The Williamses, a deeply religious couple, have adopted four children so far, and they hope to adopt at least one more child in the future. For the Williamses there have been no delays and no waiting lists. The reason is that all of the children the Williamses have adopted are disabled. One, a son, is severely retarded, and the other three, two daughters and another son, had major birth defects. All of the Williams' children are, in the euphemism employed by the adoption agencies, "difficult to place." In a world where virtually every prospective parent dreams of a bright, beautiful, and perfect child, the Williamses have chosen to offer the embrace of their parental love to children almost no one else wanted. "Our children are our greatest joy," Mrs. Williams was quoted as saying. "Caring for them is what we're on this earth for."

Of course this illustration does not say everything that can and should be said about cross bearing. It leaves unstated, for example, the explicitly theological connection between this family's faith and their action. But if cross bearing is indeed choosing to embrace suffering in the selfless service of others, this episode gives us one incident in human experience of the thing itself, a part that evokes the whole.

Again, imagine that we are creating a sermon on Jesus' statement "Let your light shine before others, so that they may see your good works and give glory to your Father in heaven" (Matt. 5:16). Where in contemporary life do we see that happening, where the "good works" of one person enable others to give glory to God? We could, as just such an example, include in the sermon the experience of Dorothy Day, the founder of the Catholic Worker movement and a Christian who spent her life serving God by serving the poor and downtrodden. Here is the example-style illustration we might provide in the sermon:

When she described what led her to Christianity and to her sense of calling, Dorothy Day often cited an experience early in her life. As a little girl living in Chicago, she went looking for a friend who lived next door. She found the door open to her friend's apartment, so she went in. She saw that the breakfast dishes had been washed and stacked beside the sink. Then she discovered her friend's mother, Mrs. Barrett, kneeling on the floor saying her prayers. When Mrs. Barrett heard Dorothy, she stopped praying long enough to tell her that her friend had gone to the store. Then she returned to her prayers. Years later, Dorothy Day remembered, "I felt a burst of love toward Mrs. Barrett that I've never forgotten."

One of Dorothy Day's biographers has written that this encounter with Mrs. Barrett saying her morning prayers was "one of the early moments that she felt a first encounter with the transcendent. This sense that there was more to life became an irresistible call beckoning her and ultimately leading her into the Church."[21]

Or suppose we are trying to illustrate the power of kindness and acceptance. We might use an example like this:

In her memoir *The Whisper Test*, Mary Ann Bird tells of the power of words of acceptance in her own life. She was born with multiple birth defects: deaf in one ear, a cleft palate, a disfigured face, crooked nose, lopsided feet. As a child, Mary Ann suffered not only the physical impairments but also the emotional damage inflicted by other children. "Oh Mary Ann," her classmates would say, "what happened to your lip?"

"I cut it on a piece of glass," she would lie.

One of the worst experiences at school, she reported, was the day of the annual hearing test. The teacher would call each child to her desk, and the child would cover first one ear, and then the other. The teacher would whisper something to the child like "the sky is blue" or "you have new shoes." This was "the whisper test." If the teacher's phrase was heard and repeated, the child passed the test. To avoid the humiliation of failure, Mary Ann would always cheat on the test, secretly cupping her hand over her one good ear so that she could still hear what the teacher said.

One year Mary Ann was in the class of Miss Leonard, one of the most beloved teachers in the school. Every student, including Mary Ann, wanted to be noticed by her, wanted to be her pet. Then came the day of the dreaded hearing test. When her turn came, Mary Ann was called to the teacher's desk. As Mary Ann cupped her hand over her good ear, Miss Leonard leaned forward to whisper. "I waited for those words," Mary Ann wrote, "which God must have put into her mouth, those seven words which changed my life." Miss Leonard did not say, "The sky is blue" or "You have new shoes." What she whispered was, "I wish you were my little girl." Mary Ann went on to become a teacher herself, a person of inner beauty and great kindness.[22]

Once more we recognize, of course, that this experience, as powerful as it is, does not approach the full depth or breadth of the meaning of grace. It is grace, but it is not everything that grace is. Instead it gives us a glimpse of grace as it finds halting expression in a real person's life. It is a fragment, a part, which allows us to feel that portion of the gospel's power that is ours to touch and then to find our faithful imaginations guided in pilgrimage toward the whole truth that lies ahead.

Because the example-style illustration points to a slice of life and claims, "This is a piece of the very thing we are talking about," its use raises a thorny theological problem. Can we ever present an episode of honest human experience, lived out in the brokenness of the world, and say, "This is the gospel in action. Here, in this incident, we can see the very kingdom we proclaim"? The answer, of course, is no, not fully. As the theologian Jürgen Moltmann maintains, "Christian proclamation cannot be supported by analogies in the cosmos or historical events. A damaged world and the history of guilt and death do not in themselves reflect any messianic light."[23] The promises of the gospel—forgiveness of sin, freedom from bondage, the triumph over evil and death, oneness with God—are just that: promises. Promises are made in the present, and, if they are believed and trusted, they make a difference in how we live now. But promises refer to the future, and their full realization lies ahead. Just so, the promises of the gospel speak of God's future, of the God who promises to renew the whole creation and of the faith of those who wait, watch, and work in hope.

It is crucial that preachers be clear that the proclamation of the gospel is, again citing Moltmann, "the Word that opens up the future,"[24] lest we replace the promises of the gospel with only the sad announcements of the possibilities available for life self-contained in the present circumstances of the world. We see this happening among those preachers who substitute "positive thinking," psychological adjustment, and "creative values for living" for the radical promises of the gospel. We also see this in the sort of preaching that implies that the reign of God can be muscled into reality through right thinking, correct behavior, or social reorganization.

More subtly, we see this as well in sermons that employ in a thoughtless manner just the sort of example-style illustrations we have been discussing. Our sermons will and should include experiences of forgiveness, reconciliation, liberation, victory, and answered prayer, but we must not do so in ways that imply to the hearers, "And if you could only think more clearly, work more diligently, believe more deeply, trust more fully, these realities would be completely in your grasp as well." We may tell, for example, of the experience of a person who recovered from a life-threatening illness, giving thanks to God for this gracious sign of healing. We must also remember, though, the many faithful people who will not experience such a healing but who cling nevertheless to the gospel promise that the disease destroying their bodies does not have the power to speak the final word. We live in a Good Friday world, where Christians must pray for reconciliation as yet unrealized, hope for liberation even as people lie captive, water the seeds of forgiveness where there is still enmity, apply the oil of healing while pain and death yet rage, and pray with all our might, "Come, Lord Jesus."

What right do we have, then, to point to any moment in human experience and say, "This discloses the truth I am speaking about"? We may do so only if we recognize that such moments are but foretastes and anticipations of the new creation. They are, to use the language of the New Testament, "signs and wonders" of the coming kingdom.

The resurrection of Christ—and the proclamation of that resurrection in the power of the Holy Spirit—is the clearest and deepest of these signs. The church, also, the gathered community of faith to which we preach, is a sign in the present of that future kingdom. As Moltmann states:

[The Church as messianic community] is the fellowship which narrates the story of Christ, and its own story with that story, because its own existence, fellowship, and activity spring from that story of liberation. It is a "story-telling fellowship," which continually wins its own freedom from the stories and myths of the society in which it lives, from the present realization of this story of Christ. It is a fellowship of hope, which finds freedom from the perspectives of its society through the perspectives of the kingdom of God. Finally, it is a fellowship which, by virtue of its remembrance of the story of Christ and its hope for the kingdom of man, liberates men and women from the compulsive actions of existing society and from the inner attitudes that correspond to them, freeing them for a life that takes on a messianic character. In Christianized societies this does not merely lead to the critical freedom of faith towards the respective social systems; it leads to the critical freedom towards the church which is tied up with the social system, and towards Christianity in general. . . . The messianic community belongs to the Messiah and the messianic word; and this community, with the powers that it has, already realizes the possibilities of the messianic era, which brings the gospel of the kingdom to the poor, which proclaims the lifting up of the downtrodden to the lowly, and begins the glorification of God through actions of hope.[25]

And finally, our life together in the community of Christ allows us to look with realistic and yet hopeful eyes toward the world as the arena where God's Spirit is even now working, making the impossible possible, creating faith where there is nothing else to believe in, creating love where there is nothing lovable, creating hope where there is nothing to hope for.[26] Trusting the promise of God to redeem the whole cosmos, we see signs of the coming triumph of God in every place where misery is alleviated, hostility is lifted, and chains of bondage are broken.

The Metaphor Type

In a simple metaphor we call something familiar by an unfamiliar name. We speak of locomotives as "iron horses," of sunset as "the dying of the light," or of much talking as "a blizzard of words." In an analogy, one thing is compared to another thing. In a metaphor, something is unexpectedly summoned to stand for something else. An analogy seeks to help us to understand. A metaphor seeks to create new meaning, to help us experience the reality of something in a new way. An analogy is the tool of good teachers; a metaphor is the instrument of poets.

In one of his poems, Wendell Berry describes how the frosts and rains of winter have pushed the stepping stones on a hillside out of line. He pictures himself walking over these stones, stepping short, then long, to the right, then to the left. The poem closes with these words: "At the winter's end, I dance the history of its weather."[27] Now, what does that mean? If he had given us a simile, say "trying to step along these random stones is like dancing," we would know the intended point of comparison. But instead he speaks metaphorically. "At the winter's end, I dance the history of its weather." Does this mean that he moves in the way dancers move? Or that his steps follow a rhythm and a pattern shaped elsewhere and not of his own making? Or that he celebrates, by his stepping, the power of winter? Or that his stepping is a kind of unconscious remembering? All of these things? Something else? There is mystery at the heart of a metaphor. It continues to tease our minds into active thought, urging us to discover more and more ways to re-vision what we thought we already saw well.

Many of the parables of Jesus are metaphors in story form. In telling these parables Jesus did not say, "Let me explain some feature of the kingdom with this little story," but rather, "Listen to this story. Live in its world. Find yourself among its characters and situations. Feel its claims upon your life. And when you have allowed its world to become your world, then, and only then, speak the phrase 'the kingdom of God.'" Because a parable grows out of a metaphor, observed C. H. Dodd, it leaves "the mind in sufficient doubt about its precise application to tease it into active thought."[28]

Sometimes sermons employ human experience in a metaphorical way. But we should caution ourselves that this is the rarest type of illustration, and in some ways the riskiest, because it sacrifices precision and clarity for the sake of imagination and multiple meanings. In analogy-style illustrations, we present a slice of life as in some ways *like* the concept we are talking about. In example-style illustrations, we present a slice of life that is itself a partial expression of the larger concept. In metaphor-style illustrations, we place experience and concept side by side and invite the hearers to make imaginative connections.

For example, in a sermon titled "From the Sixteenth Floor," Charles Rice invites the hearers to view a city from a sixteenth-floor window, high above the streets. From this vantage point we can see the busy-ness below, the people moving about like dots in motion. We pick out a person in a hospital jacket, another walking along the street wearing a purple shirt. We see "faces . . . lost in endlessly fascinating canyons, heartache obscured by well-furnished windows." Because we view this from above, though, we ironically become less aware of individual motion and more attuned to the rhythms of the whole, to the larger motivations and moral impulses. We see not just people moving about, but joy and pain, malice and fate, ugliness and beauty. We begin, as Rice guides us, to have compassion, for the cunning as well as for the dying, and even to pray for this city and its people.

After holding our gaze on the city for a long time, Rice pauses and then concludes the sermon this way:

> The gospel tells the story of Jesus' coming to Jerusalem riding upon a lowly donkey.
>
> "And when he drew near and saw the city he wept over it, saying, 'Would that even today you knew the things that make for peace'" (Luke 19:41–42). Not long after that, he carried a cross to the hilltop outside Jerusalem.
>
> Nailed up there, he had a good view of the city.[29]

"Nailed up there, he had a good view of the city." That is the last line of Rice's sermon, but that is not where the sermon ends for the hearers. Our minds go back to the time spent on the sixteenth floor. We remember the sadness we felt, and then we remember Jesus' tears. We recall our own good view of the city and its pain, and we then think about Jesus' pain and his "good view" of the city. We recite again our prayer for the city's redemption, and then see the cross as the answer to our cry. Most of all we wonder. We do not yet know all that this sermon means. We feel its redemptive power long before we can name its many truths.

Here is another metaphor-style illustration, this time from a sermon by Patrick J. Willson:

When I was six years old I played on the most marvelous playground. As I remember it now, it was all mine, though certainly other children must have been around to play on it. I still see it through my six-year-old eyes, and it stretches out forever behind our two-story house in Frankfurt, Germany, but I suppose, in truth it was only as big as several city blocks.

I remember it as a place filled with wonderful things. I climbed up and over broken brick walls, and I was a cowboy standing on a mountain. I scaled enormous slabs of concrete that slanted up out of the ground and found a dozen secret places that only I knew about. Raspberries grew on my playground, and gooseberries, and red currants: I picked them right off the vine and ate them and stained my shirt with them. In a shoe box I collected little scraps of melted glass that littered the earth. You could find all sorts of things on my playground.

One day I was digging in my playground and uncovered a little blue rubber motorcycle. I scraped the dirt away. The wheels still rolled. The little blue motorcycle could have been mine. I knew it wasn't. It belonged to someone else, to another little boy. It belonged to whoever had played on my playground before me.

I wondered what had happened to that little boy, and as I wondered, a fact I had known, assumed, and taken for granted slipped from the surface of my knowing into the very depths of my awareness. What I had dug up that day was not only a little blue motorcycle, but an awareness of the presence of evil in the world. My world. My playground, as you may have guessed, my six-year-old's garden of earthly delights, was a bombed-out section of residential Frankfurt, not yet rebuilt in those years following the Second World War. The walls and slabs I ran on and jumped from were what were left of the houses families had lived in. Raspberries and currants and gooseberries grew there because years before hands had planted, pruned, and tended them. The globs of glass I collected were windows which melted in the fires, windows mothers had watched their children from and waved at them as they played. The little blue motorcycle I rolled across my palm had rolled in the hands of some little boy who had lived in one of these houses that were no more.

What happened to that little boy, what happened to those
families, I did not and could not know. What I came to know in
that moment was that terrible things happened in this world,
that evil had also played across my playground.

In this garden there were weeds.[30]

This incident from Willson's own life could be seen as an analogy-
style illustration: just as there are weeds in this garden, there is evil in
the world. But there is too much detail, too much ambiguity in the way
this illustration unfolds, for it to serve as a simple analogy. We could
also see it as an example-style illustration. If Willson had been discussing the idea of coming to an awareness of the presence of evil, this
experience would be a good example of the thing itself. But Willson
was not trying to illustrate just one idea or experience. Rather, he was
attempting to evoke a world of many meanings, a world in which good
and evil are both present—indeed, a world in which it is impossible
to determine always what is good and what is evil. He conveyed all
this and more by employing this illustration metaphorically. His text
was the parable of the wheat and the weeds (Matt. 13:24–30), and the
sermon invited the hearers to live simultaneously in the complexity of
the parable and the complexity of our life.

Metaphor-style illustrations spin off many meanings. That is their
greatest strength, and, ironically, their greatest danger. They can, in
effect, scatter the listeners, sending them off on many different trajecto-
ries of meaning, creating confusion rather than illumination. Metaphor-
style illustrations must be so well-chosen and crafted that listeners can
mine their insights and forge the relationships between them and the
rest of the sermon, but if we have to stop and explain them or corral
them, they lose their power. They can convey the richness, diversity,
and mutifaceted character of the lived faith, but they can also evoke a
bewildered shrug of the shoulders rather than an "aha!"

Opening Doors

A sermon illustration is like a doorway opening into a larger room
of understanding and experience. A preacher must always ask about
any illustration, "Is this doorway wide enough for all the listeners to
pass through?" Suppose, for example, we choose to relate the story

of a person struggling to be ethically responsible amid the pressures, constant demands, and competitive environment of life in the corporate world. How will such an illustration be heard—indeed, can it be heard at all?—by a ninth-grader or by an unemployed person who would welcome the "constant demands" of a decent full-time job? We are tempted to say no to this question; ninth-graders worrying about algebra and people concerned about the source of their next paychecks simply cannot recognize themselves in the world of a corporate decision maker. There is a measure of truth in that, but only a measure. As a matter of fact, people have a rather remarkable capacity to enter imaginatively into the experiences of others and then to take what they have seen and heard and learned into their own lives. Indeed, it would be a serious mistake to become so concerned about speaking to every hearer's need all at once that we drain the blood out of illustrations, making them bland descriptions of life in general. There is no such thing as life in general; ironically, illustrations depend upon the honest ring of particularity—*this* life, *these* circumstances—for their ability to speak powerfully to a wide range of hearers.

We do, however, want to be sure that the range of our illustrative material reflects the rich variety of experiences present among the hearers. Sometimes this will mean that a section of a sermon will require not one illustration but two or three, each embodying a different kind of life circumstance: several doorways instead of only one. On other occasions, instead of a single complete illustration, we may choose to employ a series of images or vignettes:

> But how do we handle the problem of unanswered prayer? We pray for rain, but the drought continues. We pray for peace, and the headlines still shout of war. We pray for healing, but the dark stain remains on the X-ray. We pray for our children, and the crises continue. We pray for inner calm, but the anxiety does not diminish. We pray for light, but the shadows lengthen. How do we handle the problem of unanswered prayer?

This preacher, instead of providing a single full illustration about someone's struggle with unanswered prayer, has briefly named a series of such experiences. Not all hearers, of course, will have prayed for healing or for their children, but the chances are good that most listeners will find themselves somewhere on this list.

We must also be concerned about the cumulative effect of our illustrations. An illustration in this week's sermon about the ethical struggles of a corporate executive may well be effective, but to draw upon that world week after week soon closes the door to those on the outside. Unless we work intentionally at increasing the range of our illustrative repertoire, we will gravitate toward illustrations that reflect only the experiences of people like ourselves, who see the world the way we do. A young minister noted for her engaging sermons once asked a few trusted members of her congregation for an evaluation of her preaching. She was surprised to discover that, among their many words of praise, their one common criticism was that her illustrations were almost always about the struggles, issues, and experiences of young adults. That was, of course, the world she knew best, but cumulatively this illustrative world was taking its toll on the effectiveness of her preaching.

Just so, if most of our illustrations are about individuals wrestling with their concerns, we underline an individualistic distortion of the faith. If most are about family life, we communicate that being single is outside the Christian norm. If we never include the experiences of children, the gospel becomes adult oriented. If most of our illustrations are laden with feeling and emotion, we imply that loving God with the mind and the will is not as important as loving God with the heart. If there are often stories about men helping troubled women, we reinforce sinister gender stereotypes. Over time, the illustrative material in our sermons creates a worldview, and we must be careful to ensure that this worldview reflects the life we have been given in the gospel and not merely the culture close at hand.

Searching for the Sources

Where do we find illustrations? The pulpit is a hungry place. How do we collect the quantity of illustrative material we need for weekly preaching? There are four primary sources: the preacher's own life, the preacher's imagination, the world around us, and the media.

The Preacher's Own Life

Occasionally the best illustrative material we can find comes from our own life experiences. But is it appropriate to talk about ourselves from the pulpit? Contemporary homileticians and other students of preaching have given several answers to that question, ranging from an enthusiastic yes ("The best help we can offer is our own woundedness and a description of what has saved and healed us"—Salmon[31]), through a cautious "sometimes" ("Self-disclosure in moderation is appropriate to preaching"—Craddock[32]), to a horrified no ("To be blunt, there are virtually no good reasons to talk about ourselves from the pulpit"— Buttrick[33]). Most homileticians occupy the middle ground, recognizing both the power and the danger in self-disclosure. Some important rules have been devised: Don't always make yourself the hero; don't reveal pastoral confidences; don't embarrass a child or a spouse; don't turn the pulpit into a confessional; do tell experiences with which the hearers can identify, rather than "minister stories"; and so on.

These are good rules, but far more important than a list of rules is the matter of intent. Listeners are surprisingly savvy about discerning not only what we are saying about ourselves but also why we are saying it. If we are trying to come across as powerful or charming; if we are trying to win their sympathy or to get them to take care of us; if we are straining to say, "I may be a minister, but look, I'm really human, too"; if we are simply indulging ourselves in autobiographical egotism, most of the congregation will read us like a book. If, on the other hand, we are saying, "Here is how it is to encounter some aspect of life and the gospel; let me use my own life as an example," then through our illustrations, our hearers can be helped to name their own experiences.

An important distinction can be made between those personal experiences in which we are the primary subject and those in which we are simply the observer. An illustration that begins, "Last week, while I was waiting in the checkout line at the grocery store, I overheard a conversation between a father and his daughter," is a personal experience, but one in which we are not one of the primary actors. In such illustrations it is usually better to keep ourselves on the periphery, to maintain a stance as the narrator. Rather than intruding into the middle of the incident, telling the hearers that we were touched, dismayed, angered, saddened, or whatever by this father-daughter conversation, it is generally more effective to recount the experience in a manner that allows the listeners to be affected themselves.[34]

The Preacher's Imagination

It is certainly permissible to make up sermon illustrations, so long as we adhere to one strict rule: the preacher must always signal to the hearers that the illustration is a piece of fiction. We do not have to be clumsy about this, saying, "Now beware, I made up this next story." An introductory phrase like "Suppose," "Imagine that," or "What if" will usually suffice.

Why is this rule necessary? What is the difference, for example, in telling a true account of a man who comes to us for counseling because he is depressed and telling as true a fictional story of a man in another town who seeks counseling for depression? The latter story could have happened, and no confidences are broken in its telling. The reason we must always let the congregation know when we are relating fictional illustrations is that our only resource in preaching is the truth. We may have many flaws in our preaching. We may be less than exciting, somewhat disorganized, or even honestly mistaken about matters. All these flaws can be forgiven, but the one unpardonable sin for a preacher of the gospel is to lie. Concealing the fact that an illustration is fiction may seem like a small deception, but it makes a tear nonetheless in the essential fabric of truthfulness upon which our preaching depends.

The World around Us

The accomplished late-twentieth-century preacher Ernest T. Campbell zealously urged preachers to carry a small notepad at all times so that they could record the wealth of illustrative material encountered in the course of every day. Although now the notepad would probably be electronic, Campbell's advice still has double value: recording experiences and insights when they happen ensures that illustrative material is not lost, and the very habit of keeping an illustration journal causes preachers to be more alert and watchful about the disclosive power of everyday life.

The main problem with most published collections of sermon illustrations or sermons from the Internet is that they are canned and stylized, stories generally remote from the world of our hearers and often overly sentimental ("Gladstone and the Duke of Wellington stories" or "Little Eddie stories" some preachers call them, to call out their sentimentality). It is far better to populate our sermons with images, phrases, and experiences drawn from ordinary life: the message on the bank sign, a line from a song, a scene from the shopping mall, a video that went viral, a conversation in the stands at the high school game. Part of what preaching does is help Christian people to see life around us through the eyes of our faith, and including artifacts from the world around us serves as dress rehearsal for that kind of envisioning.

It would be a dreary way to live, of course, if we were condemned to go out the front door every day in search of sermon illustrations. There is also something sadly utilitarian, perhaps even unethical, about asking about every experience, "Can I use this in a sermon?" The principal way to avoid turning our entire lives into homiletical mills is to know very specifically what it is that we are looking for. If, for example, we are working ahead on a sermon in which the concept "kindness" will appear, some hard advance thinking about kindness will implant that idea in the creative area of our minds. Then, as we go about our business, small, otherwise unnoticed events—a gesture of a department store clerk, a hand offered on a bus, an extra plate at a table—will attach themselves to the concept. If we know what we are looking for, the chances are improved that we will find it (and, as Campbell would remind us, the chances are good that we will promptly lose it if we don't make a record of it right away).

The Media

Television, movies, plays, newspapers, the Internet, social media, magazines, books, and other media provide broad access to the world around us. It is especially important for a minister to develop the habit of regular reading and exploring of both theological and nontheological materials. This is a matter of frustration for many ministers, since the crushing demands placed upon them tend to crowd out time for "nonessential" reading and reflection. In fact, though, the reading of novels, plays, short stories, cultural analysis, and other types of literature is not a nonessential for contemporary ministry. Some cultures still communicate their crucial ideas orally, but most of us do our ministry in a world that thinks in print. A preacher in our time and place who does not read widely is like a physician, an attorney, or a teacher who does not read: quickly obsolete. Wise preachers view their reading as a part of their ministerial workload, build reading time into their schedules, and protect it.

Reading informs and invigorates ministry in a variety of ways, and it has several specific benefits for preaching. First, reading gives us access to scenes in plays, episodes in novels, news accounts, and other materials that can be employed as illustrative matter. Second, reading heightens our own creativity and sharpens our language and compositional skills. Scenes in good plays, for example, can be very instructive regarding the effective use of dialogue, since playwrights and preachers share at least one task: placing evocative human experience in concise oral form. Short-story writers and preachers share another task: shaping effective communication in a brief span. Reading plays and short stories can improve our preaching, even when we do not quote them in a sermon. Properly used, the Internet is a powerful research tool for preaching, especially if we keep our wits and our integrity about us and resist the temptation to find ready-made homiletical materials there.

Even the most diligent preachers cannot read everything they would like to be able to read. Most congregations, however, have people who read widely, and they can become active partners in the ministry of preaching. If we identify those people and let them know the sort of material we need, they can keep us supplied with a rich variety of resources.

9

Preaching and Plagiarism

> At the heart of plagiarism is concealment.
> Richard Posner, *The Little Book of Plagiarism*

> Preaching is like painting. When we see an artist's name on a painting, though we know she has many creative influences shaping her style and vision, we assume she brushed every drop of pigment on the canvas. If she were to pay someone else to paint the picture and then sign her name, something within us cries foul. This would say something false about both her and the art.
> Craig Brian Larson, "Plagiarism, Shmagiarism"

Several years ago, a student in one of my preaching courses was struggling terribly. The sermons he preached in class were plodding, disorganized, and weakly supported exegetically and theologically. He was aware that he was not meeting expectations, and he was frustrated and embarrassed by his performance. But then, in his final opportunity to redeem himself in the course, he surprised us all by preaching a stunning sermon, both profound and lyrical. It was unexpectedly excellent.

Too good, in fact. Sadly suspicious, I plugged one of his more delicious phrases into a search engine. Alas, up came the whole sermon on a church's website, preached by the pastor of that church many months before. It was an unfortunate but clear case of plagiarism. That was not, however, the whole story. My search actually produced dozens of hits, disclosing that, evidently, my student was not the only preacher to find this particular sermon compelling. A number of other preachers, all with their sermons posted online, had lifted paragraphs and pages from the original sermon, mostly without credit. In a last and unexpected twist, this much-copied sermon itself turned out to contain a long section cribbed without attribution from a column in a popular journal of religion. With a few clicks of the mouse, I had uncovered a crime wave of homiletical petty larceny.

The stealing of sermons is nothing new, of course, but there is plenty of evidence that the practice is spreading and that the kerosene on the fire is the Internet. Not only are thousands of sermons available for the snatching on church web pages, but scores of commercial sites hawk complete sermons, illustrations, outlines, images, and PowerPoint accompaniments for a fee. The proprietors of these sites are aware, naturally, that their customers may have a flicker of conscience over downloading sermons, so several sites include words of reassurance. "We know you may be worried about plagiarism," they essentially warble, "but the authors of these sermons want you to use them. And besides, these sermons are designed to stimulate your imagination as you create your own sermons. You'll still be doing the work."[1]

Right. One pastor who actively markets his sermons online told the British journal *Christianity*, "If my bullet fits your gun, shoot it,"[2] and Craig Brian Larson, writing about pulpit plagiarism at PreachingToday .com, cites a preacher who says, "When Chuck Swindoll starts preaching better sermons, so will I."[3] When it comes to preachers desperate to feed the incessant pulpit hunger, "the Internet," as one of my colleagues likes to say, "is like having a drug dealer on every corner."

But the Internet is not only the supplier, it is often the police officer too. More preachers may be stealing sermons these days, but more are also getting caught in the fine mesh of web crawlers and search engines. Four years ago, early on a Sunday morning, the parish nurse at a church in Washington, DC, ran an Internet search on the sermon title that her pastor had announced for that day, only to find a sermon with that exact title on the website of a church in Manhattan. She carried a printout of the New York sermon with her to worship, and sure enough, she heard the same sermon from the pulpit that morning, almost word for word. This was the first evidence of what turned out to be a long-standing pattern of pulpit plagiarism on the part of the pastor, and its discovery threw the congregation into turmoil.

Because of the prominence of this church and the pastor, that controversy made national news, but there have been numerous other, less-publicized local occurrences where preachers have been caught in the pincers of Google. Almost every community has a story of a church torn apart and a pastor embarrassed, if not dismissed, over "borrowing" sermons. In the future, churches may well adopt the strategy of many colleges and universities, which are combating plagiarism with powerful software programs that comb through extensive databases as well as every nook and cranny of the worldwide web, comparing student papers with possible sources and sleuthing out similarities in language. There may come a time when pastors seeking new calls or appointments will have to pass their sermons under the watchful eye of such software, as a kind of plagiarism background check.

What can we say about the ethics of preaching, without attribution, other people's sermons, in whole or in part? It is tempting to keep it simple, to cite the commandment "Thou shalt not steal" and be done with it. However, the issues surrounding pulpit plagiarism are more complex than they may appear at first glance. To begin with, the reality of the Internet is not merely a change in technology. As the music industry has already discovered, the use of the Internet carries with it major cultural shifts in how we understand the ownership and use of information.

The rules of attribution that pertain in one cultural place or moment do not necessarily apply in another. (For example, notice that there is nary a footnote in Matthew's Gospel to give credit to Mark, his main source.) Some voices are now arguing that the whole concept of intellectual property, on which many of our convictions about plagiarism rest, is a post-Enlightenment, modernist illusion that is rapidly being unmasked. The very idea that people create new things out of words and thus own them falls in the face of the evidence that every literary creation is an amalgam—known and unknown, acknowledged and unacknowledged—of previous oral and literary acts. We are now entering, goes the argument, a kind of postmodernist "open source" society in which the whole notion of plagiarism evaporates because, when closely examined, everything is a kind of plagiarism.

Several years ago, *Harper's Magazine* published an elegant essay by novelist Jonathan Lethem arguing just that. "Any text," he writes, "is woven entirely with citations, references, echoes, cultural languages, which cut across it through and through in a vast stereophony. The citations . . . are quotations without inverted commas." Then, to prove the point, and as a kind of literary joke on the reader, Lethem reveals at the end of the essay that virtually every line of his piece was cribbed from other sources. (The quotation just cited is not Lethem after all, but Roland Barthes.)

Some pastors have picked up a theological version of this open-source argument. Sermon words are gifts from God, they say, and thus fair game for any and all who wish to appropriate them. How dare preachers do anything but sing the doxology, they ask, when their sermons show up in the mouths of other pastors? Moreover, with God-given words in ripe clusters of low-hanging fruit all over the Internet, originality becomes a highly overrated virtue, perhaps even a sign of hubris. For these preachers, the goal is to create an impact upon bearers; who cares where the words come from?

"Don't be original—be effective!" urges Steve Sjogren of the Cincinnati Vineyard Community Church, in an essay at Pastors.com. "In my mind," he continues, "there is a tremendous amount of pride (let's call it what it is) when we insist on being completely original as communicators. . . . The guys I draw encouragement from—the best communicators in the United States . . . get 70 percent of their material from someone else. Remember, Solomon wrote that 'there is nothing new under the sun.'"

This vaunting of free gift over originality could be called the "Dizzy Gillespie Theory of Preaching." When Gillespie heard that Phil Woods, a young sax player, had been accused of stealing the style of famed saxophonist Charlie "Bird" Parker, Gillespie defended Woods. "You can't steal a gift," he said. "Bird gave the world his music, and if you can hear it, you can have it."

Others make a more practical argument in favor of softening the boundaries of pulpit plagiarism: borrowing a *good* sermon is far to be preferred over numbing a congregation into submission with a poor one of your own. When a pastor in my city was caught preaching cut-and-paste sermons from the web and then distributing printed copies under his own name, he repented and was given a second chance by the congregation. However, one concerned member of the congregation wrote to Randy Cohen, whose column "The Ethicist," in which Cohen provided practical ethical advice to readers, was then a regular feature in the Sunday magazine of the *New York Times*. The letter described the case and asked for Cohen's opinion. Cohen responded by roundly criticizing the pastor for preaching another's sermons without credit and, even more, for publishing them under his own name. But then he wondered, "Perhaps sermon writing should not be a job requirement." Being a pastor, Cohen said, requires many different gifts, and no one can possess them all in abundance. "If an otherwise excellent pastor is clumsy with his pen," he mused, "his parish would be better served by hearing him deliver the profound and stirring words of a more talented author."

Really? Poor preachers should simply stop the pain and treat their congregations to sermons composed by steadier hands? Surprisingly, Cohen would find agreement from no less an authority than St. Augustine, who wrote, "There are, indeed, some people who have a good delivery, but cannot compose anything to deliver. Now, if such people take what has been written with wisdom and eloquence by others, and commit it to memory, and deliver it to the people, they cannot be blamed, supposing them to do it without deception."

Complicating the plagiarism issue even more is the fact that some congregations in primarily oral cultures—for example, sectors of the African-American church and some Appalachian white churches— preserve and honor the tradition of repreaching well-known "set piece" sermons, such as "'Jesus' Funeral" or "The Deck of Cards" (a sermon in which the preacher symbolically deals out cards, one at a time, making a biblical allusion for each one). The preaching of such sermons is folk performance art, and originality of composition is not the issue. Many of the hearers would have heard these sermons time and again and, as in the case of hearing a jazz riff, would be interested mainly in how the performer improvises on the old material.

The ethics surrounding pulpit plagiarism, then, are not simple, but a good bit of clarity is achieved, I think, when we keep two factors in focus. The first is truthfulness. "Plagiarism," writes Richard A. Posner in *The Little Book of Plagiarism*, "is a species of intellectual fraud."[4] Posner goes on to name the two key ingredients of fraud in every act of plagiarism: one, somebody copies something and then claims ("whether explicitly or implicitly, and whether deliberately or carelessly") that these words are the plagiarist's original composition; and two, this deception causes the readers (or hearers) of these words to act differently than they would if they possessed the truth.

So if a preacher takes a paragraph or a page or a story from a novel, a movie, another sermon, or anywhere else and fails to signal to the congregation that this is borrowed material, then the first element of plagiarism is present. Sermons are not term papers, of course, and giving the full details about sources is not a must. A simple "as one biblical scholar has put it" or "another pastor tells a story about . . ." will usually do. Beyond this, source details should be filled in on the basis of how helpful they will be to the hearers. If it makes a difference to the hearers to know that sermon words have been borrowed from Luther or Anne Lamott or Walter Brueggemann, then say so.

Giving credit to others is not merely a matter of keeping our ethical noses clean; it is also a part of bearing witness to the gospel. No sermon stands alone, but instead takes its place in a "cloud of witnesses." The proclamation of the gospel does not spring forth from our cleverness or ability to generate novelty. To borrow words from others and to show that one's sermon dips into the deep well of shared wisdom is itself part of Christian testimony, a fresh expression of Paul's confession, "I handed on to you as of first importance what I in turn had received" (1 Cor. 15:3).

But what of Posner's second ingredient of fraud—namely, that pulpit plagiarism occurs when the preacher's deception about sources causes the hearers to behave differently than they would have had they known the truth? Perhaps as much or more than any other form of communication, preaching depends upon a cord of trust binding together the speaker and the listener, the preacher and hearer. A good sermon consists not primarily in flawless logic, soaring poetry, or airtight arguments but in passionately held truth proclaimed with conviction. To compromise the truth in ways that hearers would consider deceptive makes them reluctant to extend this necessary trust and damages the witness. For evidence, we can point to the hard disillusionment and sense of betrayal experienced by many in congregations where pastors have been caught plagiarizing sermons.

Preaching, like all forms of communication, rests upon a tacit agreement between the parties involved. When Comedy Central's "The Daily Show" or NBC's "Saturday Night Live" sends up a parody of the news, it is not necessary for the performer to say, "Now this part of what I am saying is absolutely true, but this other part is satire." The viewers already know this; it is woven into the implied agreement. When a revival preacher in a Pentecostal church in Galax, Virginia, pulls out a deck of cards and begins dealing them out and chanting,

"When I see the ace, I am reminded there is but one God, . . ." nobody needs to be told that the preacher is performing a script. This is already well known, and no deception is involved. But preachers who stand up on Sunday morning with a sermon ripped off the Internet and preach the words as if they were their own almost certainly violate the implied agreement with the congregation.

A good test of this point is to ask what would happen if the preacher told the truth? What if the preacher were to say, "Hey folks, it's been a busy week and I didn't have time to work on a sermon, and honestly, I'm not all that creative anyway. So here's a little something I found on the 'net"? The fact that the air would immediately go out of the room is a reliable indicator that the tacit agreement of the sermon event has been violated. This is why plagiarists, for all their blather about God's words being free for all, never confess their true sources and always imply that these words are coming straight from the heart. Yes, Augustine made space for preachers to memorize the words of other, more eloquent proclaimers, but note well that he added the test of truth: "supposing them to do it without deception."

In addition to the standard of truthfulness, the second factor to keep in focus is immediacy. While there is surely room in the pulpit for the "set piece" sermon and the oft-repeated illustration, finally preaching is a word from God for these people in this place at this moment. Preaching is not just about inspiration; it is ultimately about proclamation: "Today this Scripture has been fulfilled in your hearing." Moltmann, as we noted earlier, described the act of preaching as someone getting up from the assembly, standing in front of God's people, and speaking and acting in the name of Christ. The church, Moltmann says, "does not want to listen to itself and to project its own image of itself; it wants to hear Christ's voice."[5] That is, God's people want to hear Christ's voice speaking now, and to them.

Moltmann's picture points to the location of the preacher, at once joyful and agonizing. The preacher comes from the pews to stand in the pulpit. Only preachers who deliver their own sermons stand with one foot in the life of the people and one foot in the biblical text. No Internet-dependent preacher stands in this same place. No borrowed sermon, however fine, can answer the question that cries out from every congregation, "Is there a word today, a word for us, from the Lord?" This is not the same as saying that sermons must be fully original. All preachers borrow from others, and should. There is a difference between being a debtor and being a thief. All preachers stand on the shoulders of biblical scholars, theologians, and faithful witnesses from across the generations. We do not owe our congregations an original essay; we owe them a fresh act of interpretation.

Gray areas remain, of course, and judgment calls must be made. If a preacher finds a superb Fred Craddock story in a sermon by Jane Doaks, must Doaks be credited along with Craddock? If a preacher reads a wonderful sermon by Barbara Lundblad and borrows not a single word of it but adopts the structure of the sermon, should Lundblad be cited? Is the phrase "He comes to us as One unknown, without a name, as of old, by the lake side" so much a part of the culture that it is, in effect, in the public domain, or should Albert Schweitzer be explicitly credited as the author?

Preachers who strive to tell the truth, who seek to honor the communion of saints, who desire to maintain the trust of the faithful community—that is to say, preachers with ethical integrity—will wrestle with these questions and make the best decisions they can. Pulpit plagiarists, however, in the name of expediency, will grab what they wish wherever they can find it and claim it as their own. Their stolen sermons may occasionally sparkle, but in the end these sermons will be disclosed as mere rhinestones, and these preachers will have spread the banquet table of God with the empty calories of homiletical fast food.

10

From Desk to Pulpit

> Question: Why do you actors seem to make such impressions upon your audiences, while we preachers frequently leave our congregations cold?
>
> Answer: Actors speak of things imaginary as if they were real, while you preachers too often speak of things real as if they were imaginary.
>
> —An exchange between the archbishop of Canterbury and English actor Thomas Betterton

A "written sermon" is a contradiction in terms. Of course, many sermons are written down before they are preached, and some sermons are written up after they are preached, but a sermon itself occurs not in the writing but in the preaching. A sermon, by definition, is a spoken event. This distinction is important, because speaking and writing are not merely two separate but equal channels of communication. The effects of the spoken word are markedly different from those of the written word.

One difference is that speaking can be addressed to a group, whereas writing implies an individual reader, or at most a series of individual readers. The apostle Paul wrote one of his letters "to all the saints in Christ Jesus who are at Philippi," yet that letter, in its written form, could not be read by "all the saints" at once, only by individuals. However, when that letter was read aloud—that is, spoken to—the Philippian congregation, the hearing of it became a community experience. Indeed, the spoken word has the power to create community. "Preaching" and "congregation" are reciprocal terms. It is true that we preach to a congregation, but it is also true that, through our preaching, the hearers become a congregation. Consider the words of Walter J. Ong:

When a speaker is addressing an audience, the members of the audience normally become a unity, with themselves and with the speaker. If the speaker asks the audience to read a handout provided for them, as each reader enters into his or her own private reading world, the unity of the audience is shattered, to be re-established only when oral speech begins again. Writing and print isolate. There is no collective noun or concept for readers corresponding to "audience." The collective "readership"—this magazine has a readership of two million—is a far-gone abstraction.[1]

Moreover, the act of speaking, unlike writing, takes place in the active presence of those who receive the communication. Even if I am "talking to myself," I have to pretend that I am two people.[2] Writers can imagine those who will eventually read their words, but speakers do not need to imagine the hearers. They are present in the moment of speaking, and their presence exerts a shaping force on the communication. Preachers do not "own" their sermons in quite the same way that authors "own" their manuscripts. When we stand up to preach, we already know most of what we will say, and we may even place on the pulpit a complete script of our words, but we do not really have the sermon in our hands or in our minds. A sermon happens only when we open our mouths and the hearers open their ears. People may call it "our sermon," but it does not belong to us alone. It belongs as well to those who help create it by their listening. To put it theologically, a sermon is a work of the church and not merely a work of the preacher.

From Written to Oral

In earlier chapters we explored the crucial steps a preacher takes in moving toward a sermon: interpreting a biblical text, creating a form, deciding about the use of illustrative material, and so on. Even though these activities have traditionally been thought of as "preparing the sermon," it would be more accurate, given the orality of preaching, to describe these steps as preparing *for* the sermon. Since most of these preliminary activities have involved reading and writing, one final step must be taken as we go from the desk to the pulpit: the move from writing to speaking.

The first decision we must make as we prepare to speak the sermon is the choice of what, if any, written materials or electronic notes to take with us into the pulpit. There are three broad options: a full manuscript, notes or an outline, or nothing written at all. Many people have cast their ballots for one or another of these methods, alleging its superiority, but the fact is that all three are quite acceptable and can be equally effective. The way to begin thinking about this decision is not by weighing the intrinsic merits of this or that method but by keeping our overall purpose in view. In preaching, we seek to say something important to other people, and whatever prompts we take with us into the pulpit should be designed to support that action. If you are to say something important to other people, three vital elements must be brought into cooperative interaction. (1) You must be present in the speaking; (2) some significant *message* must be spoken; and (3) the *listeners* must be active partners in the event. How can written materials enhance or impede this interplay among speaker, message, and hearers?

The use of a full manuscript obviously places the emphasis on the sermon content, ensuring that the message will be intact, and that is no small virtue. The careful advanced selection of apt words, phrases, and images for sermons is an act of ministry and much to be preferred over the sloppy and haphazard use of language that can result when we search for wording on our feet. The thoughtful composition of our sermons, heedfully selecting the language best suited for this congregation's hearing, is a way of taking seriously our responsibility to the listeners.

On the other hand, the cumbersome reading of a full script can strain to the vanishing point the interaction between preacher and hearers. The experience of hearing a preacher preach to a stack of papers or a screen rather than to the hearers is deadly. Many preachers, though, have learned how to read their sermons with energy and skill, minimizing the loss of presence often associated with this method. Also, manuscript pages can be composed so that they can be used much like a set of notes. The lines can be printed like stanzas of a poem, spaces can be allocated between the sections of the sermon, brackets can be drawn around illustrative material, key phrases can be underlined or highlighted, headings or marginal notes can be attached to various portions, or other markings made to render the manuscript more a picture of the sermon's movement and less an unbroken sea of print.

Moving to the other end of the spectrum, using no written materials whatsoever places the emphasis on the presence of the preacher and, to some degree, on the participation of the hearers. Preaching without written aids is a difficult skill to master, but there is an undeniable authenticity and immediacy when the preacher speaks directly to the listeners with no written "screen" between them. This advantage is squandered, however, if the sermon seems recited from rote memory, on the one hand, or loose, rambling, and content starved, on the other. Some preachers attempt to develop the ability to preach without notes because of the amazed approval often given to this method by congregations, but the oratorical nimbleness of the preacher is a pseudo-value in the Christian context. The church finally does not need to experience the presence of the preacher; it needs rather to hear the claims of the Christian faith *through* the preacher. If the avoidance of written materials causes the content of the sermon to be lost, ultimately all is lost.

The use of notes or a sermon diagram represents a middle choice and an attempt to balance the competing needs for careful content, presence of the preacher, and hearer interaction. This method can involve something as simple as a list of key words or as elaborate as a full sentence outline. Some preachers create notes or an outline as their only written preparation; others prepare a full manuscript and then distill it into the briefer form. Again, the main risk in this method is the possible loss of precision in the use of language.

The method you choose will depend on you and your skills, the kind of sermon being preached, and the nature of the specific preaching occasion. For some preachers, a manuscript acts like a magnet, drawing their energy and presence down into the pulpit and away from the congregation. For others, anything less than a manuscript produces vain repetitions and inappropriate ad-libs. Or again, a preacher who usually brings a full manuscript into the pulpit may want to have only a few notes, or nothing written at all, for a sermon preached at a graveside or at a camp communion service. In preaching we are trying, today and in this place, to bear witness to the gospel in such a way that these people know they are directly addressed by it. So long as we remain clear about this purpose, we are free to experiment with notes, manuscripts, and the like in various settings until we find the best methods to support our preaching ministry.

And I Quote . . .

Quotations from books, essays, songs, and plays are often very helpful in sermons, but their use creates a special problem because quotations represent an intrusion of the written form into a spoken event (see also the discussion of sermon plagiarism in the previous chapter). Before we decide to employ a quotation in a sermon, we should consider whether or not a quotation is the best means to accomplish our goal. Generally speaking, there are only two good reasons for using a quotation: the credibility of the person who said it or the power of the language in which it is said. Consider, for example, this quotation from a hymn:

Should it be ours to drain the cup of grieving even to the dregs of pain, at thy command, we will not falter, thankfully receiving all that is given by thy loving hand.[3]

Those words possess their own power, but they gain even more strength when we know they were composed by Dietrich Bonhoeffer in a German concentration camp only months before his execution. Who said them is as important as what they say. Or again, consider this brief portion of a sermon on the opening verses of the Gospel of John:

If we were to search for the most beautiful and moving passage in the New Testament, we would certainly have to consider the beginning lines—the Prologue—of the Gospel of John. These verses form a hymn which soars with majestic poetic power, and its images press deeply into our minds. Speaking of these verses, the New Testament scholar Raymond Brown observed, "If John has been described as the pearl of great price among the [New Testament] writings, then one may say that the Prologue is the pearl within this gospel. . . . The choice of the eagle as the symbol of John the Evangelist was largely determined by the celestial flights of the opening lines of the Gospel."[4]

Here the preacher quotes a well-known scholar as a way of saying, "The view I am describing is also held by biblical scholars—Raymond

Brown, for example." One caution about this matter of quoting authorities: no words have more immediate credibility in a sermon than those
of the truthful preacher. If our implied message is, "You may not accept
this coming from me, but Augustine said it, Luther said it, Julian of
Norwich said it, Barth said it, Dorothy Day said it, and Einstein said it
too," then we sadly underestimate, even cheapen, the gift of authority
the Christian community grants to us in the act of preaching.

Sometimes it is the wording of the quotation, more than the person
quoted, that most makes a statement effective. Here is an example:

> It is a mistake to sharpen our minds by narrowing them. It is
> a mistake to look to the Bible to close a discussion; the Bible
> seeks to open one. . . . The Bible is no oracle to be consulted for
> specific advice on specific problems; rather, it is a wellspring of
> wisdom about the ambiguity, inevitability, and insolubility of
> the human situation. . . . The Bible makes us comfortable with
> struggle but uneasy in success. . . . [T]he Bible is a signpost, not
> a hitching post.[5]

The power of that quotation lies in the way it is stated and not primarily in the fact that William Sloane Coffin happened to be the one who
said it. When we employ a quotation like this, our responsibility to the
hearers is to let them know, in the least disruptive way possible, that we
are using the words of someone else. If the listeners would recognize
Coffin's name, or if we wish to give the statement a personal ring, or
if we simply desire to credit the source, we may introduce the quotation with a brief phrase like, "William Sloane Coffin has observed. . . ."
Otherwise we can just say, "As one minister has said," "someone has
pointed out," or the like. Elaborate oral footnotes (such as "William
Sloane Coffin, in his collection of sermons entitled *The Courage to
Love*, said . . .") tend to clutter the air and undermine the power of the
quotation itself.

One rule about quotations: they almost always lose some of their
effectiveness as they move from the page to the pulpit. They are seldom as evocative for the hearers as they were for us when we first read
them. Because of this, sermon quotations should be sparingly used,
and they should always be distilled to their essence. If, for example, we
wish to quote a provocative statement of a character in a novel, instead

of reading a whole page of the novel to give the background, we can set the scene ourselves, in our own words, and then provide the quotation.

Finding the Rhythm

Should sermons be rehearsed aloud? That question never fails to provoke a squirm of embarrassment among preachers, since the language of rehearsal smacks of performance and playacting. If we know the content of our sermon and believe what we are going to say in the sermon, why should we practice it? Would it not be more authentic simply to stand up and preach it "for real" the first time?

The primary purpose of practicing a sermon aloud, however, is not to polish our role as performer. To the contrary, it is to place ourselves in the role of the listener. Indeed, as we speak our sermon out loud, we become its first hearer, and we begin to grasp that this event is about the sermon and the hearer more than about us. Homiletician Jana Childers has argued on this point:

> Ideally, in the case of both theatre and preaching, performance means the use of self as vehicle—the disciplined giving of one's voice and body to a message, idea, or experience that needs one. Indeed many artists have found such discipline to be a corrective for an inflated ego.[6]

Listening to our own sermon being spoken makes us aware of the rhythms, movements, and intrinsic timing of the sermon in ways that studying notes or a manuscript can never do. We realize, perhaps, that a sentence that looks good on paper sounds convoluted in speech. If the hearers are to understand what we are saying, that sentence will need to be broken into shorter oral phrases. Or a description ("the many problems of our town") suddenly sounds dull and bloodless and cries out for sharper images (the abandoned factory with the rusting gate, the homeless child curled sleeping beside her mother under the highway bridge, the vodka bottle hidden in the laundry closet).

In speaking our sermon aloud, we discover places where pauses will be necessary to allow the hearers time to reflect, where our speech will need to be more rapid, or slower, if the power of that part of the sermon is to be felt. We hear ourselves describing "Goliath, whose height was six cubits and a span" in a tiny, unamazed voice that would give the impression he was really only five feet four inches tall.[7] We recognize that if the hearers are to find themselves in a story we are telling, we must learn the story well enough to say it without reading it. As we practice the sermon aloud, we see in our imaginations the faces of the people who will hear it, and our language becomes more immediate, more directed to life, more rich with grace.

Practicing the sermon also enables us to absorb it. We do not memorize it, but we learn it "by heart" and, thus, can be more present with and for the hearers in the actual event of preaching.

Speaking the Truth

The time has come for the sermon. We are standing there, and the congregation waits and listens. How should we speak? Should we be firm and convincing, or gentle and inviting? Shall we let our bodies be caught up in the energy of our message, or should we restrain our movements, letting our words speak for themselves? Should we make plenty of eye contact with the congregation, or will that only make them feel scrutinized and uncomfortable? Should we worry about our accents or our nasalization or how we always stumble over the word "Nebuchadnezzar" or the way our glasses slip down on our noses as we speak?

Obviously it would be foolish to say that the mechanics of voice and body do not matter in preaching. They do, and excellent manuals are available to assist preachers in the techniques of body and voice control.[8] It is encouraging to know, however, that flaws and idiosyncrasies in our delivery are not nearly so damaging as one might suspect. Obviously, if our voice is too soft to be heard, our speech too slurred to be understood, or our gestures violent contradictions of our message, these are serious problems that need firm attention. Hearers soon learn, though, to live with the majority of hitches and halts in delivery that most of us have. They grow to love some of them, enjoy with amusement some others, and filter out the rest. It is called grace.

Sometimes preachers are given the rather lame advice to "be natural" in the pulpit. Such advice, Robert Kirkpatrick wryly notes, "is of no more help to the preacher than is the same advice when spoken by the photographer to the over-tense or over-relaxed individual on whom his camera is trained."[9] We cannot be natural when we are not feeling natural. Preachers are not immune from nervousness, tenseness, or moodiness, and these conditions affect us when we preach. It is part of the human condition to which we, and our hearers, can and will learn to adjust.

There is an even deeper truth to learn, however, about sermon delivery and the preacher's physical presence in preaching. If we are faithfully exercising our ministry of preaching, if we are honestly bearing witness to the gospel, for and with people whom we love, over time it will show. If we are fundamentally bored by what we are doing, feel contempt for or superior to the hearers, are cynical toward what we are preaching, try to be impressive or charming, or wish we were in some other vocation, that will also show. A person who, week after week, is speaking the truth in love looks and sounds like a person lovingly telling the truth; there is finally no hiding it.

11

Conversation along the Pilgrim Way

So what do you do? You let the sermon go. You cannot hang on to your success or failure. The sermon, such as it was, is in God's hands—God's quite capable hands. Remember the parable of that small and insignificant mustard seed that grew into a great tree. For all you know, God may take your miserable sermon and find a mustard seed in it for some parishioner's consolation, or conviction, or growth.

—Marjorie Hewitt Suchocki, *The Whispered Word*

In times gone by, when many Christians made pilgrimages to holy shrines, they talked together as they journeyed. They told wonderful, sad, and even raucous stories. They disclosed their fears and their ambitions, their faith and their failings, their secret joys and hidden doubts as they broke bread at table and drank the harsh wine of wayside inns. When pilgrims embarked on their journey, they held in common only a destination; when they reached journey's end, they shared a common life.

We have now come to the final stretch of our mutual journey. Along the way I have imagined that you and I, and the others who have gone with us, were talking together as we traveled. I hope you have heard my voice and the voices of many others who have taken up the ministry of teaching those who preach. I also hope you have heard your own voice—questioning, probing, challenging, demurring, becoming your own teacher.

One of the well-traveled medieval pilgrim roads led through perilous regions of Spain to the great Cathedral of Saint James in Compostela. It is said that as the pilgrims approached the city they would focus their eyes on the horizon, straining to see the towers of the cathedral, the object of their long journey. The one who first spotted the cathedral in the distance would cry, "My joy!" and would promptly be named the "king" of the pilgrim band. In fact, many people today who have last names "King," "Leroy," "Koenig," or "Rex" owe their surnames to the sharp eyes of some pilgrim ancestor.[1]

Perhaps, as we have walked together on our pilgrim road toward a deeper understanding of the ministry of preaching, you have been casting your own eyes toward the distant horizon in the direction of our destination. Indeed, it would be gratifying to me to think that you were the first to have it in view, the one to cry, "My joy!"

Preaching Lore

Whenever preachers gather to talk shop, certain perennial topics arise. Some questions about preaching, large and small, practical and theoretical, must constantly be reopened and examined anew. These questions have no permanent answers but rather an evolving preachers' lore that has grown up around them. "What do you do about . . . ?" "My experience has been. . . ." "Have you tried . . . ?" "Do you find that . . . ?" "Whatever you do, don't. . . ." These are the sounds of preachers talking with each other about the lore of their craft as they walk together along the pilgrim way. This last portion of our journey together will be spent exploring some of those recurring questions and entering into the ongoing conversation.

How Much Advance Planning Should We Do for Our Sermons?

Preachers vary widely in their planning habits. Some preachers have well-organized minds, and with the aid of a calendar and a lectionary they plan their preaching months in advance. A few even take a week or so of study leave to sketch out a general preaching scheme for the coming year. Most of us are less disciplined, beginning the next sermon only after the present one has been delivered.

The best wisdom is that every preacher can be actively at work on five or six sermons at once. A good method is to create separate file folders or computer files for, say, the next half-dozen sermons. The biblical texts should be chosen and enough of the exegetical work done on these texts to know the general direction of each of the sermons. The preacher can then browse through these files periodically to keep the upcoming sermon themes in mind. Clippings from the newspaper, quotes from novels, pastoral experiences, and other ideas can then be entered into the files so that, when the time comes to create a sermon, its file will already contain some working material. As soon as a sermon is complete, a new file is made to take its place at the end of the line. Older homileticians called this method a "homiletical garden." The big task is in setting up the system, since exegetical work on several sermons is required. Once the garden is planted, however, it can be tilled and cultivated as a matter of routine.

How Do You Save Illustrative Material for Future Use?

Again, customs differ among preachers. Some have elaborate filing systems (hard copy or electronic). Whenever encountering a story or an incident that shows promise as preaching material, the preacher makes a judgment about its subject matter and files it accordingly. This is an orderly way to proceed, but the problem lies in the fact that good preaching material can seldom be easily categorized. It is difficult to classify, for example, a newspaper story about a wealthy man who, weary of the burdens of his riches, tossed his fortune in one-hundred-dollar bills onto a busy freeway, causing motorists to abandon their cars and chase wildly after the money. A story like that can be "about" many things, and it is hard to know where to file it.

Thus, other preachers do not file illustrative material at all; rather, they keep it in a single place and sort through it for every sermon, allowing unexpected connections to be made between the sermon content and the collected bits and pieces. A compromise solution is to file the material in its most likely slot but also to make a one-phrase record of each item in another file. The complete files keep the material in order; the one-phrase files can be used for random searches.

What about Sermons and Digital Technology?

In some ways the landscape of preaching and digital technology is changing so rapidly that it is difficult to make an observation in the morning that is not already obsolete by afternoon. When the first

edition of this book appeared nearly thirty years ago, a few congregations were experimenting with screens in worship, but hardly anyone
could have dreamed where the digital revolution would take us. Now,
in thousands of "satellite" church campuses across the land, preachers
are able to appear in several worship settings simultaneously as high-
quality projected images or holograms. It is possible that some people
have heard many sermons but rarely or ever been in the physical presence of a preacher.

Perhaps even more prevalent today than multiple screen projections is the practice of creating sermons that are skillful blends of
the image and the spoken word. Preachers of a previous generation
searched through books and journals in a quest for ideas and illustrations. In much the same way, preachers of this generation search the
Web for video clips and images to accompany the sermon. In his book
on preaching, *Unleashing the Word,* Adam Hamilton, who is the pastor of a large church that has a "video team" dedicated to the task of
enriching worship with images, gives some advice for the use of video
clips in preaching. His practical wisdom sounds much like the guidance the older homiletics books would have given about the proper
length of sermon illustrations:

> Video clips in the midst of a sermon should, as a rule, be no
> longer than one and a half to two minutes. Most video clips
> we use are under one minute. That means more time must be
> spent editing down a video interview—but here again, less is
> more. If you consider a thirty-minute sermon as standard, and
> a video is three minutes in length, 10 percent of the sermon
> was devoted to that one clip. There are exceptions, but as a
> general rule, this is too much time to devote to one clip.[2]

Some preachers and congregations cannot imagine now a sermon
that is not accompanied by images on a screen. Other preachers and
congregations cannot imagine ever going that way and perhaps even
mark off their litiurgical and homiletical identities as those "who don't
do screens."

It seems that we are on a "shake down" cruise in regard to the use of
visuals in preaching. We have learned a great deal about the technical
side of things, how to use images and to employ the technology with

increasing skill. But we are just beginning to learn about the theological and communicational implications.

In some ways, what is happening in preaching is paralleled by what is going on in teaching. Many, if not most, teachers are now employing some visual technology in their classroom instruction but are still discovering the full potential and the full peril of this new pedagogy. I spoke with the dean of a state medical school who told me that many of the professors at his school had become enchanted with the potential of PowerPoint in their teaching, filling their lectures with slides of medical photographs and parsed definitions of terms. The faculty were surprised, said the dean, when the students circulated a petition asking the faculty to turn off the PowerPoint and "just talk to us." The problem was probably not with the PowerPoint at all but instead with the way it was being used. Students were experiencing teachers who were more focused on the screen than they were on classroom interaction, and they wanted to be engaged again and addressed by their professors.

The integration of the spoken and the visual in preaching is prevalent enough and has now been with us long enough that it is clear that the practice is here to stay. But even while we are still in the experiemental phase of this, a few instances of "lore" can be named:

1. Images on a screen are indeed powerful, but not as powerful as the spoken word. There is no form of human communication as powerful as someone courageously speaking the truth in love. Some preachers, especially those who lack confidence, intuitively believe that a video clip flashed onto a screen is more interesting and compelling than anything they could ever say. Images are—or can be—powerfully informative and appealing, but they are no match for the spoken word.

For one thing, images are flat and literal. What you see is what you get. Baseball fans often comment about the difference between hearing a game called on the radio and seeing one played on television. TV is wonderful because one can actually see the action, but ironically, most people find the games to be more interesting on radio. The reason is that the television gives you everything, requiring only that you look, while the radio listener has to be fully engaged as the mind creates the action in the listener's imagination. Preachers should remember that the spoken word can take hearers to places in their imaginations where the visual cannot so easily go.

2. Images are best used in sermons to support the spoken word, not to replace it.   The best use of images in sermons is to support what is spoken, not to stand in lieu of what is spoken. For example, I recently heard a sermon in which the preacher was talking about the danger of cultural images of worth. She talked about how our culture is dazzled by youth and a certain picture of physical attractiveness, thus communicating that one is not of worth unless one is young enough, thin enough, handsome or beautiful enough. If this preacher had used a screen, this could have been a place for images from magazine covers or a short video clip from a "use this cream and the years disappear" commercial, as a support for the spoken word.

3. Keep the energy flowing between the preacher and the listeners, not between the preacher and the screen.   We have all experienced PowerPoint presentations in which the speaker stared at the screen as the slides flashed by, simply describing what was on the screen or, worse, reading copy off the screen. Material projected on a screen works best when it simply appears at the right moment, supporting what the preacher is saying. This means that what is being said in the sermon drives the appearance of the images, and not the other way around. It also means that the image on the screen should not be a distraction for the listener or for the preacher but an amplification of the energy flowing from the preacher toward those who hear.

One other caution here: in Chapter 5 in the discussion of sermon form, we warned about how the older outlining style could easily impose a kind of rigid linearity upon the sermon. Oddly, the same goes for visual computer programs like PowerPoint. Creating a stack of slides to display on a screen may reflect the latest technology, but in many ways such programs are really old-fashioned slide shows in new dress, and they may themselves enforce a "next-next-next" linearity upon the sermon even greater than the old three-point outlines. Even programs such as Prezi that are designed to overcome linearity do not fully do so. They may make the transitions between images more fluid and dynamic, but the "this-and-this-and–now-this" effect remains.

4. Less is often more.   This bit of wise lore comes from the pastor Adam Hamilton, who has much experience in the use of media in preaching. He writes:

> I have attended presentations where the philosophy of some seemed to be, "I have all this capability on my laptop and my video projector—I need to use it." The most effective speakers applied the principle: "Just because I can do this doesn't mean I should," or again, "Less is more."[3]

Should Sermons Have Titles? If So, What Kind?

Nowhere is it written in stone that sermons must have titles. Indeed, a great deal of distorted preaching has been generated by preachers assigning titles to sermons before the work on them is done (for the sake of posting on the website, in the church newsletter, or in the bulletin), only to find that careful exegesis of the biblical text demands that the sermon move in another direction. In a tug-of-war between a text and a previously announced title, the title almost always wins, and the sermon is the poorer for it.

Nevertheless, most sermons do have titles, and that means we need to think through the purpose of a title. Some people argue that titles have a semi-evangelistic purpose, since church wanderers and other seekers survey the Saturday newspaper for a tempting sermon title. I am dubious about that, but even if a small number of people scan the church ads for alluring titles, it would be unfortunate if preachers created glitzy sermon titles to snare curiosity seekers.

The main function of a title is to serve as an advance introduction to the sermon. When people read the title, they immediately begin guessing what the sermon will be about. Just like the regular sermon introduction, then, a sermon's title makes an implied promise. If we entitle a sermon "God's Answer to Suffering," we are promising nothing less than to supply that answer. Homer K. Buerlein, a lay critic of preaching, complains that some sermon titles tell too much. They don't make promises about the sermon; they "give the sermon away." Commenting on a title like "Practicing Christianity through Love of God and Humanity," Buerlein writes:

From that title, you know exactly what the preacher is going to say. You know, for instance, that a true Christian cannot love God without loving people, and vice versa. No doubt, numerous examples of each type of love will be present in the sermon.[4]

The best sermon titles, then, are probably those that orient people to the sermon and prepare them to be active listeners, without either promising too much or revealing too much of the sermon content. A simple title, like "Repentance" or "Learning to Forgive," is good, and so are titles that are intriguing yet honest, like William Muehl's "God Has No Pride"[5] or Ernest T. Campbell's "Locked in a Room with Open Doors."[6] Such titles create a sense of anticipation and readiness on the part of the hearers.

How Long Should a Sermon Be?

It is tempting to say that each sermon should be long enough to get its task done—no more, no less—but the matter is not that simple. Preaching is not just putting messages of various sizes into spoken form; preaching is ritual activity as well, and a ritual has its own internal pacing and timing. A sermon is an oral genre, and there are community expectations about its length. To illustrate, imagine that a neighbor runs into you on the street, opens the conversation by saying, "Got time for a good joke?" You are in the mood for a laugh and not in a hurry, so you nod your head, and the neighbor begins, "There were these two sailors on shore leave. . . ." An hour and a half later, the neighbor is still not finished telling the joke. Think how perplexed you would be. When you said you had time for this, you were expecting a brief, funny story. Now, there is no law stating that a joke cannot last for an hour—or a week, for that matter—but in our culture the oral genre called "joke" means a short, humorous story. Anyone who takes on the ritual role of joketeller must abide by those limits or suffer the consequences of listener mutiny.

Congregations have ritual expectations about the range of time a sermon should last. These expectations are the product of many forces, including their past experience with preaching, the specific nature of the service of worship, and the larger view of time in their culture. Some congregations expect a sermon to last only ten minutes; others expect forty-five minutes or an hour. If the preaching is too brief, the congregation will not perceive that they have heard a "real" sermon, regardless of its content. If the sermon far exceeds the expected length, the congregation will almost surely grow restless, will perhaps even shut down their listening altogether.

Preachers should take these congregational expectations seriously but not legalistically. Indeed, a congregation's ritual regarding preaching is strong but not inflexible. If, for example, the previous preacher was a person who did not value preaching very much and for twenty-five years presented two-minute "thoughts for the day" instead of sermons, we are not locked into that format even though the congregation has grown to expect it. If we choose to preach sermons of, say, eighteen or twenty minutes in length, we should not be surprised to receive some initial resistance, but the congregation will almost surely gradually adjust its expectations accordingly.

A different sort of problem is posed by the occasional sermon that falls outside the range of time expected by the hearers. Suppose we decide that a certain sermon needs an extra five minutes beyond the normal length. The chances are good that, if we simply preach that long without doing anything to prepare the congregation, they will find the extra time to be a struggle. We could, of course, announce at the beginning, "The sermon today will be a long one, so be prepared," but that would almost surely send up a groan and precipitate a sit-down strike. It is generally more effective to send a more subtle signal to the hearers that this sermon is an exception to the rule. Presumably, we have a good reason for making this particular sermon longer than usual, and, instead of merely warning them that "this will be a long one," we can offer the reason.

> In the Gospel lesson for today, Jesus told the rich ruler, "Sell all that you have and distribute it to the poor." Most of us would be happy to consider that command as applying to the ruler, but surely not to us. But is this so? Are we, too, commanded to "sell all"? What responsibility do we have toward our possessions? Those are not easy questions, and there are no easy answers. We will have to think carefully and deeply about them, and today, even more than usual, we will have to put on our thinking caps and look seriously at what our faith demands of us.

This preacher has said nothing about the length of the sermon, but a clear signal has been given that this sermon will be unusually demanding. This does not guarantee, of course, that the hearers will not become restless, but it does honestly inform them of the reason that this day's sermon will be extended.

Some homileticians believe that attention spans have been seriously eroded by television and that, as a result, sermons need to be briefer, more episodic, and more visually oriented. There is surely a measure of truth in this, but the destructive effects of the electronic media on preaching have probably been exaggerated. In fact, the shallowness of communication in our time generates a hunger for an urgent and important word. If our sermons begin to imitate the flip, superficial style of the media, we relinquish the great opportunity we have been given to speak that word.

Is It Effective to Get Out from behind the Pulpit and to Move Around among the Congregation?

As a piece of furniture, a pulpit can get in the way of communication. If it is too big, too high, or too remote, it can well hinder closeness and personal contact between the preacher and the hearers. Consequently, many preachers are leaving the pulpit behind and standing in the chancel or even moving around among the people as they preach.

While this strategy can bring the preacher closer to the people and make communication more immediate, there are several issues the preacher should consider before deciding to step out from behind the pulpit. First, the pulpit is not just a stand for notes or a screen to hide the preacher's legs (although there is practical worth there); it is a symbol of the presence of the word. To stand at the pulpit conveys an unspoken message, namely, "I am the temporary occupant of a venerable office to which I am committed and obedient." Most pastors would not administer the Lord's Supper away from the Table nor conduct baptism away from the pool or font, and we ought to consider the symbolic power of the pulpit.

Second, preachers tend to overestimate the value of physical closeness to the people. As Garrison Keillor of *Prairie Home Companion* fame once quipped, "A preacher is a person who engages in far more eye contact than people want." We sometimes forget the symbolic power we carry when we are preaching, and what seems like welcome vulnerability and intimacy to us may come across to hearers as a frightening intrusion, intimidation, or a transgression of private space.

Are Children's Sermons a Good Idea?

Some argue that children's sermons are the unfortunate result of a modern mentality that dotes on the cuteness of children. There is no more reason, the argument goes, to create a special sermon for children than there is to create one for people over sixty-five. Moreover, children's sermons tend to be banal, moralistic, and indulgent of some children's desire to perform in front of adults.

That is a harsh opinion but worth considering nonetheless. It is true that the ideal is to construct the whole of worship, including the sermon, in such a way that the entire congregation, including the children, can be involved in every element. This does not mean that the language of worship is reduced to a child's level but rather that the needs and capacities of children are taken into account throughout. A sermon, for example, can and should include some material that speaks to the world of children. The children in the congregation can participate directly in those portions of the sermon and listen more rhythmically and intuitively to other parts that are beyond their understanding. The practical problem is that this ideal is quite difficult to achieve.

Children represent perhaps the hardest group to incorporate into the full span of worship, and the best way to consider a children's sermon is as a frank admission of our failure to create genuinely multigenerational worship. So, yes, children's sermons are, for many congregations, a good idea, so long as they do not serve as a substitute for the continuing search for more embracing forms of worship. Moreover, special attention can be given to children in worship other than through a children's *sermon*. Indeed, it reinforces a misunderstanding about worship to imply that the sermon is the only crucial element. Including children's prayers, hymns, responses, or offerings, instead of only children's sermons, overcomes this narrowing of liturgical focus.

If we do decide to preach children's sermons, however, we should consider some cautions:

1. They should be real sermons: that is to say, they should be proc-
   lamations of the gospel and not lessons on conventional morality.
2. They should be addressed to the children, and not through the
   children to the overhearing adults.
3. We should not assume that children are a monolithic group.
   Cognitive abilities change rapidly during childhood, and there
   is no such thing as "speaking at the level of a child." There are
   many such levels. The widespread custom, for instance, of giving
   "object lessons" ("these eyeglasses, children, are like the Bible")
   depends on the child's capacity to think abstractly, an ability very
   young children simply do not have. Some children's sermons
   should just be the telling of stories, including Bible stories, without any attempt to make a point. Understanding a "point" again
   requires the capacity for abstract thought.
4. We should be cautious about the practice of asking open-ended
   questions of the children, not only because this sends their parents into anxiety but also because of the potential for embarrassing the child. A child's serious response may amuse the
   congregation, whose unexpected laughter can be perplexing or
   even frightening.

How Do We Handle the Dry Periods in Our Preaching?

Preachers inevitably experience periods of drought in their preaching,
times when sermons come even more painfully than usual and creativity ebbs. These times should neither surprise nor dismay us. In some
ways, the best counsel is to acknowledge that all preachers have them,
to expect them, and to allow them to run their course.

Many times, though, dry periods in our preaching signal empty
moments in our own growth in faith. The best response, then, is not to
fret about sermon technique but rather to set out in some new direction in our understanding of and commitment to the gospel. Some
preachers, when they sense that their preaching is losing vitality, set
themselves to the task of preaching a series of sermons on issues, doctrines, or biblical texts with which they are less familiar. This approach
forces them onto new ground, where they must read, study, wrestle,
and pray as they prepare to preach.

How Do We Get Out of Stylistic Ruts in Our Sermons?

If we are not careful and diligent, our sermons may begin to sound alike. We may find ourselves employing similar, and thus predictable, forms for every sermon or using characteristic formulas of speech. Some preachers almost always begin their sermons with a contemporary story; others overuse rhetorical questions as means for engaging the hearers ("So what does this ancient text have to say to us today?"); still others have their pet phrases ("dear friends," "peace and justice concerns," "spirit-filled Christians").

Because these patterns are ours and reflect the ways we think and speak, they are usually difficult to spot. Sometimes we can become aware of them by reviewing, several weeks after the fact, manuscripts or tapes of sermons that we have preached. The delay in time provides the sense of distance we need to cast a critical eye on our own work. Far better, though, is to ask some impartial observer with an editorial knack (generally a trusted friend or colleague outside of our congregation) to comb through a sample of our sermons looking for oft-repeated techniques and clichés of form and language. This can be a threatening exercise, of course, but the reward of vitality in our preaching is worth the risk.

Should We Balance Pastoral Sermons with Prophetic Ones?

Preachers recognize that some sermons are addressed more to personal needs and issues, while others apply more to public issues and the concerns of the larger society. They believe, accurately, that the Christian faith addresses both kinds of issues, and so they seek to keep their preaching in balance.

It would be a mistake, however, to make too sharp a distinction between "pastoral" and "prophetic" sermons, as if personal issues could be separated from their placement in the social context, and vice versa. The gospel does not speak to isolated individuals and then swivel to speak another word to the world of politics and social systems. The gospel speaks to the totality of human life, to people as they strive to be faithful among the many and complex interconnections of their lives.

In chapter 2 we learned that when preachers go to Scripture they take the people with them, and that what is heard in the text is affected by the circumstances of those who will hear the sermon. It is absolutely crucial that preachers understand that we are standing before Scripture on behalf of the people in the full realities of their lives—personal and political. Consider, for example, what one South African minister who worked, suffered, and preached eloquently against the government policy of apartheid heard when he listened, on behalf of his congregation, to the text in Revelation 13:11–18 that describes the beast that looks like a lamb but speaks like a dragon:

> It looks like a lamb, John warns, but it speaks like a dragon. It says peace! peace! where there is no peace. It speaks about reconciliation without the confrontation and the cost. The dragon which looks like a lamb is full of compassion for the anguish of the oppressor as he makes yet another "unavoidable" decision to kill the innocent. And yet it cannot hear the voice of God in the cries of the poor and the needy. It is the voice of those who believe that the sins of the church should be buried by history instead of confessed and forgiven. It is the voice of those who are so concerned about what may happen to white South Africans one day, after apartheid will have come to its inevitable end, that they show no concern at all about what is being done to black South Africans right now. It looks like a lamb, but its voice is the voice of a dragon. It is the voice that protests, even now, as the blood of our children stains the streets, "Apartheid is a Christian policy!" But the truth is out and cannot be suppressed: apartheid is not Christian; it is a blasphemy, an idolatry, and a heresy.[7]

Because of the place in history occupied by this preacher and his congregation, he heard the text speaking a true and powerful word against the oppressive powers of the government. This is clearly a political, prophetic word, but it is not a nonpastoral word. It is an inspiring, encouraging word to lift the hearts and nourish the souls of those who must live each day in the terrors of that situation.

Here is what a preacher in another context heard when he stood on behalf of the people before the parable of the Unforgiving Servant (Matt. 18:23–35):

We forget that sin is what you and I do, too. That we too owe a debt. Take a moment right now, and think back over just the past month in your life. Think about the times you have spoken sharply to your husband or wife or parent or child. Think about the things you have done you really don't want anybody else to know about. The things out of pure selfishness. Remember taking that shortcut at work? Enjoying somebody else's embarrassment [or] pain? And then multiply the month's failure by twelve for the months of the year and that again by the number of years in your life. And you begin to understand what Jesus meant by giving the unmerciful servant such an enormous, unmanageable debt.[8]

Now, this hearing of Scripture is admittedly far more inward and less sharply political than the word the South African preacher heard. The sermon portion is populated by images of personal analysis and self-reflection. And yet even here there are forces pushing beyond the merely private life of an individual into the more systemic worlds of family, work, and social responsibility.

So rather than arbitrarily dividing our preaching into pastoral and prophetic categories, we take the fullness of the life of the people into the encounter with Scripture and then tell the truth about what we hear. Sometimes our sermons will take a more pastoral tone, sometimes a more prophetic one, but these are not two distinct kinds of preaching. Even so, we must constantly guard against our inevitable tendency to silence the full witness of Scripture. For many of us—let us admit it— this means a tendency to force the gospel in personal, inward, and individualistic directions. Walter Brueggemann has written on this matter:

[A] tendency to which good preaching is opposed is a kind of subjectivity that assumes we are free or able to conjure up private worlds that may exist in a domesticated sphere without accountability to or impingement from the larger public world. Such a powerful deception among us seems to offer happiness, but it is essentially abdication from the great public issues that shape our humanness.[9]

What that means, among other things, is that even if we are preaching in a suburban context where the immediate concerns are job, home, school, and personal crises of one kind or another, we cannot pretend that we do not participate in the same world in which South Africans, Iraqis, Rwandans, and others live. We are involved in the struggles against the principalities and powers, both through our faithfulness and through our sinful cooperation with those forces of evil. We must take that circumstance with us as we go to the text, and then we must bear witness to the fullness of the gospel even though the cost be great.

A Parting Word on the Pilgrim Way

That which was from the beginning, which we have heard, which we have seen with our eyes, which we have looked upon and touched with our hands, concerning the word of life— the life was made manifest, and we saw it, and witness to it. (1 John 1:1–2)

Appendix A

"The Eye of the Storm"[1]

Edmund Steimle

A Christmas Eve Sermon on Luke 2:1–20

I think I shall never forget the time when Hurricane Hazel, back in the fifties, was sweeping through eastern Pennsylvania and hit Philadelphia, where we were living at the time, head on. Unlike most hurricanes, which lose much of their force when they turn inland, this one hit with all the fury of a hurricane at sea: drenching rains, screaming winds, trees uprooted, branches flying through the air, broken power lines crackling on the pavements. It was frightening. Then suddenly there was a letup, a lull. Shortly all was still. Not a leaf quivered. The sun even broke through briefly. It was the eye of the storm. "All was calm, all was bright." And then all hell broke loose again: branches and trees crashing down, the screaming winds, the torrential rain, the power lines throwing out sparks on the pavement. But that was a breathless moment—when we experienced the eye of the storm.

Christmas Eve is something like that, like the experience of the eye of the storm. At least the first Christmas night. So Luke reports: "And she gave birth to her first-born son and wrapped him in swaddling cloths, and laid him in a manger, because there was no place for them in the inn." The Christmas crèche and the Christmas pageantry picture it so today: "All was calm, all was bright."

Mary . . . resting now, after the pain of the contractions and the delivery without benefit of anesthetic. The child . . . sleeping peacefully in the swaddling cloths and the straw. At least we like to think him so. "Silent night, holy night." Of course, maybe his face was all contorted reds and purples with the frantic bleating of a newborn child, fists clenched, striking out at this new and strange environment after nine months in the warmth and security of the womb. But no. Let's picture him sleeping, exhausted perhaps from his frantic protests. "All is calm, all is bright. . . . Silent night, holy night." The eye of the storm.

For make no mistake, he comes at the center of a storm—both before and after the birth. The storm before: From devastation of a flood expressing the anger of God with a people whose every thought and imagination was evil, to his anger at the golden calf, to the destruction of Jerusalem and the Exile in Babylon, to Jonah desperately trying to run away from this God, to the narrow legalism of the Pharisees, to the oppression of the Roman occupation. He comes at the eye of the storm before.

And what followed this "silent night, holy night"? The storm after: the massacre of the innocent male children two years old and under by Herod in his frantic effort to deal with the threat of this child sleeping in the manger. And as he grew up, his family thought him a little bit nuts, his hometown neighbors threw him out of the synagogue when first he tried to preach. Then the sinister plots to do away with him, the angry mob crying for his blood on that first Good Friday, and the end? Death to the child.

What we tend to forget on Christmas is that these lovely stories of the birth—the manger, the shepherds, the angel chorus in the night sky, the wise men following the star and presenting their rare and expensive gifts—are not children's stories. If you think it takes children to make a Christmas, then you don't belong in church tonight. These are adult stories for adult Christians. Oh, let the children delight in them of course—and get out of them what they may. But they were written down by adult members of the early Christian community for other adult members of the Christian community.

Moreover, they are postresurrection stories, that is, they grew up in the tradition after the resurrection. Who knows where they came from? They came into being in the years following the resurrection as negro spirituals came into being, as mature Christians pondered the mystery of the beginnings of this life whom they had seen die and rise again from the dead. They knew about the storm which preceded the birth. And they knew even more—first hand—about the storm that followed. They were not carried away by "the romantic fantasies of the infancy." Like one standing in the eye of a hurricane, they were aware of the storm that went before and that followed.

And so tonight you and I come here, not wanting, I hope, to block out or forget the storms around us. Because if we do, we miss the whole point. We too are aware tonight of the storms which surround this "silent night, holy night."

We are aware of the confusion and destruction around us in the world. The violence in the Middle East, southern Africa, and Northern Ireland, the hunger in the Third World. Or closer to home, the muggings on the streets, the unemployment (a grim and passive kind of violence), the ghettos, the injustice to the blacks, the inner cities gutted by poverty and inflation and the massive indifference—sloth is the old-fashioned word for it—on the part of so many of us who do not live in the gutted inner cities. Moreover, we are aware of the precarious future which haunts all of us. People are dying this Christmas night as people die on every night. As one day, one night, you will die and I will die. And before that the inner loneliness which no one of us can entirely shake, and the specter of hopelessness which haunts us—for peace in the world, for the end of inflation, for families breaking up, for our nations as they drift along often so aimlessly, and for ourselves and our future.

The point is, we don't forget all this on Christmas Eve—or block it out. Like a person standing in the eye of a hurricane, we are aware of it all. If you want to forget it all tonight—OK! Go home and listen to Bing Crosby dreaming of a white Christmas. And there's a place for that—but not here!

For what other message on Christmas Eve is worth listening to? What peace? What hope? If it is simply a forgetting—when we can't forget, really—then we're reducing the Christmas story to a bit of nostalgia and indulging ourselves in the sentimental orgy which Christmas has become for so many, or we are reduced to the deep depression which grips so many others on Christmas Eve.

No. The Bible—praise God—tells it like it is. They saw the birth of the child as the eye of the storm—a peace which passes all understanding because it is not a peace apart from conflict, pain, suffering, violence, and confusion; that's the kind of peace we can understand all too well. But it's a peace like the peace in the eye of a hurricane, a peace smack in the middle of it all, a peace which indeed passes all understanding.

So in this hour, this night, worshiping at the manger of the child when "all is calm, all is bright," we rejoice in the hope born of the conviction that the storm, the destruction, the violence, the hopelessness, does not have the last word. But God—who gives us this "silent night" in the middle of the storm—he has the last word.

So rejoice . . . and sing the carols . . . and listen to the lovely ancient story and light the candles . . . and be glad—with your families, your friends, with the God who is above all and through all and in you all, who comes to us miraculously in this child, this night, when "all is calm, all is bright."

Appendix B

"The Lost and Found Department"

Barbara Brown Taylor

> Which one of you, having a hundred sheep and losing one of
> them, does not leave the ninety-nine in the wilderness and go
> after the one that is lost until he finds it? When he has found it,
> he lays it on his shoulders and rejoices.
>
> Luke 15:4–5

You could call the fifteenth chapter of Luke "the gospel within the gospel." Beginning with the parables of the lost sheep and the lost coin, and ending with Luke's story about the prodigal son, it is good news all the way. Everything that was lost is found. The lost sheep is returned to the flock, the lost coin is recovered by its owner, the lost son is restored to his father, and the parties go on all night long. God's talent for finding us proves greater than our talent for getting lost, and there is joy in heaven as well as on earth.

We love these stories because we imagine ourselves on the receiving end of them. I listen to the parable of the lost sheep and it is about *me*. I am the poor, tuckered-out lamb, draped across my dear redeemer's shoulders so full of gratitude and relief that I vow never to wander away from him again. Or I am the silver coin, lying in some dark corner of the universe until the good woman who will not give up on me sweeps me into the light. They are stories about me, and I treasure them, but in their original context they sounded like anything but good news to their hearers.

At the beginning of the fifteenth chapter, Jesus is criticized for the third time by the Pharisees for spending his days with sinners—lepers, tax collectors, women of the night—and not only for talking with them, but for eating with them as well, in open defiance of Jewish dietary laws. Not content with dining in their unclean homes, he has gone beyond the pale by "receiving" them—returning their hospitality and receiving them as any host would receive a guest. The sinners, needless to say, are fascinated by his treatment of them. Whatever this man has to say, they want to hear more. They draw near to him, while the scribes and Pharisees choke on their rage.

From a modern perspective, it is hard to see what the fuss is all about. Jesus the good shepherd is just doing his job. Jesus the good housekeeper is just making sure every corner has been swept, and my democratic heart goes out to all the unfortunate souls whose lives he touches. Then again, I tend to imagine good old-fashioned sinners. What is so awful about a tax collector, after all? Or a hooker with a heart of gold? Nothing, if this is a nostalgic story about the past. But if it is to bear the weight of the present and the future, then it deserves better treatment.

It deserves real characters, for one thing, real Pharisees and real sinners brought face-to-face with a real Jesus. I do not know how they look to you, but I imagine Jesus down at the plasma bank on Boulevard, standing in line with the hungover men waiting to sell their blood, or maybe down at the city jail shooting the breeze with the bail bondsmen who cruise the place like vultures. I imagine him at the Majestic Diner on Ponce de Leon Avenue with a crack dealer, a car thief, a prostitute with AIDS, buying them all cheese omelettes when I come in with the sixth-grade confirmation class and sit down a couple of booths away.

I imagine the kids getting a load of this and then beginning to ask me questions: "Is that who we think it is?" or "How come you warn us to stay away from people like that and there he is?" Then I imagine myself saying something to them about how those who are well do not need a physician or about how the good shepherd cares more for the one than for the ninety-nine, but the words get stuck in my throat. I could tell them this morning's parables, I suppose, but I am afraid they might get the message: that to be lost is to be precious in the sight of God, and that their good behavior rates less joy in heaven than the alleged repentance going on at that nearby table. How do you tell kids something like that? It is like telling them to get lost.

That is how it sounds to the scribes and Pharisees, anyhow. They are God-fearing believers, devoted disciples who do not merely talk about the life of faith. They live it, giving God's law their full respect and scrupulous obedience. It is not an easy life, but they are willing to live it because they mean to set an example. They mean to offer a healthy alternative to the ways of the world, showing people it is both possible and pleasing to live according to God's will.

They are not uninterested in sinners, but they believe that the best way to help them is to hold up a high standard, inviting them to achieve it and letting them know where they fall short, until finally they are challenged to become the best they can be. Some people have what it takes and some, tragically, do not, but there is nothing to be gained by mixing the two. It is the kind of message that appeals to people. It makes the rules clear and rewards those who obey them, admitting the winners to the ranks of the educated, the employed, the righteous, and sending the losers back to try, try again. They each stick with their own kind and they know who they are. The righteous know that they give heaven reason to rejoice and the sinners know that they grieve the heart of God, if God knows or cares who they are at all.

Then Jesus comes along and starts messing around with the system, treating sinners like special cases and making them think they are as important as other people. He socializes with them, which is as good as condoning their behavior, and thereby robs them of their motivation to do better. Why should they buy anything from the Pharisees that Jesus is giving away for free? All they have to do is wander off from the flock, pursuing their own whims, and the good shepherd will go off after them, leaving the ninety-nine to fend for themselves. It is not only bad shepherding; it is bad pastoral care. It is bad theology. If you receive sinners and admonish the righteous—when the system is clearly set up to work the other way around—then what will happen to the community of faith? What about the good people? What about us?

These two parables are full of problems, not least of which is that they do not seem to mean what Jesus says they mean. According to his explanations, they are about heaven's joy over one repentant sinner, but the lost sheep does not repent as far as I can tell and the lost coin certainly doesn't. They are both simply found—not because either of them does anything right, but because someone is determined to find them and does. They are restored thanks to God's action, not their own, so where does repentance come in at all?

Three possibilities occur to me. First, that Jesus was just making it all up as he went along and got his wires a little crossed. The stories mean what he says they mean and we should not get hung up on the details. Second, that Jesus told the stories exactly as we have them and was content to let us figure them out for ourselves, but that their open-endedness made his editors so anxious that the explanations were added later so that we would not, um, misunderstand them. Third, that they are not parables about lost sheep and lost coins at all, but parables about good shepherds and diligent sweepers.

"Which one of you," Jesus says, "having a hundred sheep . . ." He is not inviting the Pharisees to imagine themselves sheep but to imagine themselves shepherds, leaving their carefully tended flock in order to chase one stray through the wilderness. Isn't it interesting the way we listen to parables like this one and can always find some way to wind up on the sheep's end of things instead of the shepherd's?

If you are willing to go with the third possibility—if you are willing to be a shepherd—then the story begins to sound different. The accent in what Jesus says falls on a different syllable. Repentance is not the issue, but rejoicing; the plot is not about amending our evil ways but about seeking, sweeping, finding, rejoicing. The invitation is not about being rescued by Jesus over and over again but about joining him in rounding up God's herd and recovering God's treasure. It is about questioning the idea that there are certain conditions the lost must meet before they are eligible to be found, or that there are certain qualities they must exhibit before we will seek them out. It is about trading in our high standards on a strong flashlight and swapping our "good examples" for a good broom. It is about discovering the joy of finding.

A few summers ago, my husband Ed and I went on a ten-day hike in the wilderness with fifteen other people and a trip leader, none of whom we knew ahead of time. We were a motley crew from all over the United States, and as the days passed it became apparent that all walkers are not created equal. Some of us charged ahead while others of us lagged behind, and while we encouraged one another along, we soon learned that we could only travel as fast as our slowest member.

Her name was Pat. She was the eldest member of the group, and the heaviest, and the most unpleasant. She liked to walk alone at the rear of the group, which was just as well, since she had an irritating habit of listening in on other people's conversations and then breaking in to correct their grammar, geography, history, botany, or any of the other subjects about which she knew so much. She liked a full hour for lunch and threatened to be sick if she were rushed. Most of the spots our trip leader picked to stop were too sunny, or too wet, or too steep for her, but she would plunk herself down anyway and announce that she would "make do."

Around the fifth day out we got good and lost, walking for close to ten hours over three mountains before we made camp. When we arrived—after dark, in the rain, in the middle of nowhere—Pat was not with us. We compared notes and discovered that no one had seen her since noon, when she had thrown rocks at the person assigned to bring up the rear of the group and told him to leave her alone.

Delighted, he had complied, but that meant no one had seen her for almost eight hours. We were all trembling with exhaustion and soaked to the bone; no one could even imagine heading back up the last mountain in order to find her. But it was the trip leader's job, so he did it. Armed with hot soup, a jacket, and a first-aid kit, he disappeared into the dark while the rest of us milled around, trying to stay away from the idea of what it would be like to be lost in the wilderness without a match or a map or a friend.

We paced and dozed until close to midnight, when Pat stumbled into camp hanging on to her shepherd. Those of us who had despised her at noon fell all over her in the dark, petting her and hugging her and welcoming her home, pressing mugs of hot chocolate into her hands and oatmeal cookies into her pockets. No one thought to ask her if she was going to be a nicer person from now on, or whether she had learned her lesson. We were too glad to have her back. Imagining her out there in the dark, we had all felt more than a little lost ourselves, so finding her was as good as being found.

Pat acted rather nonchalant about the whole thing, if you ask me, but the next morning she was up and dressed and on the trail before any of us, and from that day on she was part of the flock. Not everybody's favorite member, by any means, but part of the flock. Maybe it was getting lost that changed her—although she denied even a moment's fear during her ordeal—but then again, maybe it was being found that did the trick. Maybe it was our welcome home that made the difference, that convinced her she was part of the flock, but at any rate it was hard to separate her repentance from ours, or the repentance from the rejoicing. We all kept better track of each other from then on, and took turns walking with Pat, who surprised everyone by bursting into song one night and leading us all in a medley of old camp tunes.

Maybe some of us are destined to be shepherds and others of us to be lost sheep, but when I am working so hard to find and stay found, it is difficult not to judge those who seem to capitalize on staying lost. I want to believe that they are not merely lost people, but that they are bad people, because then I could write them off and save myself some grief. I want to concentrate on the good people, the ones who want to be found, or who are busy finding others. I think about heaven ignoring those good folks in favor of one sinner who finally says, "I'm sorry," and I want to sue God for mercy.

Then I hear someone behind me who calls me by my name, and big brown hands grab me by the scruff of the neck, hauling me through the air and laying me across a pair of shoulders that smell of sweet grass and sunshine and home, and I am so surprised, and so relieved to be *found* that my heart feels like it is being broken into, broken open, while way off somewhere I hear the riotous sound of the angels rejoicing.

Appendix C

"Why Bother?"

Cleophus J. LaRue

Acts 17:16–23

Splattered across the front doors of a trendy restaurant in Palo Alto, California, were these words: "This is a bad place for a diet!" That most visible, in-your-face warning suggested to me that there are certain places where some requests are out of order and certain times where some appeals are in poor taste. No matter how noble, how worthy, how life-giving they are in and of themselves, there are certain times and certain places where it is simply unseemly to speak of some things.

In like manner it appears to me that we could splatter across the pages of our text this day a similar warning: This is a bad place for the gospel. Whether one regards

Introduction:
Interestingly, the sermon begins with an "analogy-style" illustration (see the discussion of this style in chapter 8). The restaurant in Palo Alto, which advertises itself as "a bad place for a diet," is analogous to first-century Athens, which is presented as "a bad place for the gospel."

In addition to naming a basic theme that will run through the whole of the sermon, namely that the proclamation of the gospel must often be performed in trying circumstances (see the discussion of the purpose of sermon introductions in chapter 7), this introduction also creates a bit of suspense in the sermon. The

Acts as a bona fide historiography or simply a piece of well-crafted Hellenistic literature, the gospel in Athens comes off sounding like a bunch of misguided, out-of-place "hooey."

listener wonders, "What does he mean? How was Athens a bad place for the gospel?" and the listener waits to hear what the preacher will say about that.

***Connector** (silent)*
The sermon has been introduced and the preacher is about to go into Move #1. This is a place where the sermon takes a turn and where often a "connector" would be inserted (see the discussion of "Connectors" in chapter 7). LaRue could have said "How was Athens a bad place for the gospel?" or "In the first place, Athens was a bad place for the gospel because. . . ." But instead of a verbal connector, LaRue simply pauses slightly. He is wagering here that the hearers already have the question hanging in the air, "And how is Athens a bad place for the gospel?" thus eliminating the need for the preacher to verbalize it as a connector. If he's right, a pause works fine to mark this turn.

Athens had seen and heard it all. In Paul's day, this once great and proud city was still considered the cultural and intellectual capital of the Roman Empire. It was a city steeped in art, literature, and learning. Of longstanding it had its names and its heroes and thus was not easily impressed by the new

Move # 1
LaRue plans to lay out three reasons why Athens was a bad place for the gospel. Here in Move # 1, we get the first one, namely that Athens had heard and seen it all, and, therefore, it was not likely to be impressed by the "upstart Christian gospel."

or the now. It was the place where Socrates, Aristotle, and Plato had lived and taught. And still counted among its sacred places was the Academy of Plato, the Lyceum of Aristotle, the porch of Zeno the Stoic, and the garden of Epicurus. The voices of her poets had been heard throughout the civilized world and the hands of her artists had filled her streets and temples with images of the gods. It was said of Athens that while strolling her streets you were more likely to meet a god than you were a man or a woman. Her myriad buildings and works of art stood in silent testimony to her former glory and grandeur. Even though Luke goes to great lengths to create for us this scene where Paul is standing face-to-face with the philosophers in their own town and on their own turf, the upstart Christian gospel still comes off as out of place. It just doesn't seem to fit in Athens. The gospel seems to be out of its league in Athens. Athens is a bad place for the gospel.

The gospel seems all the more misplaced when one considers . . .

Notice how he starts this Move with a topic sentence, "Athens had seen and heard it all," which names the theme and sets the listeners' compass bearings for what is to follow in this Move.

Notice also how the Move closes with the phrase, "Athens was a bad place for the gospel." This is, of course, the theme named in the Introduction and the theme being elaborated in this whole swath of the sermon. LaRue is skillfully marking the end of the Move and keeping the listeners on track, helping them to follow the flow of the sermon.

Connector
Here LaRue announces, with a Connector, that the sermon is about to go to Move # 2. Notice how he does this. When he says, "The gospel seems all the more misplaced. . . ," the sermon advances both forward and downward. It

advances forward because this Connector indicates that, having heard reason # 1 for why Athens was "a bad place for the gospel," we are now about to hear reason # 2. This Connector advances the sermon downward because it uses the qualifying phrase "all the more. . . ." In other words, LaRue tells the hearers that reason # 2 doesn't merely provide another click in the ratchet; it also increases then tension and intensifies the downward argument about why Athens is not a good place for the gospel.

. . . how Paul got to Athens in the first place. Athens is a temporary stopover. He did not arrive there by way of some well-thought out missionary plan, but he arrived there through happenstance and rerouting born of necessity because the work God had called him to do had not gone well in other places; it had not gone as he had prayed or planned. He arrived in Athens not on a set schedule but on a wing and a prayer trying to rearrange what unforeseen circumstance had wrought. He does not enter the city fresh and friendly but he enters disheveled, unkempt, bedraggled, woebegone, battle-scarred and road weary. And because he is already

Move # 2
Here LaRue names the second reason why Athens was not the best place for the gospel, namely the happenstance way that the gospel arrived in town. It arrived on a "wing and prayer" and was represented by a "road weary" evangelist.

in a bad mood, he is immediately repulsed by what he sees. He does not see a city filled with beautiful works of art, but rather a city full of idols.

Yes, he probably could have been in a better mood. And, yes, he probably would have been better received had he feigned some initial aesthetical appreciation for the works of art he found in the home of Hellenism's literati and intelligentsia. But when you've been stoned in Lystra, jailed in Philippi, threatened in Thessalonica, and hounded out of Boreoa, it is understandable that you might not be in a sightseeing mood when your friends finally drop you on the outskirts of Athens.

May I say here parenthetically, brothers and sisters in the faith, that sometimes we do our best work under life's most austere and trying circumstances. We do our best work when life is hard and the load is heavy, our best work when life finds us in a situation where we would prefer not to be and hope not long to stay. Like Paul, when life finds you there, do not bemoan your plight, but lift up your head and your heart and go forward with the work God has assigned you to do.

Sermon Parenthesis

Here LaRue momentarily halts the steady march forward of the sermon in order to make a parenthetical comment. In one sense, this parenthesis doesn't technically belong in the sermon. Observing that "sometimes we do our best work under life's most austere circumstances" is a pastoral insight that doesn't quite follow at this point in the sermon. The preacher is stepping off the sermon path to pause and to offer a bit of wisdom. However, we don't yet know the destination of this sermon, but when we get there we will realize that, in this parenthetical comment, LaRue has given a foreshadowing of the sermon's ending.

So Paul ends up in Athens, not through some grand plan, but through happenstance. Even in the face of the uncertainty, tension, and anxiety that crowd his existence, he continues to press his case for the gospel of Jesus Christ. But his arguing and preaching are not well received in Athens. When the people of Athens first heard Paul speak, they asked with some derision and not a little contempt, "What does this babbler want to say?" What does this seed picker, this one who picks up just enough of an argument to speak about it in a superficial manner, what does he have to say? In Athens God's international gospel globetrotter, our first theologian, and the greatest preacher this side of Jesus Christ, comes off sounding like an outgunned pipsqueak taking on a fight he must surely know he cannot win.

Even when invited to address the Aeropagus court his speech/sermon does not go well. After that powerful sermon about the unknown God, there were no mass conversions and no triumphalist claims of victory. The word Luke chose to describe the impact

Move 3
In the Move, LaRue gives the third reason why Athens is a bad place for the gospel: even the first string Christian evangelist couldn't dent it. Here is Paul, "our first theologian, and the greatest preacher this side of Jesus Christ," and even he met with derision.

of Paul's preaching in Athens was not "all" or "many" but "some." Luke said "some" scoffed, others said we will hear you again, but "some" believed.

He's in hoity-toity Athens, he did not intend to be there, he is not in a good mood, he is not well received, his preaching is so-so. The question just jumps out at you—Why Bother? Why put yourself through this, Paul? These people are not interested in hearing the gospel. This is a bad place for the gospel. You are just spinning your wheels trying to get them to see life from God's point of view. Why don't you leave these high-faluting, know-it-all Athenians alone and go on to Corinth where you might be appreciated?

But do not give up so quickly, for there is some good news in the Athens experience . . .

Connector

Here we have an example of an extended and rather elaborate Connector. So far we have been given three strong and cumulative reasons why Athens is a bad place for the gospel, and now the sermon is about to change direction.

Notice that the first thing this Connector does is to reprise these three reasons: Athens is "hoity-toity," Paul didn't plan to be there and he's in a bad mood, and his preaching was poorly received. LaRue sums up the distance the sermon has traveled with the the question, "Why bother?" But the work of this Connector is not just to sum up where the sermon has been, it also signals where the sermon is about to go. Thus far, the sermon has been moving in a negative direction—down, down, down—but now it is about to take a major pivot upward. With the words, "But do not give up so quickly, for there is some good news in the Athens experience . . . ," the hearers are put on notice that the sermon is making a major change in direction, and a hopeful one at that.

Running like a thread throughout the Luke-Acts schema is the notion of a universal offer of salvation. It was begun by the Messiah who preached good news to the poor and outcast of his day and picked up by his prophetic successors. Thus in Acts the gospel is proclaimed to poor widows and proconsuls, to jailers and sailors, merchants and military officers, kings and philosophers. Even in unreceptive Athens, the message is clear: The gospel is to be preached to all! Paul has to preach in undesirable places, under less than ideal circumstances, and so do we because of God's universal offer of salvation.

The gospel is to be proclaimed to all even if only received by some. I sometimes worry that those who consider themselves most faithful in our day seem the least sure about the universal appeal of the gospel. I worry that those who consider themselves to be the lone inheritors of the Christian witness seem the most determined to turn this gospel to some truncated, privatized religious hope palatable only to the few and the feeble-minded.

The gospel is to be proclaimed to all. We can all say that when ministry finds us in Jerusalem on the day of Pentecost where thousands of souls are added to the

Move 4

In this rather long Move, LaRue draws upon his exegesis of his biblical text from Acts, as seen in the context of the whole sweep of Luke-Acts. He sees his text participating in a major theological theme in those documents, namely the universal offer of salvation in Jesus Christ, and, in particular, that "the gospel is to be proclaimed to all even if only received by some." LaRue announces that it is the hearers who are called to be the proclaimers of this gospel. In addition to advancing the flow of the sermon, this Move also has the value of anchoring the sermon explicitly in the authority of the biblical text. The idea that a single sermon text should be viewed in larger context and tested theologically is discussed in chapter 3, specifically in steps "E" and "I" of the Basic Exegetical Process.

church, but the true challenge is to say it when ministry finds us on the hard streets of a disinterested Athens. Somebody's got to go to Athens where they look at you strange and dismiss you out of hand, where they laugh at you to your face and lie on you quick, fast, and in a hurry. Somebody has to speak the good news in a bad place.

This gospel is to be proclaimed to all. It has universal appeal and power. It's not up to us to enforce it or to effect it. We are to tell it. The power is not in us, but in God. Some of us act as if we do not trust the gospel to work its way through tough situations. But be it Athens or Jerusalem the gospel is to be proclaimed to all.

That is what we are to do, tell the good news of what God has done for us in Jesus Christ, the good news of the coming reign of God, the good news of the power of the gospel to change and transform lives even in this 21st century. It is to be proclaimed to all, even if only received by some.

Granted . . .

Connector
Here is a one-word connector. LaRue drops his voice and inflects it with a bit of a worried tone when he says the word "granted." This signals to the listeners that, once again, the sermon is changing direction. He is about to spend

a Move anticipating an objection that might be in the listeners' minds about the hopeful turn made in the previous Move.

... it's going to be more difficult to get a hearing in this day because we all live in a time of what Microsoft researcher Linda Stone calls CPA—continuous partial attention. Owing to modern technology we can answer email, talk to the children, and hold a conversation on our cell phones at the same time with no one thing fully claiming our attention. It will be more difficult to get a hearing now because very little fully claims our attention.

It will be more difficult now because a recent publication on the proliferation of fast food in America confirmed what many of us suspected all along: that the McDonald Golden Arches have now replaced the Christian cross as the more widely recognizable symbol in the world. "Just As I Am" has been replaced by you deserve a break today. It will be more difficult now because of the many implications of the postmodern era with its dismissal of metanarratives and its debunking of truth with a capital T.

But . . .

Move 5
In this Move, LaRue describes some of the resistance that the gospel receives in our own time and culture. By doing so, he sets up a tacit symmetry between ancient Athens, which was "a bad place for the gospel," and our own setting.

Connector
Here is another one-word Connector—But . . . See how much

is accomplished, however, by this single word. After starting an upward sweep with Move 4, the sermon dipped downward again in Move 5. The word "But" placed here not only halts that downward movement but also signals that the sermon is about to move upward again—which is exactly what happens in the next Move.

Move 6 and Ending
This is not only the next Move in the sermon; it is also the last Move of the sermon, that is, this is the Ending (see the discussion of Endings in chapter 7). The preacher has asserted throughout the cumulative development of this sermon that the gospel is to be proclaimed to all, even if it is only received by some, and that the hearers are the ones called to do this proclaiming. The function of this whole sermon, as we shall see, is to encourage the hearers in this call, and that is what this Ending Move seeks to do.

Notice how what was named as a parenthetical statement earlier in the sermon, and which seemed at the time to be off-topic, now re-emerges as a part of this Ending Move.

Notice also the rhythmic phrases in the last paragraph—"born in Bethlehem, brought up in Nazareth, baptized in the Jordan," etc.

. . . tell it we must, for there is power in the telling of that old, old story. Too oft times we want to be deep and profound in our telling, but I encourage seminarians just to get the basic story straight. For there is power, wonder-working power in the telling of that old Story of the Crucified One.

Tell them of Jesus Christ, tell them that he was born in Bethlehem, brought up in Nazareth, baptized in the Jordan, tempted in the wilderness, preached in Galilee, was arrested in Gethsemane, tried in Caesar's court, died on Calvary's cross, and rose from Joseph's tomb. Tell it! Tell it when you are up and tell it when you are down. Tell it when all is well and tell it when all is hell. Tell it when you are well received, and tell it when you are absolutely not believed. Tell it until sinners are justified. Tell it until hell is terrified. Tell it until Jesus is magnified. And tell it until God is satisfied. Amen.

> *This feature is known, especially in African American preaching, as a "run," and part of the rhetorical power of a run is to underscore an affective appeal.*

Having made our way through this superb sermon all the way to the end, we are now in a position to look back on the sermon and name the Focus and the Function (for a discussion of Focus and Function, see chapter 5) and to see the overall design, or Form (for a discussion of Form, see chapters 5 and 6):

Focus: Because the gospel is universal, we are called to proclaim it to "all," even when it is resisted, rejected, and received by only "some."

Function: To encourage the hearers in the call to be proclaimers of the gospel to all people, regardless of the circumstances.

Form: *Why Bother?*

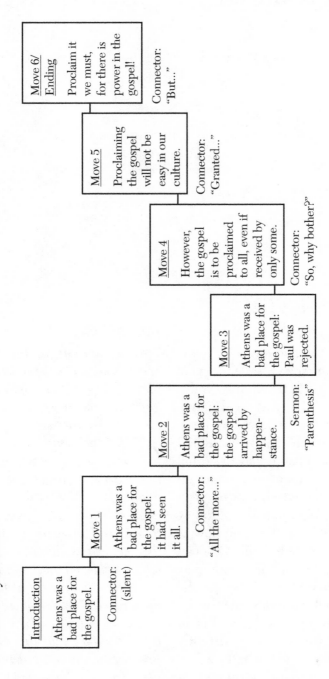

Introduction

Athens was a bad place for the gospel.

Connector: (silent)

Move 1

Athens was a bad place for the gospel: it had seen it all.

Connector: "All the more…"

Move 2

Athens was a bad place for the gospel: the gospel arrived by happen-stance.

Sermon: "Parenthesis"

Move 3

Athens was a bad place for the gospel: Paul was rejected.

Connector: "So, why bother?"

Move 4

However, the gospel is to be proclaimed to all, even if received by only some.

Connector: "Granted…"

Move 5

Proclaiming the gospel will not be easy in our culture.

Connector: "But…"

Move 6/ Ending

Proclaim it we must, for there is power in the gospel!

Appendix D

Special Effects

Ginger E. Gaines-Cirelli

Acts 2:1–21

"Forget the Church, Follow Jesus." That was the theme of a *Newsweek* cover story[1] several years ago. The story, by Andrew Sullivan, makes plenty of good points about the ways the so-called "institutional church" has been sullied by all sorts of bad behavior. You'll find no argument from me on that. But the notion that one can "forget the church and just follow Jesus" struck me then and now as being just a little too glib. One can reasonably argue that Jesus may not have had in mind the specific institutional varieties of church that we see or experience. But in the scriptures Jesus consistently calls people to "come and see," to "follow," and to do the things that

Introduction
This sermon beginning is clear, even though it is somewhat complex. The preacher applies several layers of meaning, one after the other, to get the sermon going.

The first layer consists of the somewhat startling opening words: "Forget the church, follow Jesus." At this point, the hearers can only assume that this is the preacher's view, and this generates genuine, if somewhat perplexed, interest. Does the preacher really want us to "forget the church?" We're all ears!

Then Gaines-Cirelli lets us in on the fact that this is not the preacher's opinion but instead an idea from a Newsweek *author.*

310

he himself did. Jesus creates a community by calling people and sending people and sharing life with people. Jesus, as a practicing Jew and itinerant Rabbi, lived and taught within the "organized religion" of the day and participated in the life of the Temple. He railed against the injustices being practiced within his religious tradition, but he did not abandon it. To follow Jesus inherently involves being in community— not only because this is the model set for us by the man himself, but also because when Jesus left we were given the work to carry on— to be Jesus' hands and feet and voice—Christ's body—on earth. That is simply not something that we can do alone. To be the Body of Christ, requires the myriad gifts that each of us bring.

The second layer of meaning is to give this idea from the magazine writer due consideration. The writer, says Gaines-Cirelli, has some "good points," and the fact that the institutional church has been sullied gets "no argument" from the preacher.

But after a moment of agreement, the preacher then turns to make a protest. The "forget the church, follow Jesus" idea is "a little too glib," and it doesn't take into account that Jesus himself lived within the "organized religion" of his day and did, in fact, create a community of people who are called and sent to carry on his own mission.

In sum, then, the preacher has raised a provocative question: should we forget the church or not? She has stated her own view but acknowledged that the question has two sides. This Introduction has guided us into the rest of the sermon, which is an attempt to answer this opening question.

It is tempting sometimes to "forget the church," as promulgated by the *Newsweek* piece . . .

Connector

In the Introduction, the preacher has already stated her conviction that the church is necessary. But now she invites the hearers to enter into a reflective debate with her own view. This Connector marks that reflective turn. It signals that the sermon is now going

After all, the church *is* a "broken, compromised, human organization." But who here today isn't at least a little bit compromised or broken? "As the old joke runs, I would like to find and then join the perfect church, but as soon as I join it, it will be imperfect." There is a story told about G. K. Chesterton that the *London Times* once sent out an inquiry to famous authors, asking the question, "What's wrong with the world today?" and Chesterton responded simply,

> "Dear Sir, I am. Yours,
> G.K. Chesterton."[2]

As flawed as the church is, we do well to remember that Jesus is clear that the mission is to be a healing and saving station for the sick and broken, not a trophy case for the strong and righteous. And thanks be to God—since that means that people like me and you can fit in here. We, all of us, are drawn into this messy reality of community in Christ. And it is in this context that we are offered healing grace and given opportunities—often because of the messiness of the church—to practice

to step back and to admit that the "forget the church" attitude is indeed "tempting."

Move 1

This Move embodies the debate mode in that it speaks in two voices, or perhaps in the one voice of a divided mind. In the opening sentence of the Move, the first voice speaks: "Yeah, we should forget the church because it is indeed a 'broken, compromised, human organization.'"

But then, the second voice begins to speak, saying, "But wait . . . , yes, it is true the church is broken, but so are we!" Jesus always intended the community of faith to be "a saving station for the sick and broken." Only in a community like this can we be truly included and "fit in." Only in a community like this can we be given grace and be challenged to practice being more human.

being more and more human, patient, generous, brave. We practice here so that we can manage it elsewhere once in a while.

Connector (silent)
The sermon is about to take a turn here. The preacher is ready to enter a second phase of the internal debate she has established between her own position and that of the Newsweek writer. She could have used a formal Connector here to signal this turn in the road, something like, "There's another angle on this to consider." But since this internal debate has a soliloquy-like quality, Gaines-Cerilli chooses not to insert a formal Connector but instead to pause slightly to mark the shift in the inner debate.

Students of systems theory will know that any organization is deeply affected by the conditions, personalities, and actions of the founding leader or group. That is to say, what happens in the beginning imprints itself upon the proverbial DNA of the community for years to come—for better or for worse. This is good news in our case, because even in the midst of all the brokenness of the institutional church, we are assured today that we have good DNA. Because what we know as the church

Move 2
In Move 1, the preacher began an inner debate over the issue of whether we should "forget the church" or not. In that first Move, the structure of the debate went from the negative (i.e., the church is broken, so forget it") to the positive (i.e., but that brokenness is actually a good thing for us broken people. Don't forget the church!). In Move 2, however, the order is reversed. Now the preacher will go from the positive (i.e., because of Jesus, the church has inclusion

started within the context of the covenant relationship between God and Israel, was renewed and reformed through the person and work of Jesus Christ, and then enlivened and embodied through the outpouring of the Holy Spirit. Not bad as "founding pastors" go! The church has full inclusion in its DNA, because when the promised Spirit appears in our story today, folks from "every nation under heaven" are there and Joel's prophecy, used by Peter to interpret the event, specifically speaks of women and men, young and old, and of "slaves"—those who would be understood to be on the margins of society. Upon "all flesh" the Spirit of the Lord falls. And when the Spirit is poured out into receptive people, signs and wonders happen. People speak and are understood, hear and understand one another. The thing that divided them is overcome. Unity happens—a unity that defies all human understanding. This is in our DNA . . .

In light of this, the brokenness of the church and of the world seems even more discouraging. After all, it has been more than 2000 years since all this went down and we still have the long list of broken places, exclusion, and radical disunity. A deeply broken justice system, racial and ethnic

in its DNA. This is what the Pentecost story is all about. The Spirit falls on "all flesh.") to the negative (i.e., this is all the more reason to be discouraged. 2000 years later, the church still goes against its DNA. So, "forget the church."

divides, Muslims and Christians killing each other in Nigeria, Israel and Palestine locked in a seemingly endless conflict, ISIS exploiting every possible religious tension, churches everywhere continuing to fight over who is "in" and who is "out" while thousands get fed up and say, "forget the church."

Connector (silent)

This is an important moment in the sermon, and, therefore, a crucial place in the structure of the sermon. Remember, over the last two Moves, the preacher has engaged in an inner debate between her own theological view of the church and the real temptation to agree with the Newsweek writer and to throw up our hands in discouragement about the church. She has skillfully constructed that debate, going from negative to positive, then riding the positive for a while, only to come crashing down to the negative again. So, after the first two Moves, the hearers are left with a discouragement about the church, a discouragement shared by the preacher. What now?

The preacher is going to make a fascinating theological turn right at this point, and that turn needs to be signaled by a strong Connector. It could have been a formal one, something like, "So, here we are this morning, in church. But we are tempted to say, 'Forget the church!' What are we supposed to do?" But Gaines-Cirelli has chosen to make this Connector a silent one, a pause in the delivery. When no words are spoken at a major juncture in the sermon, the silence should be filled with other indications that the sermon is changing directions. The pause should be longer than usual, and the preacher's body should turn slightly, in this case to signal that we are moving out of the soliloquy mode and the inner debate about the question and on to action.

As a Christian pastor, I must admit that there are times when I find myself tempted to believe that it is up to me to fix the church. I come by this temptation honestly, living as we all do in a culture permeated with what I call the "I can do all things (without Christ or anyone else)" bug. I can self-help my way to a brighter future . . . I can get what I want if I just work hard enough . . . I can save myself . . . Individualism and self-sufficiency permeate everything. In addition, we have created amazing technologies that can make us feel like we can do anything, control anything, fix anything. I am told it is possible

Move 3
In this Move, the preacher shares that she has the impulse to try to "fix the church." The implication, of course, is that the hearers may also have this impulse as well.

to experience virtually anything "virtually." Maybe this is why it is so tempting to think that we can control or create any reality that we desire.

Every year in my worship planning, I catch myself wanting to make Pentecost happen . . . to create the special effects—you know—the sound of a mighty rushing wind, maybe with one of those giant fans at the back of the sanctuary—and to light enough candles to set the place on fire . . . and then I realize that scenario wouldn't happen . . . they're kind of mutually exclusive . . . And then I realize that the special effect that I *really* want to create is not so much the stuff that Hollywood can produce—those effects like wind and fire. What I really want to create are the real miracles of Pentecost:

- All people receiving the gifts of the Holy Spirit— regardless of age, gender, race, orientation, or anything else—and those gifts leading them to see God's vision and to dream God's dream . . .
- People who are REALLY different speak in ways that are not only heard but understood

Move 4
Move 4 is an Example-style illustration (see the discussion of this style in chapter 8). In this example, Gaines-Cirelli describes how her "fix the church" impulse (presented in the previous Move) takes concrete form in planning for worship on Pentecost. Not only does this example give the listeners a "for instance" of the idea presented in Move 3, it also ties together the biblical text and the occasion of worship on Pentecost. Because she is giving an example of what she talked about in the previous Move, no Connector is needed.

- People who are really different listen and recognize that others are speaking their language at a deep level
- Those who have experienced the saving love of Jesus having the courage to share that experience with others
- A great conversion to love and justice and generosity and peace and mutuality—the formation of a new community with those things at the center

These are the "special effects" I want for this congregation, for the whole church, for the world.

And sometimes I really do labor under the illusion that it's up to me. But . . .

Connector
In the previous two Moves, the preacher named and described the "fix the church" impulse and gave an example of what this impulse looks like in Pentecost worship planning. Now she is, with the help of the biblical text, about to turn the sermon against this notion that we can somehow fix the church. Notice how she does this in this brief Connector. We have been sailing along with her, desiring the same "special effects" she has been describing. But now, she slips in the word "illusion,"

reinforced by the word "But," to signal that we have been running in the wrong direction and are about to enter a new trajectory.

... these miracles we read about in Acts 2 didn't happen through human ingenuity—because someone figured out a new technology for communication, or because a pastor dreamed up an innovative program, or because a congregation has such a great history and so many good and capable people. Pentecost happened—and happens—through the unmerited grace of God, happens—through the unmerited grace of God, the love of Jesus, and the outpouring of the Holy Spirit. God is the one whose "effects" are so special that people aren't just impressed by them, but are transformed, empowered, set free, brought back to life, and drawn into a new kind of community. I can't make those things happen. This church can't make them happen. And, frankly, when I remember that, I'm able to see and remember that not only is it not up to me, but God has the Pentecost Experience quite in hand. Then and now.

But . . .

Move 5
The preacher is now going to make the major two-sided theological claim of the sermon, namely that the church's experience of Pentecost is about the power of God, not our efforts to fix the church or make the "special effects" of Pentecost happen. Our role is to open ourselves to the experience and to respond with our lives. She makes the first half of this claim, that is, what God is doing at Pentecost.

Connector
In the previous Move, Gaines-Cirelli has described Pentecost as the action of God, not human

effort. Now she wants to state the other side of the coin, namely that the fact that God acts in power doesn't eliminate human responsibility. She signals this on-the-one-hand but on-the-other shift with a one-word Connector: "But . . ."

. . . that doesn't mean that you and I have no responsibility, no role to play. The original Pentecost miracle wouldn't have happened if the disciples blew Jesus off when he told them to stay in Jerusalem and to patiently wait, deciding instead to attend to their own agenda. It wouldn't have happened if the apostles, the women, and other disciples with them (Acts 1:12–14) were not open to receive the strange and wonderful gift of the Spirit's presence—an openness likely prompted by the prayers to which they were so devoted (Acts 1:14). It wouldn't have happened if others who heard the sounds of the wind and the people speaking their language hadn't responded with curiosity and open hearts. All of this is to say that, while the words of Jesus are our invitation and guide and the Spirit is always the instigator and power source, we have to decide how to respond. Some on the first Pentecost chose to "sneer" and label what was happening as embarrassing, bad behavior. But thousands

Move 6
Now in this Move, the preacher picks up the second half of the theological claim, namely that, even though Pentecost is God's act, not ours, we still have responsibility. We have to be present and open to experience Pentecost and then we have to decide whether to "sneer" at or to join "the Jesus movement."

of others—"about three thousand souls"—decided to respond by joining the Jesus movement. "And they devoted themselves to the apostles' teaching and fellowship, to the breaking of bread and the prayers." (Acts 2:42) They became part of an intentional community, what we call the church.

Connector (silent)

The sermon is now moving toward its conclusion. The hearers can sense that the plane is about to come in for a landing. All that remains is one more Move, a summing up of what we have learned. This is not a new direction for the sermon, just a completion of the journey, so the preacher has chosen to mark this with only a pause.

Abandoning the church is not going to help the world become more whole, peaceful, or just. *Being* the church—grounded in our true DNA, the love, example, grace, unity-in-diversity, and power of the Holy Trinity—is what will really make a difference.

The call, as one God-dreamer describes it is to . . .

. . . surrender to the mystery of the fire of the Spirit that burns within, . . . live in ever greater fidelity to the omnipresent

Move 7/Ending

This whole sermon has been devoted to figuring out what the story of Pentecost says to the probing question raised at the outset: should we "forget the church" or not? In this ending Move, the preacher pulls all the threads together to provide a summary answer to that question, namely that instead of abandoning the church, we can be the church, responding to the Pentecostal power of God by being God's new people. The fact that the preacher

Word of God, [and] enter into the center of it all, the very heart and mystery of Christ, into the center of the flame that consumes, purifies, and sets everything aglow with peace, joy, boldness, and extravagant, furious love.[3]

wants the hearers not merely to understand this claim but also to believe it and live it is expressed in the fact that the sermon ends with an emotional crescendo.

When we get right down to it, each one of us has to decide whether we are willing to get close enough to be set on fire with God's love or get picked up by an unruly wind that will carry us into relationships and activities we couldn't have imagined and may not fully understand. Each one of us has to decide whether we will hang back with those who sneer or take a step into the new life in Christ we receive when our hearts are open—risking ridicule from the "sneerers." Each one of us has to decide whether to *truly* follow Jesus which will mean getting mixed up in the mixed bag of the church with people who are flawed and wonderful just like you and me.

You and I don't have to try to create special effects. You ARE God's special effects. We ARE God's special effects! We are here. And God creates the best special effects ever—better than *Star Wars*, *The Matrix*, *Lord of the Rings*, and the *Avengers*

combined! The best special
effects ever are when the Spirit
keeps overflowing and seeping
into the tiniest cracks in human
hearts and minds, filling the
brokenness, softening the cyni-
cism, and forming and reforming
people like you and me, here and
there, now and again, into an ever
more faithful, open, engaged, loving, and grace-filled church—the
kind of church no one could forget . . . or would want to.

We are now in a position to look back on this excellent sermon and
to name the Focus and the Function (for a discussion of Focus and
Function, see chapter 5) and to see the overall design, or Form (for a
discussion of Form, see chapters 5 and 6):

Focus: Even though we are discouraged by the church and tempted
to leave it, Pentecost shows us that the church's power and
life are God's work, not ours. We are called to be present,
to surrender to God's power, and to respond by following
Jesus.

Function: To encourage this openness and response to the God of
Pentecost.

Form: *Special Effects*

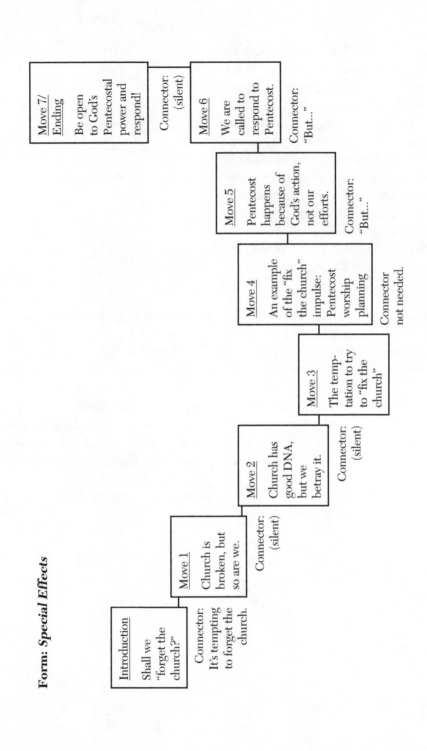

Introduction

Shall we "forget the church?"

Connector: It's tempting to forget the church.

Move 1

Church is broken, but so are we.

Connector: (silent)

Move 2

Church has good DNA, but we betray it.

Connector: (silent)

Move 3

The temptation to try to "fix the church"

Connector not needed.

Move 4

An example of the "fix the church" impulse: Pentecost worship planning

Connector: "But..."

Move 5

Pentecost happens because of God's action, not our efforts.

Connector: "But..."

Move 6

We are called to respond to Pentecost.

Connector: (silent)

Move 7/ Ending

Be open to God's Pentecostal power and respond!

Notes

Introduction

1. Jürgen Moltmann, *The Church in the Power of the Spirit: A Contribution to Messianic Ecclesiology* (New York: Harper and Row, 1977), 303.
2. Ibid., 206.
3. Craig Dykstra, "The Formative Power of the Congregation," *Religious Education* 82, no. 4 (Fall 1987): 532.
4. Ibid., 537.
5. Ibid., 540.
6. William H. Willimon, *What's Right with the Church* (San Francisco: Harper & Row, 1985), 121.
7. Moltmann, *The Church*, 303.
8. Karl Barth, *The Doctrine of Reconciliation, Church Dogmatics* IV/2, trans. G. W. Bromiley (Edinburgh: T & T Clark, 1958), 124–25.
9. Moltmann, *The Church*, 110.

Chapter 1: What Does It Mean to Preach?

1. See Mary Donovan Turner and Mary Lin Hudson, *Saved from Silence: Finding Women's Voice in Preaching* (St. Louis: Chalice Press, 1999), for a compelling description of the metaphors of "voice," "finding voice," and "claiming voice" especially, but not exclusively, in the experience of women preachers.
2. William H. Willimon, *What's Right with the Church* (San Francisco: Harper & Row, 1985), 107.
3. Karl Barth, "The Need and Promise of Christian Preaching," in *The Word of God and the Word of Man* (New York: Harper and Row, 1928), 126.
4. Theresa Rickard, "The Preacher as Midwife" (M.Div. thesis, Union Theological Seminary, 1993), 3.
5. Nancy Murphy, in her *Reasoning and Rhetoric in Religion* (Valley Forge, PA: Trinity Press International, 1994), notes how advances in the practice of preaching often precede advances in the theory of preaching, and that good homiletical theory is often in the role of catching up to good preaching practice, "making the practice more consistent in quality and more teachable," 102.

6. In her important book *A Healing Homiletic: Preaching and Disability* (Nashville: Abingdon Press, 1996), homiletician Kathy Black points out how the language of speaking and hearing can sometimes function in destructive ways. For example, to employ the metaphor of people being "deaf" to the gospel implies that deafness is a moral choice, which can sound a note of condemnation to those for whom deafness is a physical impairment. Black helpfully reminds us that the gospel can be received in many ways, not just through hearing. Nevertheless, the speaking and hearing quality of preaching is not merely an arbitrary form. The event of speaking and hearing carries an immediacy, a communal participation, and a sense of involvement and interaction that are theologically significant and not necessarily present in other types of communication. See Stephen Webb's discussion of the theology of sound and hearing, what he calls "Theo-acoustics," in *The Divine Voice: Christian Proclamation and the Theology of Sound* (Grand Rapids: Brazos Press, 2004), esp. chap. 2.

7. Mary Catherine Hilkert, *Naming Grace: Preaching and the Sacramental Imagination* (New York: Continuum, 1997), 192.

8. Karl Barth, *The Doctrine of the Word of God*, *Church Dogmatics* I/1, trans. G. T. Thomson (Edinburgh: T & T Clark, 1936), 57 (emphasis mine).

9. D. W. Cleverley Ford, *Ministry of the Word* (Grand Rapids: Wm. B. Eerdmans Publishing Co., 1979), 104.

10. Karl Barth, in Emil Brunner and Karl Barth, *Natural Theology*, trans. Peter Fraenkel (London: Centenary Press, 1946), 127.

11. Dietrich Ritschl, *A Theology of Proclamation* (Richmond, VA: John Knox Press, 1960), 132, 133.

12. Ford, *Ministry of the Word*, 103.

13. James Harris, *Preaching Liberation* (Minneapolis: Fortress Press, 1995), 11.

14. Jürgen Moltmann, *The Church in the Power of the Spirit: A Contribution to Messianic Ecclesiology* (New York: Harper and Row, 1977), 303.

15. Robert C. Tannehill, *The Sword of His Mouth: Forceful and Imaginative Language in Synoptic Sayings* (Philadelphia: Fortress Press, 1975), 1.

16. Amos N. Wilder, *Early Christian Rhetoric: The Language of the Gospel* (London: SCM Press, 1964), 26.

17. Meir Sternberg, *The Poetics of Biblical Narrative: Ideological Literature and the Drama of Reading* (Bloomington: Indiana University Press, 1985), 47.

18. Ford, *Ministry of the Word*, 107–8.

19. Karl Rahner, "Priest and Poet," in *Theological Investigations*, vol. 3 (Baltimore: Helicon, 1967), 313.

20. Karl Rahner, "Nature and Grace," in *Nature and Grace* (New York: Sheed and Ward, 1963), 134.

21. On the relationship of preaching to culture, see Daniel Patte, *Preaching Paul* (Philadelphia: Fortress Press, 1984). Patte observes that Paul, as a preacher, faced a situation similar to that of the contemporary preacher: His message, the kerygma, was couched in Jewish apocalyptic terms, but his hearers were participants in a culture, Hellenistic, for which those terms were alien. Patte argues

that Paul's preaching neither avoided the Hellenistic context nor reduced the kerygma to culturally amenable concepts. Rather, Paul repeated the kerygma in its Jewish vocabulary but accompanied this with the declaration that this kerygma was being fulfilled in terms of the hearers' own experience. Paul's preaching, then, occurred at the intersection of two languages, two "worlds": the kerygmatic and the specifically cultural-experiential.

22. James R. Nieman and Thomas G. Rogers, *Preaching to Every Pew: Cross-Cultural Strategies* (Minneapolis: Fortress Press, 2001), 156.

23. Augustine, *On Christian Doctrine* I.36.40, as quoted in Nieman and Rogers, *Preaching to Every Pew*, 156.

24. Nieman and Rogers, *Preaching to Every Pew*, 156.

25. Heinz Zahrnt, *The Question of God: Protestant Theology in the Twentieth Century*, trans. R. A. Wilson (New York: Harcourt, Brace & World, 1969), 118, 117.

26. Karl Barth, *The Preaching of the Gospel*, trans. B. E. Hooke (Philadelphia: Westminster Press, 1963), 74.

27. J. Randall Nichols, *The Restoring Word: Preaching as Pastoral Communication* (San Francisco: Harper & Row, 1987), 16.

28. James A. Wallace, *Preaching to the Hungers of the Heart: The Homily on the Feasts and within the Rites* (Collegeville, MN: The Liturgical Press, 2002), 27.

29. Ibid., 3.

30. Clement Welsh, *Preaching in a New Key: Studies in the Psychology of Thinking and Listening* (Philadelphia: Pilgrim Press, 1974), 15–16.

31. Nichols, *The Restoring Word*, 6.

32. G. Lee Ramsey Jr., *Care-full Preaching: From Sermon to Caring Community* (St. Louis: Chalice Press, 2000), 10–11.

33. Harry Emerson Fosdick, "What Is the Matter with Preaching?" *Harpers Monthly*, no. 157 (July 1928), 134.

34. Edmund Holt Linn, *Preaching as Counseling: The Unique Method of Harry Emerson Fosdick* (Valley Forge, PA: Judson Press, 1966), 15–16.

35. E. Brooks Holifield, *A History of Pastoral Care in America: From Salvation to Self-Realization* (Nashville: Abingdon Press, 1983), 34. See also Ramsey, *Care-full Preaching*, 13–17.

36. Gary D. Stratman, *Pastoral Preaching: Timeless Truths for Changing Needs* (Nashville: Abingdon Press, 1983).

37. Nichols, *The Restoring Word*, 189. Robert C. Dykstra explicitly names a pastoral hermeneutics, a way of interpreting both the Bible and contemporary experience, as the definitive mark of pastoral preaching: "Pastoral preaching, I submit, is distinguished less by the communicational style or skill of the person in the pulpit, less by sensitivity to deep concerns in the pews, less by focusing on the pressing issues of the day, however pivotal these may be to the preaching event. Pastoral preaching is distinctly marked, rather, by the pastor's personal willingness to pursue enticing leads peculiar to every biblical text or human circumstance that allude to the divine preoccupation with happy endings amid

human tragedy" (*Discovering a Sermon: Personal Pastoral Preaching* [St. Louis: Chalice Press, 2001], 6).

38. Ramsey, *Care-full Preaching*, 16. Ramsey is representative of a new generation of pastorally oriented homileticians who attempt to overcome both the individualism and excessive psychologizing of earlier versions of pastoral preaching. Ramsey advocates pastoral sermons that are attentive to theological issues and, instead of addressing discrete individuals, are aimed at building up the whole church as a caring body of disciples.

39. Joseph Sittler, *The Anguish of Preaching* (Philadelphia: Fortress Press, 1966), 38. See also the discussion of this point in Morris J. Niedenthal, "Focusing the Listener's Story," in Edmund A. Steimle, Morris J. Niedenthal, and Charles L. Rice, *Preaching the Story* (Philadelphia: Fortress Press, 1980), 78–80.

40. John S. McClure, *The Round-Table Pulpit: Where Leadership and Preaching Meet* (Nashville: Abingdon Press, 1995), 30–33. McClure has developed the themes of this book in a more philosophically full manner in *Other-wise Preaching: A Postmodern Ethic for Homiletics* (St. Louis: Chalice Press, 2001).

41. McClure, *The Round-Table Pulpit*, 37.

42. Ibid., 57.

43. Lucy Atkinson Rose, *Sharing the Word: Preaching in the Roundtable Church* (Louisville, KY: Westminster John Knox Press, 1997), 4.

44. In the preface to *Sharing the Word*, Rose essentially rejects twenty centuries of homiletical thought when she says, "If what I do is preaching, it is not reflected in the literature that describes and defines preaching. And if what I read about preaching is true, then what I do is not really preaching" (p. ix). She means for us to take this, I am fairly certain, as a rhetorical gambit, but I choose to take her at face value. Indeed, I think the approach she describes in the rest of the book is, in fact, "not really preaching." What she calls for is closer to congregational testimony, a Christian practice to be sure, and one related to the witness of preaching, but distinguishable in content, context, genre, and method from preaching.

45. George A. Lindbeck, *The Nature of Doctrine: Religion and Theology in a Postliberal Age* (Philadelphia: Westminster Press, 1984), 118.

46. Ibid.

47. Jana Childers, *Performing the Word: Preaching as Theatre* (Nashville: Abingdon Press, 1998), 11.

48. Elizabeth Achtemeier, *Preaching as Theology and Art* (Nashville: Abingdon Press, 1984), 52.

49. Ibid.

50. Charles L. Rice, *The Embodied Word: Preaching as Art and Liturgy* (Minneapolis: Fortress Press, 1991), 94–95.

51. Ibid., 98.

52. Steimle et al., *Preaching the Story*, 12–13, 15.

53. Peter Berger as quoted in Clyde E. Fant, *Preaching for Today*, rev. ed. (San Francisco: Harper & Row, 1987), 45.

54. A phrase David Kelsey applies to Barth's view of the Bible. Quoted in Lindbeck, *The Nature of Doctrine*, 120–21.

55. William Beardslee, "Uses of the Proverb in the Synoptic Gospels," *Interpretation* 24 (January 1970): 65, as cited in Richard L. Eslinger, *Narrative and Imagination: Preaching the Worlds That Shape Us* (Minneapolis: Fortress Press, 1995), 22.

56. David Buttrick, *Homiletic: Moves and Structures* (Philadelphia: Fortress Press, 1987), 12.

57. Perhaps the most prolific and persuasive advocate of narratively plotted sermons is Eugene Lowry. See his *The Homiletical Plot* (Atlanta: John Knox Press, 1980), *Doing Time in the Pulpit* (Nashville: Abingdon Press, 1985), *How to Preach a Parable: Designs for Narrative Sermons* (Nashville: Abingdon Press, 1989), and *The Sermon: Dancing on the Edge of Mystery* (Nashville: Abingdon Press, 1997), especially chap. 4. See also my own earlier work, "Shaping Sermons by Plotting the Text's Claim Upon Us," in *Preaching Biblically*, ed. Don M. Wardlaw (Philadelphia: Westminster Press, 1983), 84–100.

58. Barbara Brown Taylor, *The Preaching Life* (Cambridge, MA: Cowley, 1993), 81–83.

59. Charles L. Campbell, *Preaching Jesus: New Directions for Homiletics in Hans Frei's Postliberal Theology* (Grand Rapids: Wm. B. Eerdmans Publishing Co., 1997), 190, 193, 216.

60. Stanley Hauerwas, A *Community of Character: Toward a Constructive Christian Ethic* (Notre Dame, IN: University of Notre Dame Press, 1981), 66.

61. H. Richard Niebuhr, *The Meaning of Revelation* (New York: Macmillan Co., 1941, 1960), 35.

62. Hendrikus Berkhof, *Christian Faith: An Introduction to the Study of the Faith* (Grand Rapids: Wm. B. Eerdmans Publishing Co., 1979), 17.

63. Reinhold Niebuhr, *Leaves from the Notebook of a Tamed Cynic* (Louisville, KY: Westminster John Knox Press, 1990), 15.

64. Paul Ricoeur, "The Hermeneutics of Testimony," in *Essays on Biblical Interpretation*, ed. Lewis S. Mudge (Philadelphia: Fortress Press, 1980), 131.

65. Ibid., 128–29.

66. In his brilliant book *Confessing Jesus Christ: Preaching in a Postmodern World* (Grand Rapids: Wm. B. Eerdmans Publishing Co., 2003), David J. Lose argues for a confessional model of preaching. Although Lose argues that the preacher who confesses the faith is, by definition, more personally involved with the gospel than is the witness who points to the truth of the good news, I ultimately find very little difference between the two images. Perhaps the confessional image does emphasize more the personal belief of the preacher while the witness image is more eschatological in that the witness can testify to aspects of the faith that are not yet fully a part of the witness's own conviction or experience. The witness can see them, can point toward them, can know proleptically that they are true, but does not yet claim them as full personal conviction.

67. Lindbeck, *The Nature of Doctrine*, 121.
68. Sandra M. Schneiders, *The Revelatory Text: Interpreting the New Testament as Sacred Scripture* (San Francisco: HarperSanFrancisco, 1991), 137.
69. Ricoeur, "The Hermeneutics of Testimony," 131.
70. Richard K. Fenn, *Liturgies and Trials* (New York: Pilgrim Press, 1982), 27.
71. Anna Carter Florence, *Preaching as Testimony* (Louisville, KY: Westminster John Knox Press, 2007), xix.
72. Ibid., xx.
73. Buttrick, *Homiletic*, 451.
74. Moltmann, *The Church*, 224.

Chapter 2: The Biblical Witness in Preaching

1. Yngve Brilioth, A *Brief History of Preaching*, trans. Karl E. Mattson (Philadelphia: Fortress Press, 1965), 9.
2. George Arthur Buttrick, "The Bible and Preaching," in *The Interpreter's One-Volume Commentary on the Bible*, ed. Charles M. Laymon (Nashville: Abingdon Press, 1971), 1255.
3. David G. Buttrick, "The Use of the Bible in Preaching," *The New Interpreter's Bible*, vol. 1 (Nashville: Abingdon Press, 1994), 188.
4. James Barr, *The Scope and Authority of the Bible* (Philadelphia: Westminster Press, 1980), 55.
5. See David Kelsey, *The Uses of Scripture in Recent Theology* (Philadelphia: Fortress Press, 1975), 208.
6. Walter Brueggemann, *Inscribing the Text: Sermons and Prayers of Walter Brueggemann*, ed. Anna Carter Florence (Minneapolis: Fortress Press, 2004), 17.
7. Ibid., 13.
8. Ibid., 19.
9. Barr, *The Scope and Authority of the Bible*, 55.
10. J. Christiaan Beker, *Suffering and Hope* (Philadelphia: Fortress Press, 1987), 25.
11. Pontifical Biblical Commission, "The Interpretation of the Bible in the Church," *Origins* (January 6, 1994), 520.
12. For a splendid description of the ancient practice of prayerful biblical reading, called *lectio divina*, and its use in the preparation of sermons, see James A. Wallace, *Preaching to the Hungers of the Heart: The Homily on the Feasts and within the Rules* (Collegeville, MN: The Liturgical Press, 2002), 181–89.
13. Burton Z. Cooper and John S. McClure, *Claiming Theology in the Pulpit* (Louisville, KY: Westminster John Knox Press, 2003), 2.
14. David Bartlett, *Between the Bible and the Church: New Methods for Biblical Preaching* (Nashville: Abingdon Press, 1999), 35.
15. Ibid., 36.
16. Majorie Hewitt Suchocki, *The Whispered Word: A Theology of Preaching* (St. Louis: Chalice Press, 1999), 50–51.
17. Bartlett, *Between the Bible and the Church*, 36.

18. Cooper and McClure, *Claiming Theology in the Pulpit*, 10–19, 135.
19. Leonora Tubbs Tisdale, *Preaching as Local Theology and Folk Art* (Philadelphia: Fortress Press, 1997), 60.
20. Ibid., chap. 3.
21. Ibid., 61.
22. Leander E. Keck, *The Bible in the Pulpit* (Nashville: Abingdon Press, 1978), 62.

Chapter 3: Biblical Exegesis for Preaching

1. See John H. Hayes and Carl R. Holladay, *Biblical Exegesis: A Beginner's Handbook* (Atlanta: John Knox Press, 1982), 23–28. This guide to biblical study is one of the best available, and the reader will find here a full description of the standard exegetical approaches plus a rich bibliography of resources.
2. Lamin Sanneh, *Whose Religion is Christianity? The Gospel Beyond the West* (Grand Rapids: Eerdmans, 2003), 58–59.
3. In biblical studies, discussions of the relationship of social setting to hermeneutics are usually focused upon broad ideological and class categories, rather than upon the more finely tuned congregational situations that are so important for preaching.
4. Fred B. Craddock, *Preaching* (Nashville: Abingdon Press, 1985), 99.
5. See Eugene Lowry's description of both the promise and the perils of lectionary preaching in *Living with the Lectionary* (Nashville: Abingdon Press, 1992). See also William H. Todd Jr., "Protagonist Corner: A Word for the Fashion Conscious, or the Limits of the Lectionary," *Journal for Preachers* 11, no. 1 (Advent 1987): 35–37.
6. Gail R. O'Day, "The Gospel of John: Introduction, Commentary, and Reflections," *The New Interpreter's Bible*, vol. 9 (Nashville: Abingdon Press, 1995), 843.
7. For a more general discussion of the apparent bias of some lectionaries, see Justo L. González and Catherine G. González, *Liberation Preaching: The Pulpit and the Oppressed* (Nashville: Abingdon Press, 1980), 38ff., and William D. Thompson, *Preaching Biblically* (Nashville: Abingdon Press, 1981), 20.
8. R. Alan Culpepper, "The Gospel of Luke: Introduction, Commentary, and Reflections," in *The New Interpreter's Bible*, vol. 9 (Nashville: Abingdon Press, 1995), 35–38.
9. Keith F. Nickle, *Preaching the Gospel of Luke: Proclaiming God's Royal Rule* (Louisville, KY: Westminster John Knox Press, 2000), viii–ix.
10. Sharon H. Ringe, *Luke*, Westminster Bible Companion (Louisville, KY: Westminster John Knox Press, 1995), vii–ix.
11. See Hayes and Holladay, *Biblical Exegesis*, 24.
12. For a fine treatment of the exegetical role of the liturgical seasons, see Walter J. Burghardt, *Preaching: The Art and the Craft* (New York: Paulist Press, 1987), especially chap. 7.
13. Ronald J. Allen, *Interpreting the Gospel: An Introduction to Preaching* (St. Louis: Chalice Press, 1998), 125–26.

14. See the discussion about polarities in biblical texts in Thompson, *Preaching Biblically*, 54–56.
15. J. Randall Nichols, *Building the Word: The Dynamics of Communication and Preaching* (San Francisco: Harper & Row, 1980), 128.
16. Ibid.
17. Ibid., 129.
18. Craddock, *Preaching*, 123.
19. Hayes and Holladay, *Biblical Exegesis*, 45.
20. Ibid., 46.
21. Craddock, *Preaching*, 118.
22. O. C. Edwards Jr., *The Living and Active Word: One Way to Preach from the Bible Today* (New York: Seabury Press, 1975), 22.
23. For a fine guide to the sociological analysis of texts from the Synoptic Gospels, see Bruce J. Malina and Richard J. Rohrbaugh, *Social-Science Commentary on the Synoptic Gospels* (Minneapolis: Fortress Press, 1992). For a more general introduction to the usefulness of sociological analysis to preaching, see Richard L. Rohrbaugh, *The Biblical Interpreter: An Agrarian Bible in an Industrial Age* (Philadelphia: Fortress Press, 1978). Rohrbaugh gives numerous examples of foolish preaching that resulted from a blindness to the social setting of biblical texts or, worse, from a stubborn twisting of those texts to make them fit comfortably into the social conventions of the preacher's own time.
24. Walter Brueggemann, "The Social Nature of the Biblical Text for Preaching," in *Preaching as a Social Act: Theology and Practice*, ed. Arthur Van Seters (Nashville: Abingdon Press, 1988), 131.
25. Luke Timothy Johnson, *The Writings of the New Testament: An Interpretation*, rev. ed. (Minneapolis: Fortress Press, 1999), 331.
26. Robert C. Tannehill, "The Gospels and Narrative Literature," *The New Interpreter's Bible*, vol. 8 (Nashville: Abingdon Press, 1995), 56–70.
27. Ibid., 58.
28. Nichols, *Building the Word*, 126–27.
29. Bruce C. Birch, et al., *A Theological Introduction to the Old Testament* (Nashville: Abingdon Press, 1999), 120–25.
30. Ibid., 123.
31. Ibid., 124.
32. Ibid., 130.
33. Bernhard W. Anderson, "The Problem and Promise of Commentary," *Interpretation* 36, no. 4 (October 1982): 342, 343.
34. Elisabeth Schüssler Fiorenza, "Response (to Walter J. Burghardt)," in *A New Look at Preaching*, ed. John Burke, Good News Studies 7 (Wilmington, DE: Michael Glazier, 1983), 52.

Chapter 4: The Focus and Function of the Sermon

1. Anna Carter Florence, *Preachiong as Testimony* (Louisville, KY: Westminster John Knox Press, 2007), xiii.

2. David James Randolph, *The Renewal of Preaching* (Philadelphia: Fortress Press, 1969), 19.

3. Ibid., 1.

4. Fred B. Craddock, "Inductive Preaching Renewed," in O. Wesley Allen Jr., ed., *The Renewed Homiletic* (Minneapolis: Fortress Press, 2010), 45.

5. Ibid., 51.

6. Fred B. Craddock, *As One without Authority* (Nashville: Abingdon Press, 1971), 124–25. At the heart of Craddock's argument is the distinction between "inductive" and "deductive" movement in sermons. A similar distinction was made a generation earlier by W. E. Sangster in *The Craft of the Sermon* (London: Epworth Press, 1954), 71–79.

7. Craddock, "Inductive Preaching Renewed," 45.

8. Ronald E. Sleeth, *God's Word and Our Words: Basic Homiletics* (Atlanta: John Knox Press, 1986), 44.

9. Cleophus J. LaRue, *I Believe I'll Testify: The Art of African American Preaching* (Louisville, KY: Westminster John Knox Press, 2011), 23.

10. Haddon W. Robinson, *Biblical Preaching: The Development and Delivery of Expository Messages* (Grand Rapids: Baker Book House, 2001), 39.

11. Eugene L. Lowry, *Doing Time in the Pulpit: The Relationship between Narrative and Preaching* (Nashville: Abingdon Press, 1985), 79, 80.

12. Craddock, *As One without Authority*, 105.

13. Ibid., 100.

14. Richard L. Eslinger, *A New Hearing: Living Options in Homiletic Method* (Nashville: Abingdon Press, 1987), 124–25.

15. David H. Kelsey, *The Uses of Scripture in Recent Theology* (Philadelphia: Fortress Press, 1975), 91.

16. Ibid., 208.

17. Lowry, *Doing Time in the Pulpit*, 80.

18. David G. Buttrick, "Interpretation and Preaching," *Interpretation* 25, no. 1 (January 1981): 58.

19. O. C. Edwards Jr., *Elements of Homiletic: A Method for Preparing to Preach* (New York: Pueblo Publishing Co., 1982), 63.

Chapter 5: The Basic Form of the Sermon

1. Halford E. Luccock, *In the Minister's Workshop* (New York: Abingdon-Cokesbury Press, 1944), 118.

2. This sermon outline is an expanded version of one described in Harold T. Bryson and James C. Taylor, *Building Sermons to Meet People's Needs* (Nashville: Broadman Press, 1980), 94.

3. Merrill R. Abbey, *Communication in Pulpit and Parish* (Philadelphia: Westminster Press, 1973), 161–64.

4. Fred B. Craddock, *As One without Authority* (Nashville: Abingdon Press, 1971), 56.

5. See, for example, Fred B. Craddock, *As One without Authority*, and *Overhearing the Gospel* (Nashville: Abingdon Press, 1978); Milton Crum Jr., *Manual*

on Preaching (Valley Forge, PA: Judson Press, 1977); Eugene L. Lowry, *The Homiletical Plot: The Sermon as Narrative Art Form* (Atlanta: John Knox Press, 1980), *Doing Time in the Pulpit: The Relationship between Narrative and Preaching* (Nashville: Abingdon Press, 1985), *How to Preach a Parable: Design for Narrative Sermons* (Nashville: Abingdon Press, 1989), and *The Sermon: Dancing the Edge of Mystery* (Nashville: Abingdon Press, 1997); Richard A. Jensen, *Telling the Story: Variety and Imagination in Preaching* (Minneapolis: Augsburg Publishing House, 1980); Edmund A. Steimle, Morris J. Niedenthal, and Charles L. Rice, *Preaching the Story* (Philadelphia: Fortress Press, 1980); Ralph L. Lewis and Gregg Lewis, *Inductive Preaching: Helping People Listen* (Westchester, IL: Crossway Books, 1983); Richard L. Eslinger, *A New Hearing: Living Options in Homiletic Method* (Nashville: Abingdon Press, 1987), and *Narrative Imagination: Preaching the Worlds That Shape Us* (Minneapolis: Fortress Press, 1995); Don M. Wardlaw, ed., *Preaching Biblically* (Philadelphia: Westminster Press, 1983); David Buttrick, *Homiletic: Moves and Structures* (Philadelphia: Fortress Press, 1987); Paul Scott Wilson, *The Four Pages of the Sermon: A Guide to Biblical Preaching* (Nashville: Abingdon Press, 1999); and Joel B. Green and Michael Pasquarellow III, *Narrative Reading, Narrative Preaching* (Grand Rapids: Baker Academic, 2003).

6. Craddock, *As One without Authority*, 53.
7. Ibid., 156.
8. Ibid., 66.
9. Lowry, *The Homiletical Plot*, 76.
10. Ibid., 29–30.
11. Ibid., 31.
12. Ibid., 50.
13. Stephen Farris, *Preaching That Matters: The Bible and Our Lives* (Louisville, KY: Westminster John Knox Press, 1998), 122.
14. Paul Scott Wilson, *The Four Pages of the Sermon* (Nashville: Abingdon Press, 1999). See also Paul Scott Wilson, *Preaching and Homiletical Theory* (St. Louis: Chalice Press, 2004), 91–100.
15. Wilson, *Preaching and Homiletical Theory*, 97–98.
16. Ibid., 98.
17. Fred B. Craddock, *Preaching* (Nashville: Abingdon Press, 1985), 173–74.
18. David G. Buttrick, "Interpretation and Preaching," *Interpretation* 25, no. 1 (January 1981): 55–56.
19. Buttrick, *Homiletic*, 294.
20. Ibid., 320–21.
21. This description of Buttrick's move system is adapted from my review of *Homiletic* in *Theology Today* 45, no. 1 (April 1988): 109–10.
22. Richard Lischer, "Preaching and the Rhetoric of Promise," *Word and World* 8, no. 1 (Winter 1988): 69.
23. Ibid., 70.
24. Ronald J. Allen, *Hearing the Sermon: Relationship/Content/Feeling* (St. Louis: Chalice Press, 2004), 53.

25. Edmund A. Steimle, "The Eye of the Storm," in Steimle et al., *Preaching the Story*, 121–25.
26. Barbara Brown Taylor, "The Lost and Found Department," in *The Preaching Life* (Lanham, MA: Cowley, 1993), 147–53.
27. Ibid., 147.
28. Ibid., 148.
29. Ibid., 150.
30. Ibid.
31. Ibid., 151.
32. Ibid., 153.

Chapter 6: Refining the Form

1. For a more complete discussion of systemic sermon unity, see Thomas G. Long, "Pawn to King Four: Sermon Introductions and Communicational Design," *Reformed Review* 40, no. 1 (Autumn 1986): 27–35.
2. William H. Willimon, "Love in Action," sermon preached at the Duke University Chapel, February 14, 1988.
3. Henry H. Mitchell, "To Think on These Things," sermon preached on the National Radio Pulpit in the July–September 1978 series (New York: National Radio Pulpit, 1978), 53.
4. Barbara K. Lundblad, "Growing Old and Passing On," sermon preached on the Lutheran Series of the Protestant Hour, May 19, 1985 (New York: Lutheran Church in America, 1985), 34–35.
5. Edmund A. Steimle, "Last Call," sermon preached on the Lutheran Series of the Protestant Hour, July 1, 1973 (New York: Lutheran Church in America, 1973), 14–16.
6. Annette Sowell, "Through It All, There Is God," in Joseph R. Jeter Jr., *Crisis Preaching* (Nashville: Abingdon Press, 1998), 150–51.
7. Thomas G. Long, "Sermon: Figs Out of Season," in *Preaching Biblically*, ed. Don M. Wardlaw (Philadelphia: Westminster Press, 1983), 99, 100.
8. John Vannorsdall, "A Day Far Spent," sermon preached in the Lutheran Series of the Protestant Hour, May 3, 1981 (New York: Lutheran Church in America, 1981), 10.
9. James A. Sanders, *God Has a Story Too: Sermons in Context* (Philadelphia: Fortress Press, 1979), 20.

Chapter 7: Beginnings, Connections, and Endings

1. Gerald Kennedy, *His Word through Preaching* (New York: Harper & Brothers, 1947), 58.
2. George E. Sweazey, *Preaching the Good News* (Englewood Cliffs, NJ: Prentice-Hall, 1976), 95.
3. J. Randall Nichols, *Building the Word: The Dynamics of Communication and Preaching* (San Francisco: Harper & Row, 1980), 102–3.
4. Ilion T. Jones, *Principles and Practice of Preaching* (Nashville: Abingdon Press, 1956), 153.

5. Nichols, *Building the Word*, 101.

6. David Buttrick, *Homiletic: Moves and Structures* (Philadelphia: Fortress Press, 1987), 85.

7. See also Thomas G. Long, *The Senses of Preaching* (Atlanta: John Knox Press, 1988), 65–68.

8. Robert McAfee Brown, "Freedom and Political Responsibility," in *Proclaiming the Acceptable Year: Sermons from the Perspective of Liberation Theology*, ed. Justo L. González (Valley Forge, PA: Judson Press, 1982), 117.

9. John R. Fry, "Blindness," in Fry, *Fire and Blackstone* (Philadelphia: J. B. Lippincott Co., 1969), 45.

10. Cynthia A. Jarvis, "Let Us Pray: Why Do We Pray?" an unpublished sermon preached August 4, 1985, at Nassau Presbyterian Church, Princeton, NJ.

11. John Killinger, *Fundamentals of Preaching* (Philadelphia: Fortress Press, 1985), 84.

12. Adapted from Edmund A. Steimle, "Do Not Cling to Me," sermon preached in the Lutheran Series of the Protestant Hour, April 22, 1973 (New York: Lutheran Church in America, 1973), 13–14.

13. Walter J. Burghardt, "Who Touched Me?" in Burghardt, *Sir, We Would Like to See Jesus: Homilies from a Hilltop* (Ramsey, NJ: Paulist Press, 1982), 99.

14. Buttrick, *Homiletic*, 90.

15. Killinger, *Fundamentals of Preaching*, 83.

16. Buttrick, *Homiletic*, 84–85.

17. See the excellent discussion of "connective logic" in Buttrick, *Homiletic*, 70–74.

18. Some homileticians would add a third question to the set: *Who?* Who provides the conclusion, the preacher or the hearer? In his presentation of the inductive method of preaching, Fred Craddock suggests that the hearer may well be the better choice, that "the listener completes the sermon. . . . What is here suggested . . . is that the participation of the hearer is essential, not just in the post-benediction implementation but in the completion of the thought, movement, and decision-making within the sermon itself. The process calls for an incompleteness, a lack of exhaustiveness in the sermon." Fred B. Craddock, *As One without Authority* (Nashville: Abingdon Press, 1971), 64. Craddock is pointing to the possibility, even the desirability, of a certain open-endedness in sermon conclusions. If the preacher resists the temptation to wrap everything up, the hearers are given the freedom to finish the sermon for themselves and to "make it their own." This is a valuable suggestion, so long as we do not insist on it for all sermons and also remember that the preacher still bears responsibility for providing both the resources and the guidance for the hearers' completion of the sermon. An open-ended conclusion, in other words, is different from dumping a box of sermonic Tinkertoys into the middle of the sanctuary and telling the hearers, "Make what you want to out of this."

19. John Vannorsdall, "A Small Parade," sermon preached in the Lutheran Series of the Protestant Hour, March 31, 1985 (New York: Lutheran Church in America, 1985), 8.

20. Barbara K. Lundblad, "Longing for Breath," sermon preached in the Lutheran Series of the Protestant Hour, May 26, 1985 (New York: Lutheran Church in America, 1985), 40.
21. Henry H. Mitchell, "To Run and Not Be Weary," sermon preached on the National Radio Pulpit, Summer 1978 (New York: National Radio Pulpit, 1978), 45.
22. Richard John Neuhaus, "Change for the Kingdom's Sake," in *Preaching in the Witnessing Community*, ed. Herman G. Stuempfle Jr. (Philadelphia: Fortress Press, 1973), 53–54.
23. Baron von Hugel, as quoted in Robert E. C. Browne, *The Ministry of the Word* (London: SCM Press, 1956), 50.

Chapter 8: Images and Experiences in Sermons

1. See, for example, the remarks of the fourteenth-century homiletician Robert of Basevorn on "the winning-over of the audience" in the essay "Ornamentation," in *Theories of Preaching: Selected Readings in the Homiletical Tradition*, ed. Richard Lischer (Durham, NC: Labyrinth Press, 1987), 219–23.
2. See, for example, Ilion T. Jones, *Principles and Practice of Preaching* (Nashville: Abingdon Press, 1956). This typical textbook of the 1950s speaks confidently of preaching as "a redemptive deed" with the purpose of persuading others "to know and feel the gospel truth." The practical sections of the book, however, embody an almost exclusively ideational, rationalistic approach to sermon construction, including the use of "illustrations."
3. W. E. Sangster, *The Craft of the Sermon* (London: Epworth Press, 1954), 208.
4. George E. Sweazey, *Preaching the Good News* (Englewood Cliffs, NJ: Prentice-Hall, 1976), 194.
5. Jones, *Principles and Practice*, 139.
6. At least one recent homiletical textbook, John Killinger, *Fundamentals of Preaching* (Philadelphia: Fortress Press, 1985), 107–10, provides a list of the purposes of illustrations clearly dependent on similar lists in earlier textbooks, except that the element of persuasion is omitted. It is characteristic of more recent homiletics to view persuasion in terms of manipulation and, thus, as a negative characteristic when applied to preaching. For an alternate view, see Ronald E. Sleeth, *Persuasive Preaching* (Berrien Springs, MI: Andrews University Press, 1981), and Lucy Lind Hogan and Robert Reid, *Connecting with the Congregation: Rhetoric and the Art of Preaching* (Nashville: Abingdon Press, 1999).
7. Jones, *Principles and Practice*, 137.
8. Sangster, *The Craft of the Sermon*, 206.
9. Sweazey, *Preaching the Good News*, 193.
10. Charles Haddon Spurgeon in *Lectures to My Students*, as quoted in John R. W. Stott, *Between Two Worlds: The Art of Preaching in the Twentieth Century* (Grand Rapids: Wm. B. Eerdmans Publishing Co., 1982), 240.
11. Stott, *Between Two Worlds*, 240–41.

12. Some contemporary homileticians, convinced that the word "illustration" is irreparably tainted by its rationalistic past, advocate its banishment from the vocabulary of preaching. Others, like David Buttrick, continue to use it, but only in a restricted sense and along with other descriptive terms, like "image," "metaphor," and "example." See David Buttrick, *Homiletic: Moves and Structures* (Philadelphia: Fortress Press, 1987), 113–51.

13. Fred B. Craddock, *Preaching* (Nashville: Abingdon Press, 1985), 204.

14. William Sloane Coffin, "The Courage to Love," in Coffin, *The Courage to Love* (San Francisco: Harper & Row, 1982), 9.

15. James S. Stewart, "Beyond Disillusionment to Faith," in *Best Sermons, 1962*, ed. G. Paul Butler (Princeton, NJ: D. Van Nostrand Co., 1962), 24. The full text of this illustration is cited as an example of a "Geographical or Topographical Illustration" by John Killinger in *Fundamentals of Preaching*, 113–14.

16. Elizabeth Achtemeier, "Of Children and Streets and the Kingdom," in *Best Sermons 1*, ed. James W. Cox and Kenneth M. Cox (San Francisco: Harper & Row, 1988), 288–89.

17. Buttrick, *Homiletic*, 133.

18. Ibid., 133–34.

19. Ibid., 134.

20. Robert E. C. Browne, *The Ministry of the Word* (Philadelphia: Fortress Press, 1958), 39.

21. Thomas G. Long, *Testimony: Talking Ourselves into Being Christian* (San Francisco: Jossey Bass, 2004), 81. Robert Ellsberg, as quoted in Gerry McCarthy, "The Social Edge Interview: Author Robert Ellsberg," *The Social Edge. Com: A Monthly Social Justice and Faith Magazine*, www.thesocialedge.com (November 2003).

22. Mary Ann Bird, as quoted in Leonard Sweet, *Strong in the Broken Places: A Theological Reverie on the Ministry of George Everett Ross* (Akron, OH: University of Akron Press, 1995), 93. This example is also cited in Long, *Testimony*, 85–86.

23. Jürgen Moltmann, *The Church in the Power of the Spirit: A Contribution to Messianic Ecclesiology* (New York: Harper & Row, 1977), 222.

24. Ibid., 220.

25. Ibid., 225.

26. Ibid., 191.

27. Wendell Berry, "A Dance," in *The Collected Poems of Wendell Berry, 1957–1982* (Berkeley, CA: North Point Press, 1985), 202.

28. C. H. Dodd, *The Parables of the Kingdom* (London and Glasgow: Fontana Books, 1961), 16.

29. Charles L. Rice, *Interpretation and Imagination: The Preacher and Contemporary Literature* (Philadelphia: Fortress Press, 1970), 126.

30. From Patrick J. Willson, "Weeds in Our Garden," an unpublished sermon preached on July 19, 1987, at Shades Valley Presbyterian Church, Birmingham, AL.

31. Bruce C. Salmon, *Storytelling in Preaching: A Guide to the Theory and Practice* (Nashville: Broadman Press, 1988), 54.
32. Craddock, *Preaching*, 209.
33. Buttrick, *Homiletic*, 142.
34. Cf. Craddock, *Preaching*, 208–9.

Chapter 9: Preaching and Plagiarism

1. I recently had the same startling experience that other preachers have no doubt had. I discovered that some of my own sermons, written and published years ago, were available, without my knowledge or consent, on some of the "sermons for sale" websites. Contrary to what many people think, authors do not always own the rights to the material they have published, and the publication rights to these sermons are no longer mine. But the sermons in a deeper sense are still "my sermons," and while I would love for other preachers to find ideas in them or even to borrow material from them, I would be chagrined to know that someone preached them as their own and without attribution.
2. Rick Warren, as quoted in Thomas White and John Yeats, *Franchising McChurch: Feeding Our Obsession with Easy Christianity* (Colorado Springs, CO: David C. Cook, 2009), 115.
3. Craig Brian Larson, "Plagiarism, Shmagiarism: The Why and When of Giving Credit," *Preaching Today*, http://www.preachingtoday.com/skills/themes/purity/200503.48.html.
4. Richard Posner, *The Little Book of Plagiarism* (New York: Pantheon, 2007), 104.
5. Jürgen Moltmann, *The Church in the Power of the Spirit: A Contribution to Messianic Ecclesiology* (New York:Harper and Row, 1977), 303.

Chapter 10: From Desk to Pulpit

1. Walter J. Ong, *Orality and Literacy: The Technologizing of the Word* (London: Methuen, 1982), 74.
2. Ibid., 176.
3. Dietrich Bonhoeffer, "New Year, 1945," in *Letters and Papers from Prison*, ed. Eberhard Bethge, trans. Reginald H. Fuller (New York: Macmillan Co., 1953), 249.
4. Raymond E. Brown, *The Gospel According to John*, I–XII, Anchor Bible, vol. 29 (Garden City, NY: Doubleday & Co., 1966), 18.
5 William Sloane Coffin, *The Courage to Love* (San Francisco: Harper & Row, 1982), 7–8.
6. Jana Childers, *Performing the Word: Preaching as Theatre* (Nashville: Abingdon Press, 1998), 49.
7. Charles L. Bartow, *The Preaching Moment* (Nashville: Abingdon Press, 1980), 37.
8. See, e.g., Bartow, *The Preaching Moment*; Al Fasol, *A Guide to Self-Improvement in Sermon Delivery* (Grand Rapids: Baker Book House, 1983);

Richard F. Ward, *Speaking from the Heart: Preaching with Passion* (Nashville: Abingdon Press, 1992); and *Speaking of the Holy: The Art of Communication in Preaching* (St. Louis: Chalice Press, 2001); Childers, *Performing the Word*; and an older but still valuable work, Robert White Kirkpatrick, *The Creative Delivery of Sermons* (New York: Macmillan Co., 1944).

9. Kirkpatrick, *The Creative Delivery of Sermons*, 11.

Chapter 11: Conversation along the Pilgrim Way

1. James A. Michener, *Iberia: Spanish Travels and Reflections* (New York: Random House, 1968), 892.
2. Adam Hamilton, *Unleashing the Word: Preaching with Relevance, Purpose, and Passion* (Nashville: Abingdon Press, 2009), 53.
3. Ibid., 50.
4. Homer K. Buerlein, *How to Preach More Powerful Sermons* (Philadelphia: Westminster Press, 1984, 1986), 25.
5. William Muehl, *All the Damned Angels* (Philadelphia: Pilgrim Press, 1972), 15.
6. Ernest T. Campbell, *Locked in a Room with Open Doors* (Waco, TX: Word Books, 1974), 20.
7. Allan A. Boesak, *Comfort and Protest: Reflections on the Apocalypse of John of Patmos* (Philadelphia: Westminster Press, 1987), 105.
8. Ronald D. Sisk, "How to Forgive," in *Best Sermons 1*, ed. James W. Cox (San Francisco: Harper & Row, 1988), 312.
9. Walter Brueggemann, "The Social Nature of the Biblical Text for Preaching," in *Preaching as a Social Act: Theology and Practice*, ed. Arthur Van Seters (Nashville: Abingdon Press, 1988), 147.

Appendix A

1. Edmund A. Steimle, "The Eye of the Storm," in Thomas Long and Cornelius Plantinga, eds., *A Chorus of Witnesses: Model Sermons for Today's Preacher* (Grand Rapids: Eerdmans, 1994) 237–42.

Appendix D

1. Andrew Sullivan, "The Forgotten Jesus," *Newsweek*, 159/15 (April 9, 2012), 26–31.
2. https://www.chesterton.org/wrong-with- world.
3. Brennan Manning, *The Furious Longing of God* (Colorado Springs, CO: David C. Cook, 2009), 125.

Index of Scripture References

341

Index of Names and Subjects